Cinderella Boy

ALSO BY
KENNY A. NOBLE

Rite of Passage

The Mentor

Chef Boy or Me

Devotions for Spiritual Growth

Cinderella Boy

A biography about overcoming childhood abuse

Kenny A. Noble

A
—
W

ANGEL WINGS
PUBLISHING

SEYMOUR, INDIANA

to Sue
the one person who helped me
find normality in life.

Cinderella Boy

AUTHOR'S NOTE

This is my story—my testimony, written the way I perceived life as a child and later as a teenager. For a few experiences, I relied on my mother for information and details, but most incidents are embedded in my mind like scratches on a steel plate that have never worn away. Although, I chose to write this story in fiction format, everything written is true. Nothing is fabricated.

Naturally, I could not remember the exact dialogue of each incident, but I have been careful to remain true to the spirit of the moment. All events have been arranged in chronological order as much as possible, but some experiences have been condensed into a few days when in fact they may have occurred weeks or even months apart.

As I recorded my story, memories were like an emotional minefield, and at times, and I was forced to leave off writing for a while in order to get my emotions back in control. Revisiting the past opened old wounds, and the memories became nearly as painful as the real-life incidents. As a result, it has taken more than a thousand hours spread out over a twelve-year period to finish this project. But even though the writing has been painful at times, I have often been reminded just how fortunate I am to have survived my youth.

I confess, it is humbling to be so transparent in this book, but I've done so purposely in hope that my testimony will be a witness of God's deliverance. Based on my childhood beginning and subsequent teenage years, I think most would agree that it would have been abnormal if my adult life had turned out as anything other than criminal. Yet, he who watched over the sparrows intervened in my life and altered my destiny. For that, I am so grateful.

Above all else, my sincere wish and my reason for writing my story is in hope that my testimony will provide the inspiration you need for victories in your own life. The help and deliverance God gave me is certainly available for you also.

God Bless,
Kenny A. Noble

THE CONDITIONS UNDER WHICH MY LIFE BEGAN

Before I formed thee in the belly I knew thee;... Jeremiah 1:5

My wife and I brought my dying mother home to care for her during her last few days. Sue sat with her during the day, and I slept on the floor beside her bed at night. At fifty-four years old, I thought Mom was much too young to die of cancer, but then, her life had been rough from the very beginning.

She was only twelve years old when her parents divorced and began to pass her back and forth between them every two weeks. Apparently, a young daughter crimped their single lifestyle, and neither parent wanted her. Then like a knight in shining armor, her first serious boyfriend proposed marriage. Both parents encouraged the relationship, and Mom married the young man one day after her thirteenth birthday.

A year and a half later, fourteen-year old Virginia had her first baby—a little girl. Not long after, her husband surprised her with the news that he had joined the Army. He shipped out to Korea and left her to support herself and the baby alone.

Eventually, Virginia became involved with a local married man, and by the time she was seventeen, I was born. The affair continued, and two years later I had a baby brother. Finally, she filed for child support and refused visitation rights until her boyfriend agreed to support his two sons.

Her actions only spurred his anger, and the last time my father came to see me, he came drunk, he came angry, and he came with a butcher knife. According to Mom, I was his favorite, and in his drunken stupor, he reasoned that if he could not visit his own son, then no one else should be allowed to do so, either. The only thing that saved my life that day, was Mom's quick thinking. She hid me up inside the kitchen cabinets along with the dishes until he finally left.

A few days later, as she took a shortcut through an alley, he tried to run her down with his vehicle. That was the last time she saw him.

When Mom's husband returned home from the Army and discovered her sin and two new boys in the family, he enlisted the help of her father, and the two of them lured Virginia out into a country cabin in the Medora Knobs. There her husband suddenly appeared and pried his own daughter from the teenager-mother's arms. He disappeared along with his daughter, and it was years before Mom was able to track him down and see her daughter again.

Society was tough on a teenage mother during the nineteen-fifties, and when a man eight years her senior showed interest in Virginia, she quickly jumped into marriage once again.

This is where my story begins ...

THE BEGINNING

Hear, O LORD, when I cry with my voice: have mercy also upon me, and answer me. Psalm 27:7

FIVE-YEAR OLD KENNY, stood trembling in the darkness as he ate his sandwich at the kitchen table. The window fan hummed a steady tone of rebellion against the wind that disrupted its natural power. Steve stood beside Kenny, and tried to gulp down his own sandwich. Both boys shuddered each time their stepfather spoke.

In the next room, Junior sat in the recliner where he watched television and cursed at the boys between commercial breaks. He wore nothing but white briefs and a handle-bar T-shirt, which revealed several large tattoos on his muscular arms. "You kids hurry up in there. It's your bedtime." His voice was deep and gruff.

Kenny wanted to make Junior like him, but he did not know how. He never talked back to his stepfather, he always did his chores on time, and he tried to stay out of his way. But when Junior was not cursing Kenny, he sat glaring at him with his black eyes that were ugly with hatred.

Kenny leaned close to Steve's ear. "Just tell him you got to go to the bathroom."

Tears dripped from Steve's cheeks. "I'm scared."

"Tell him."

"I can't hold it no more." Steve squeezed his knees together and whimpered, followed by the sound of something dripping on the floor.

"You should have told him," Kenny said. He kept his eyes on Junior and quietly switched places with Steve in order to block Junior's line of sight. Slowly, he reached over and pulled down Steve's shirt tail, but it did not hide the dark stain on Steve's pants.

Profanity from the other room sent shivers of fear up Kenny's spine. "You boys quit stalling and eat those sandwiches. You been in there long enough." A string of curse words followed, but Junior's eyes never left the television screen. He took long puffs on his cigarette which left a haze of smoke hovering above his head.

Virginia sat on the sofa with her legs curled up under her while she stared at the television screen, seemingly oblivious to her husband's angry rants at the boys.

A light rap sounded on the screen door, and Ronnie stepped inside the living room. Tall for a thirteen year old, Ronnie kept his blond hair cut in the short flattop style of nineteen-sixty. "Mom wants to know if you still need a babysitter for Kenny and Steve." Ronnie was Kenny's distant cousin.

Junior took another deep draw on his cigarette and blew out a long string of smoke. "How much she want?"

Ronnie took a step back toward the screen door and puckered his face as if he had not considered the question. "Whatever you want to pay, I guess. Mom said, she don't mind taking care of the boys." He shoved his hands deep inside his pockets and smiled at Kenny.

Junior placed his cigarette in the ashtray and folded his arms crossed his chest. "I want her to keep them all the time, day and night." He glanced at Virginia as if he expected her to challenge him. When she did not respond he added; "We'll pick them up on the weekends, … when we can."

"Be right back." Ronnie turned and disappeared out the screen door. He lived only four blocks down on fourth street.

Junior picked up his cigarette. "If we get those brats off our hands, we can do some things and enjoy ourselves."

Virginia glanced his direction and nodded.

"We got to live, too," he said.

"I know."

"Can't do anything when you have two kids on your hands."

"Whatever you think best," she mumbled.

"You boys done?" Junior called. It was a statement more than a question. "Get in there and get ready for bed."

Kenny winced at the sharpness in Junior's voice. Nearly numb with fear, he left the remainder of his bologna sandwich on the table, and hesitantly led Steve across the living room floor toward their bedroom. Steve followed in Kenny's shadow, his head down, both hands pulling on his shirttail.

"What have you done, Steve?" Virginia asked. "You've wet all over yourself, haven't you? Get into the bedroom right now. Why didn't you tell me you had to go?"

Steve stood frozen in place like a cornstalk on a still day, his legs spread apart, trembling.

"Kenneth, you're supposed to watch out for him," Junior said. "Why didn't you tell us he had to go to the bathroom?" He gritted his teeth a moment and stared at Kenny before he took another puff on his cigarette.

A string of curse words followed punctuated by small clouds of smoke from his lips. "Why in God's name do we have to put up with this?" He crumbled his empty cigarette pack and dropped it into the ashtray. "Kenneth Allan, go to the store and get me a pack of cigarettes. Hand me my pants so I can give you the money."

Virginia shifted her position on the couch. "I'll go."

"No, let him go."

"Kenny's too young to cross the road by himself."

"He's almost six," Junior said. "He should be useful for something." He grabbed the pants Kenny held out to him. "Here's a quarter. Don't lose it either."

"Watch for cars," Virginia said. "Ewing Street is busy. Look both ways before you cross."

Kenny hurried out the door. He was glad to get away from Junior a few minutes. At the corner of fourth and Ewing street, he stopped and looked both directions like his mother had taught him. When the road was clear, he swallowed hard and ran across the road toward the A&P grocery, the quarter squeezed tightly in his fist.

Inside the store, he circled the check-out counter and took his place in line. As the customer in front of him talked with the cashier, Kenny toyed with his quarter on the checkout conveyor belt. Finally, the man said goodbye to the cashier and left.

She activated the conveyor belt, which caused Kenny's quarter to quickly roll down a crack inside the giant apparatus. He froze in place. A lump formed in his stomach. He was in trouble.

The cashier gestured for him to step forward to checkout.

"My quarter went down the crack," he said quietly as he pointed.

"Nothing I can do about it." She gestured for the next person in line to step forward.

"I got to have my quarter back," Kenny pleaded, nearly in tears.

The cashier ignored him and rang up the next customer's groceries.

Kenny was not sure how long he stood there in confusion while customers passed by him, but suddenly he looked up to find his mother staring down at him from the end of the counter. Her eyes flashed anger. "What's taking you so long?" she asked, her hands fisted on her hips.

The cashier looked at her and then at Kenny. "He lost his quarter down the conveyor belt."

Kenny stood speechless.

Virginia snapped her fingers. "Come on. We're going home."

Kenny ran to keep up. Even though losing the quarter was an accident, Junior would likely punish him.

Back at the house, Virginia took Kenny straight to the bedroom. There was no misunderstanding her rough actions and quick movements. She was angry. Normally, Junior would have filled the air with cursing and angry complaints, but this time he seemed unsure how to respond to Virginia's mood. That would soon change.

"Where's my cigarettes?" he called from the living-room chair.

"Get them yourself. Kenny lost your quarter." She let her tone rise, as she tossed pajamas on the bed for the boys. "Kenny, you help Steve get dressed for bed."

Kenny pulled Steve's wet clothes off of him and helped him dress in his pajamas.

Steve wiped his eyes and sniffed.

"Don't cry, Steve," he whispered. "We're going to bed now."

Steve's face crinkled up as his voice cracked. "Am I still in trouble?"

Before Kenny could answer, Junior appeared in the doorway. "Kenneth, you sleep in the bathtub tonight. That's the best place for you."

Kenny remained silent. Talking back was never allowed. But bedtime was welcome every night, because once in bed, he was free from Junior's oppression until morning.

"Don't make him do that," Virginia called from the other bedroom.

"You don't need to be doing his wet-bed laundry," Junior growled as he pointed at Kenny. "Leave them pajamas off, and sleep in your underwear. No sense getting your pajamas wet too."

Virginia came to the doorway. "If he wets the bed, I just won't wash his covers. He can sleep in his wet bed covers again."

Junior snapped his head around and glared at Kenny. "You heard what I said. You sleep in the tub in your underwear. Maybe, it'll teach you to appreciate a clean bed."

Virginia released a sigh and disappeared into her bedroom without another word.

Junior remained in the doorway and stared at Kenny a moment, his black eyes glistening like deep pools of water. "Get your brother in bed and turn out the light, and then you do what I told you. You hear me?" his voice low and gruff.

Kenny nodded. His heart beat heavy against his chest. "Yes sir." He finished helping Steve get his pajamas on and tucked the covers around his little brother once Steve was in bed.

"Wait," Steve whispered and stretched out his arms toward Kenny.

Kenny hurried back to the bed where he hugged and kissed his brother goodnight.

After he turned out the light, Kenny removed all of his clothes except for his underwear and then quietly made his way through the darkness into the bathroom. He climbed inside the porcelain tub and turned on his side. The tub was cold.

"You in the bathtub?" Junior called from the darkness.

"Yes." Kenny could not stop shivering.

"Let him sleep on that cot," Virginia said.

"I'm trying to raise that boy right, and he has to learn."

"He's only five. Little boys do have accidents."

"Accidents? He wets the bed every night. Why didn't Ronnie come back? I thought Edna was going to take those two."

Kenny curled up in the fetal position and crossed his arms as he whispered a prayer to Jesus. Only a few nights ago his mother had told him about angels and how Jesus sent angels to watch over each child. In Kenny's mind, angels frightened him, especially with their antlers.

When he had explained how he felt, his mother had laughed and assured him angels did not have antlers. According to her, they looked like normal people except for their wings. A few nights later, he opened his eyes to find two angels dressed in white at the foot of his bed. He screamed in fear, which brought his mother running.

"Angels will not hurt you," she promised. "They are God's helpers—like Santa's elves. Angels only do good things."

He believed her. No one had told him that Angels would be dressed in white, but he had seen them at the foot of his bed. They had seemed real, and whether they were his imagination or he had truly seen them, he never forgot seeing them that night.

As he shivered inside the cold tub, he squeezed his eyes shut even tighter and prayed for Jesus to send one of those angels to keep Junior from bothering him any more tonight. With his knees pulled up against his chest and his arms wrapped around his legs, he tried to get comfortable, but the tub was too cold, and he could not stop shivering.

Every time his parent's bed squeaked, the knot in Kenny's chest grew tighter for fear Junior was coming to punish him. He kept whispering prayers to Jesus until finally the world around him faded away, and he drifted off into sleep.

*   *   *

A NOISE AWAKENED KENNY in the middle of the night. He opened his eyes and nearly screamed. Someone dressed in a white gown hovered above him. He slid lower toward the foot of the tub and tried to make out the image in the darkness.

"Kenny?" the voice was only a whisper. "Go in the other room and sleep on that army cot. Keep quiet and tiptoe." It was his mother.

He climbed from the tub and quietly made his way through the darkness. The wooden floor creaked beneath his feet as he walked to the living room where she had placed the cot. The old army cot was a rickety wooden frame held together with a giant piece of stained canvas.

Face down on the canvas, he pulled his arms under his chest and closed his eyes. Without a cover, he was still cold, but the cot was warmer than the tub.

Sleep came quickly, and he did not know anything until Junior's resonant voice jarred him awake the next morning. "Get up. You've done it again."

Instantly, Kenny rolled off the cot and stood facing Junior, his arms at his side. He had moved so quickly, dizziness overtook him a moment, but even in his stupor he was aware of his wet underwear. A large puddle of urine was on the hardwood floor beneath the cot.

It was the same every night. He slept so soundly he never knew when he had to pee. He swallowed hard, not sure what Junior wanted him to do.

Junior pointed to the puddle. "Get down there and put your face in that." He spit his words out like poison. "You like to get punished, don't you?"

Kenny obeyed, but he did not reply to the question. The puddle of urine was cold and smelly.

"Get your nose in it." Junior put his foot on Kenny's head and pushed his face hard into the puddle. "Stay right there and don't you move until I tell you. You're getting a whipping for this."

Kenny remained perfectly still. Junior's footsteps retreated to the other room. The iron stove door squeaked, followed by the sound of Junior tossing chunks of coal inside the stove. A moment later, the rattle of the coal bucket and Junior's footfalls faded as he went outside and closed the back door.

Bed wetting always got Kenny in trouble. Many times, he had tried to stay awake at night, but it was impossible. He always fell asleep. He even refused to drink liquids, but nothing he did kept him from wetting in the bed at night.

Junior stomped back into the room, the floor shaking beneath his feet. "Where is the key to the coal shed?"

Kenny raised his head from the puddle. "I don't have it," his voice weak.

Junior stepped closer, his face scarlet and the two veins in his forehead pulsing. He swore graphically. "Don't tell me you didn't have it. It's not on the shelf where it's supposed to be, and you're the only one who fills the coal bucket. What'd you do with it?"

"I put it back on the shelf." He cringed as Junior moved even closer.

"You want me to give you a belting again? Stop lying to me."

Virginia stepped into the room. "Maybe Steve picked it up."

"Steve wouldn't bother it. He doesn't even know it's there." Junior turned and went back outside slamming the door shut behind him. Minutes later he came stomping back into the house again and did not stop until he approached the spot where Kenny was still prone on the floor, his face in the puddle.

"Get up," Junior said.

Kenny stood, trembling.

Virginia came into the room. "Now, what's wrong?"

"That kid left the coal shed unlocked." Junior cursed.

"Don't get so upset. He'll remember the next time."

Junior worked his jaw. "Someone stole all our coal. Every piece is gone." He grasped Kenny's arm and dragged him to the bedroom. "I've had enough of you for one day."

Kenny collapsed on the floor.

Junior pulled his belt from his waist and reached down for Kenny's arm. He was too late.

Kenny quickly slid under the bed out of Junior's reach.

"Get back out here, you—"he released a string of curse words as he knelt on the floor and reached under the bed for Kenny.

Kenny slid to the other side of the bed, out of Junior's reach.

Junior stood back up and hurried to the opposite side of the bed. He was too late again.

Kenny quickly escaped Junior's reach again by sliding back to the far side of the bed.

"Virginia, get in here and help me." Junior's voice held a ruthless edge that made Kenny's hair stand on end.

She came into the room and knelt on the opposite side of the bed where Kenny waited. She stretched out her hand. "Come here, Kenny."

Kenny yielded and went to his mother's arms. Virginia promptly handed him over to Junior who jerked him by the arm and dragged away from the bed.

Virginia left the room without a word.

Junior locked onto Kenny's wrist, and shook him like a dust mop as he went into a frenzy swinging the belt at Kenny's bare legs and back side, over and over again. All the while Kenny screamed and cried as if he was dying.

When Junior finally stopped, he dragged Kenny to the corner of the room and released him. "Stay right here in this corner and don't move until I tell you to."

Kenny sobbed uncontrollably. His body throbbed all over. The pain would subside, but the hurt in his heart was different. His mother had betrayed him. He wept several long minutes as his body shook from spasms of pain.

His mother often told him not to pay attention to Junior's cruel words, that he was just a rough talker, and he really didn't mean the things he said. At first, Kenny tried to believe her, but he finally realized she only said those things to make Kenny feel better. Junior made no secret about how he hated Kenny, but he never explained why he hated him.

Kenny tried to be good, but Junior always found a reason to curse and punish him. Every day, Kenny prayed for God to make Junior like him, but so far, nothing he did helped. The sobs faded, and without realizing it, he drifted off to sleep on the wooden floor.

*   *   *

SEVERAL DAYS LATER, Kenny's mother awakened him early. "Get up, we're going for a long drive," she said. With Steve on her hip, she took the boys outside and put them in the backseat of the car. Junior was already in the front seat waiting.

"Where we going," Kenny asked.

"To Daddy's new job. We're going to stay with him this week."

The drive took several hours and Kenny slept most of the way. It was barely daylight when they arrived at their temporary home. The house's broken window glass was covered with plastic, and the screen door was held by only one hinge. Junior carried the suitcases inside the house before he hurried back out to the car and sped away.

Kenny fell asleep on the old sofa in the living room until his mother wakened him for breakfast. "What kind of cereal do you want this morning," she called from the kitchen.

"I want Popeye cereal," Kenny said. He found a red rubber ball buried inside the sofa cushions. When he dropped it on the wooden floor it bounced and rolled behind the sofa.

He wiped the sleepiness from his eyes and crawled behind the sofa where he discovered the ball had rolled onto a piece of screen wire that covered a large hole in the floor. He crawled closer to reach the red ball.

"Let's eat breakfast," his mother called again. "I got your puff wheat—I mean Popeye cereal ready."

Kenny didn't get a chance to answer. Without warning, the screen wire gave way, and he dropped into the dark hole below the floor. With no time to cry out, he fell down, down, down until his feet caught on a narrow ledge inside the old well housing.

Too frightened to cry, he braced his hands against the side of the concrete pipe and looked down. The dark reflection of water stared up from the hole below. He turned his head upward until he could see the opening above him.

His mother was already on her knees staring down at him, her expression a mask of terror. "Jesus!" she cried. "Oh Jesus, please." She positioned herself flat on the floor and extended her arm down into the hole. "Grab my hand, honey. Be careful."

Kenny kept his legs spread apart and reached up as high as he could, but his mother's hand was too far away. Below him the twinkling dark eye of water blinked at him like an evil monster. How far down it was to the water he could not be sure, but he kept his feet planted on that narrow flange where two sections of the well housing were joined together.

If he moved, he would slip and fall into the mouth of the monster below. His heart pounded like a rabbit trying to get out of its cage. "Jesus help me," he whispered.

Suddenly, his mother disappeared from the opening, frantically praying for God's help. "God, I'll serve you with all of my heart if you'll save my boy. Please God, help me." Soon she reappeared and lowered a sheet down into the hole. "Kenny honey, grab onto this and I'll pull you up. Hold on as tight as you can."

Kenny grabbed the end of the bed sheet and held on tight. But when his mother pulled him upward and his feet began to lift from his secure perch, it frightened him, and he let go of the sheet. "I'm scared, Mommy."

"Try it again, and hold on tight. You've got to." After several failed attempts, she pulled the bed sheet back up. "Stay as still as possible while

Mommy gets help. Do you hear me?"

"Uh-huh." Kenny tried not to look down again. Everything went quiet. The clammy dampness around him caused him to shiver. After a moment, he could not resist glancing at the hole below him, which made the lump in his chest tighten. The reflection stared back at him like a one-eyed monster, and he feared the monster might reach up and grab him by the feet and pull him down.

"Mom?"

No answer.

He called out several more times, but the pounding footsteps he'd heard earlier along with her praying voice were gone. Tears rolled down his cheeks. Why had she left him? The words she had spoken a few nights before came back to him; "Jesus is always with you. You never have to be afraid, because he will take care of you and send his angels to protect you."

"Jesus," he cried. Tears blurred his vision as he closed his eyes. "Jesus, help me."

Finally, the sound of footfalls on the floor above gave him hope. Several voices talked at once. When he looked up, a stranger stared down at him.

The man reached down into the hole. "Hi Kenny." The man smiled. He did not seem afraid at all. "Don't worry. I'm going to get you out of there." The man extended his hand down toward Kenny. "Can you reach my hand?"

Kenny slowly reached up as high as he could, careful to not let his feet slip. The man's hand was too far away.

The man said something to those around him. "Okay Kenny, get ready. You'll be able to reach me now."

Two other men lowered the man upside down into the hole where he clasped onto Kenny's wrist. Slowly, they pulled the upside-down-man back up out of the hole along with Kenny. The man didn't release his grip on Kenny until he was safely away from the hole in the floor. Kenny spotted his mother on her knees with her arms outstretched toward him, and he ran straight into her arms.

"Thank you, Jesus," she cried. Her cheeks were wet with tears. She kissed him over and over and hugged him so hard he could barely breathe. After a moment, she released Kenny and thanked the men for their help.

"This old house should be condemned," one man said. "That hole needs covered up. If we can find some boards, I'll come back and nail them over that hole so this doesn't happen again."

"Thank you, but we're not going to stay here. My husband will take me back home tonight, and if he doesn't, then I'll take a bus. Who knows what else is wrong in this house."

The men all nodded. Each man patted Kenny on the head on his way out the door.

"Don't you worry, honey," his mother said. "We're not staying here any longer. We're going back home. I don't like this house at all, do you?"

Kenny shook his head. His mother had been right, Jesus had been with him in the well, just like she had promised. Jesus had answered his prayer and protected him. He decided right then he would always talk to Jesus every day. Maybe Junior would like him now when he heard how Jesus had protected him.

When Junior came home that evening, Virginia met him at the door and quickly explained what had happened. "We're not staying here," she said. "I'd rather sleep in a tent than to see my boys in danger."

"He shouldn't have been nosing around behind the sofa," Junior said. "Maybe this will learn him not to get into things."

"He's a child. Besides, why would they have a well under the house anyway?" Virginia asked.

"The house looks like that room was added on a long time after the rest was built. I'd say the well was in the front yard at one time, and they built the room right over it," Junior said.

"They should have covered the opening. Kenny could have drowned. I'm calling Edna again tomorrow. She'll keep the boys for us."

Junior nodded. "You're finally coming to your senses. That's the best idea you've had, yet. Tell her I'll pay her whatever she wants. I like kids, but that one is too much for me."

Virginia frowned and shook her head. "Admit it, you don't like kids at all."

At her insistence, Junior drove the family back home that same night. At bedtime, she insisted Kenny sleep on a pallet on the floor next to her bed. She reached down and held his hand until he fell asleep.

* * *

HAPPY FEELINGS BUBBLED inside Kenny's chest as he walked around his Aunt Edna's house. His parents had dropped the two boys off at her house early in the morning along with a box of clothes, and then they had both abruptly left while the boys were in the other room.

"Are you going to miss your mother?" Edna asked.

Kenny shook his head. "Steve will miss her.

"Won't you miss her?"

"Steve's the baby. But I'm bigger."

Everything was peaceful inside Edna's house, and it smelled good, too. Kenny walked into any room he wanted and no one said anything to him. If he wanted to sit in a chair, he could do it. He didn't have to sit on the floor in this house. From now on, he was going to pray every day that Jesus would never make him go back and live with Junior again.

"How old are you, boys?" Edna had a double chin that danced each time she turned her head or talked.

Kenny raised his open palm. "I'm five-years old, but Steve's only three. I'm going to be six pretty soon."

"Why didn't you bring your toys with you," Edna asked.

Kenny was silent a moment as he looked at Steve and shook his head. "We don't have any toys. Except, Steve has a doll."

Walter, Edna's husband, called from the other room. "I need your help in here, Edna. This bed frame takes two people to put it together."

Edna turned and went to help her husband. "We need an extra bed anyway," she said.

"How long we keeping them?" Walter asked quietly.

"As long as we can." Edna lowered her voice. "Virginia said Junior is mean to them—especially to Kenny. I'll adopt them, if she'll let me."

Walter laughed. "You're too close to retirement to raise another set of kids."

"I know, but as far as I'm concerned, this is just as much the work of the Lord as preaching a sermon on Sunday. Those boys will grow up to be just like Junior if somebody don't take them in. And we both know how awful that would be."

Walter nodded as he picked up a hammer and tapped on the bed frame. "Never saw a meaner man than Junior."

Edna stepped to the door way. "You boys want some cake?"

Kenny nodded and arched his brow as he looked at his brother.

Steve grinned.

"Let's go to the kitchen table. You like cake?" she asked as she picked Steve up and set him in a kitchen chair.

Steve rolled his tongue to the side of his cheek, but didn't answer.

Edna raised her hand in gesture for Kenny to take the other chair.

Kenny suddenly jerked backward. "What'd you jerk for?" Edna asked. "Nobody's going to hit you in this house. Does Junior hit you?"

Kenny stared at the yellow cake with chocolate frosting in the center of the table. He did not answer. He did not want to talk about Junior, and he hoped he never saw him again.

Aunt Edna cut two large servings of cake, which she placed on saucers and slid in front of each boy. Next, she poured two glasses of milk.

Walter walked through the kitchen and back again.

"You boys keep staring at Walter like he's the boogie man," Edna said. "Don't worry about him. Walter likes kids. You won't see much of him anyway. He works long hours at Cumins Engine factory. When he comes home, he so tired he usually sits in the recliner in front of the television until bedtime.

Edna went back into the other room. "You boys eat all you want," she called. "I'm going in here to sit down a while. I feel like a busted can of biscuits today."

Ronnie, Edna's son, joined the boys at the table. "Your mom make you cake at home?" Ronnie asked.

Both boys shook their heads.

Ronnie grinned. "You ever had cake before?"

Kenny lifted a shoulder as he stuffed his mouth with cake. "Don't remember. We had doughnuts before." The boys quickly gobbled up the cake on their plates and sat staring at the cake pan.

Ronnie laughed. "You want more?"

Kenny looked at his brother. "Steve wants more."

Ronnie called out to Edna. "Mom! They want more cake."

"Give them all the cake they want." Edna stepped to the doorway and grinned. "Those boys are happier than a two tailed puppy."

"Christmas is coming soon," Ronnie said. "What do you want for Christmas, if you could have anything in the world?"

Kenny answered immediately. "I want a hubcap."

"A hubcap? What for?"

"To play," Kenny said. "I want to be in the parade. He began to pound on the table with the palms of his hands.

Ronnie laughed. "You mean a drum. You want a drum for Christmas."

Kenny talked around his mouthful of cake. "When I grow up, I'm going to be in the parade, too."

The boys spent several months with Edna and her family, and Ronnie became like an older brother who always looked out for them. Kenny took care of Steve every waking moment and could not stand to be separated from him. He had never forgotten the day the man took his big sister from his mother's arms. She never came back again, but he thought about her and sometimes it made him cry. Steve was all he had left, and he did not want to lose him too.

The two brothers became the focus of attention among Edna's family, and their new home provided a temporary glimpse of normal life. The daily kindness everyone in the household showed the boys was something Kenny had never experienced. There was no yelling, never curse words, no slaps on the face, and no chores to do. He could laugh and talk anytime he wanted, and at mealtime, he could eat all he wanted. No one would say anything to him.

Just as important, he could go outside in the backyard and play—something he was never allowed to do before. All he had to do was ask Aunt Edna, and she would let him do anything he wanted. If he was hungry or thirsty, he had only to ask and she would fix him something, even if it was not mealtime. Uncle Walter treated him nice too, but Kenny never quite got over his fear of men.

The happy feelings often rose up inside Kenny's chest, but as soon he remembered how Junior might come any moment and take him away, fear returned and chased the happy feelings away.

That dreaded day came too soon for Kenny. Virginia and Junior showed up without warning and took the boys back home. A dark knot swelled up inside Kenny's chest, and he immediately grew quite. He did not want to go back home, and he certainly did not want to leave his Aunt Edna. Yet, he understood if he spoke his mind he would be in trouble with Junior.

Virginia and Junior took the boys to a new house where they had moved on Highway 31 near the railroad tracks. The new house had a large backyard, and Virginia promised that the boys could play outside sometime.

Junior was just as hateful to Kenny as he had been in the past, and Kenny quickly learned life was better if he stayed out of Junior's sight. Every day he continued to pray for Jesus to send him back to live with his Aunt Edna.

* * *

THE NEW HOUSE HAD A SMALL DESK in the boy's bedroom where Kenny learned to play office. He cut out grocery coupons from old newspapers, and pretended the coupons were money. That is, until Junior called out for Kenny to do something for him.

As soon as Junior called his name, Kenny had to immediately dropped everything he was doing and rush to stand at attention before Junior. To do anything less resulted in a reprimand—or worse. Often, Junior wanted a glass of water or milk. Sometimes, he wanted his cigarettes, but the most common request was to turn the television knob to a different channel.

It was completely different from life with his Aunt Edna. At her house he had not been made to do chores, and had not been required to wait on others; instead, Aunt Edna did things for him. He missed her, and he could not wait until the day came when he could live with her for good. Every day as he fell asleep he prayed Jesus would make a way for him to get away from Junior and go back to live with her.

Junior did not like to watch television, which meant he was often bored in the evenings. When he became bored, he turned his attention to tormenting Kenny. Junior had a disgusting prank where he made Kenny get on his knees and press his nose against Junior's buttock and wait until Junior released gas. Junior chuckled and acted as if it was funny, but Kenny hated it. He did his best to hold his breath, but he could hold it only so long.

Occasionally, Virginia tried to intercede for Kenny, but Junior always overpowered her. As soon as possible, Kenny always hurried back to his room and hid. It would take only a few minutes until Junior needed something again, and Kenny would run and stand before him to wait for his next instructions.

Junior was as short tempered as a rattlesnake, and he didn't care who knew it. According to him, the responsibility of raising another man's children was a curse. His most common complaint came from a newspaper article. According to the source, the cost of raising a child to age eighteen was almost fifty-thousand dollars.

"That's the reason, I can never get ahead," Junior growled. "And I've got two kids I'm paying for. That's fifty-thousand for each one." He told this story everywhere he took the boys.

Junior made certain Kenny fell into a routine of doing chores from morning to evening. Kenny was too small to reach the kitchen sink or stove, but Junior insisted he stand on a chair to cook eggs and wash dishes. By the time Kenny finished washing breakfast dishes it was nearly noon and time to repeat the process. Numerous chores gave Kenny little time for play.

Autumn arrived, and Kenny was old enough to enroll in first grade. This was the second time his mother had tried to enroll him in school. The first time, Junior informed Kenny he was putting him in boy's school where he would be kept prisoner. It frightened Kenny, because Junior described it as a terrible place where they kept only bad boys. It was not until years later that Kenny understood Junior's lie. It had not been a boy's prison at all; instead, it was a public grade school.

But now Kenny was finally old enough to begin first grade in public school, and he considered school as God's deliverance from Junior. For eight hours at school each day, Kenny escaped his enslavement and experienced a normal life among children his own age.

"Kenneth Allan, get in here."

Kenny's heart sank every time he heard Junior call his name. He hurried into the living room, his head hanging, his posture stooped. He didn't dare look up and meet Junior's eyes.

Junior pointed at the floor.

Kenny picked up a roll of toilet paper to clean the carpet where the dog had messed. Grandpa Lambert had brought two Cocker Spaniel puppies for the boys, but they were never house trained.

"As soon as you're done there, I want to you start washing those dishes in the sink," Junior said.

Virginia shook her head. "He can't reach the sink. I'll do them later."

Junior arched one brow. "That's what God gave us chairs for. The boy can make himself useful. I'm not raising no lazy brats."

"I'm cold," Virginia said, as if she wanted change the subject. "It didn't get as warm today as they said it would. Why don't you start a fire in the stove."

Junior nodded. "Soon as I finish this cigarette." He took a long draw and then exhaled. "Kenneth, go out in the garage and get that glass jug of kerosene by the door."

Kenny left his spot where he was scrubbing the carpet and hurried out to the garage. Two glass jugs of fluid sat side-by-side near the door. They both looked the same except the fluid inside one was darker than the other. Kenny chose one and took it inside the house.

"Set it by the stove," Junior said.

Kenny obeyed and then went to the kitchen and scooted a chair in front of the sink. He didn't mind working and doing chores, but Junior made it worse because he always tormented Kenny while he was working. Junior never talked to Kenny very long without telling him how much he disliked him.

If only he could live with his Aunt Edna. He planned to go back someday, because he had learned that Jesus answered prayers. If he did not go back soon, then he would escape from Junior when he was older. He would run away and live with Aunt Edna.

Junior picked up a few sticks of kindling and tossed them inside the wood stove. Next, he opened the glass jug and doused the wood with the fluid. After he placed the jug on the carpet near his feet, he struck a match and tossed it inside the stove.

Kaboom!

The house shook like an earthquake had struck it. In the blink of an eye, a giant light jumped from inside the stove to the floor like lightning. The room was quiet for several seconds.

Junior blinked his eyes and stared at Kenny a long moment. "What did you do? You dirty—" He released a long string of curse words as he beat at the embers burning his clothes. The fire had singed away his eyebrows until they were nearly gone. A washtub-size fire burned on the carpet in front of the stove where Junior had spilled the liquid.

Virginia hurried to the sofa where she grabbed an afghan and tossed it on the floor to smother the fire. Immediately, the fire ignited the afghan and grew even larger. She began to pray out loud as she stomped at the afghan.

Junior finally got his senses back. "Get everyone out of the house."

"You boys get outside," Virginia called.

Kenny walked to the door. "Come on Steve. We have to get outside."

Four-year-old Steve crawled under the kitchen table, hooked his arms around two of the chair legs and pulled them in close to himself.

Kenny refused to leave the house without his brother. "Come on, Steve. We have to go.

Steve only shook his head and stared at the growing flames in the living room.

"Steve. Come out of there," Virginia shouted.

Kenny dropped to his knees. "Steve," he talked softly. We have got to go outside right now."

Steve crawled out from under the table and took Kenny's hand. Together they walked out the door and down the steps into the garage.

Once the boys were outside, Virginia grabbed the burning afghan and dragged it across the floor through the kitchen and gave it a hard toss out into the garage. The afghan rolled under the car and kept burning. "Oh God!" she cried out, and ran outside to move the car. "The keys." She stopped mid-step and went back in the house.

Junior blocked her path at the doorway. "Get out in the yard, now." He followed her outside where he jumped into the car, started it, revved the engine and spun gravel as he backed the car out of the garage and away from the house. The afghan burned until the flame died down and left nothing but smoldering ashes.

Virginia scooped Steve up in her arms, took Kenny by the hand, and led them out into the yard near a cedar tree where they waited. "Should I go to the neighbors and call the fire department?" she shouted.

Junior didn't answer. He disappeared inside the house. After a few minutes, he came to the door and gestured for them to come inside. "The fire's out." He looked freakishly evil with his eyebrows burned away.

"And you young man are going to get a whipping." Junior waggled his pointed finger at Kenny.

Kenny's muscles stiffened. What had he done? The fire was not his fault. Why was Junior blaming him?

"We have to get the smoke smell out of the house." Virginia raised the windows. "What did Kenny do?"

"I told him to bring me the jug of kerosene, but he gave me the jug of gasoline. It's a wonder I wasn't blown completely out of the house." His dark eyes glared at Kenny like hot coals.

Kenny picked up the roll of toilet paper from the floor and walked passed Junior. When he did, Junior flinched as if he was about to slap Kenny.

Kenny cried out and stepped backward.

Virginia usually said nothing when Junior punished Kenny, but this time she spoke up. "He's a six-year old boy."

"He should have known," Junior said.

'You can't expect him to know the difference between gasoline and kerosene. "

"Gas and kerosene are two different colors. You can easily tell the difference just by looking at them." Junior nearly shouted.

"Then why didn't you notice it was gas when you picked it up?" she asked.

Junior gritted his teeth and glared at her a moment. Finally, he grabbed his cigarettes and lighter. "The landlord will charge us for this."

That evening after dinner, Junior sat on the sofa watching television while Kenny remained in the bedroom and cut out newspaper coupons. He sat at his desk deep in his imagination when he heard the dreaded call.

"Kenneth Allen, get in here." The sharpness in Junior's voice made the hair of Kenny's skin prickle. He immediately dropped what he was doing and hurried to the living room to stand before Junior.

Virginia sat curled up in the chair while Junior sat in the middle of the sofa wearing only his underwear. Steve played with his dolls on the floor.

When Kenny appeared, Junior stared at him a long moment like a cobra stares at a bird just before it strikes. "Go into my bedroom closet and pick out the belt you want me to whip you with."

Kenny swallowed back a flutter of panic but did not move or speak.

"Go. You have a whipping coming for what you've done."

"You can't whip him for that fire," Virginia said.

Junior cocked one brow and glared at her. "I'm whipping him because he wet the bed last night."

She sighed and looked down at her magazine.

"He does that on purpose," Junior said. "And he's going to learn to mind me. I'm going to break his stubbornness if it's the last thing I do."

Kenny swallowed against the now softball sized lump in his chest as he turned and walked to the bedroom to retrieve the belt. As he opened the closet door to choose a belt, he prayed for Jesus to help him. "Please Jesus, don't let it hurt so much. I'll try to be good. I really will."

Back in the living room, Junior took one last drag on his cigarette and stood. "Get in the bedroom and strip off all your clothes." He followed Kenny into the bedroom. As soon as Kenny was naked, Junior grabbed him by the wrist and began belting him on the backside and legs as Kenny danced and screamed for mercy.

When it was finally over, Junior tossed the belt on the floor and took several deep breaths as he stared at Kenny. "Put your underwear back on and get to bed. I don't want to see your ugly face anymore tonight." He left the room and shut the door behind him.

Kenny trembled as he put on his underwear and climbed into bed. The sobs did not stop for several minutes. He wasn't sure why he had gotten a whipping tonight, but he was grateful it was over. The soreness would worsen for another day or two and then it would begin to subside.

At least, he would have peace until morning, when Junior would call his name and make him get up and stand near the table. It was Kenny's job to pour Junior's coffee when he wanted it and retrieve his clothes for him.

At six years old, Kenny wasn't clear on exactly how Junior wanted things, and when he did something wrong, the normal punishment was a backhand across the face—usually a double slap. Kenny soon learned to allow his head to roll with each slap and not resist. It made the pain easier to bear.

Each morning at a specific time, it was Kenny's job to go to his parent's bedroom and waken his mother. He would then get her a cup and saucer from the cabinet and place them on the table along with the cream and sugar. As soon as she sat down at the table and Kenny poured her coffee, he would leave the room and begin his chores, which included making the beds, dusting, and sweeping the floor.

Virginia poured her sugary coffee into the saucer to let it cool before she sipped it. "I don't understand why you have to go back towards town every Friday night when Columbus is the opposite direction."

The beard growth on Junior's chin rasped as he rubbed it and looked away. "Because," he raised his voice. "I have to pick up Joe."

"But you said Joe moved to Columbus."

"He did, but he lives in town now."

"Why can't Joe drive here and meet you at our house so you can ride together from here?"

Junior's temper suddenly flared, and he slammed his hand on the table. "For God's sake woman, why do I have to explain everything to you? Don't you trust me?"

Virginia arched her brow and took another sip of her coffee. "Forget I said anything," she said quietly.

Junior cursed.

"I have to go get ready if we're going to town." She slid her chair back from the table and disappeared into the bedroom.

Kenny dusted in the living room and tried to stay quiet and unnoticed.

"Go make your bed and wake Steve up," Junior said.

Kenny hurried to the bedroom where the two boys slept. "Steve, it's time to get up." He helped Steve into the clothes he had worn the day before and followed him into the kitchen. At the table, he fixed Steve a bowl cereal and milk before he went back to his chores.

An hour later, the family was in the car where Junior was backing from the garage. Virginia picked up something from the floor board of the car. "Where did these come from?" Her cupped hand revealed a pair of large blue ear rings.

Junior's mouth fell open, but no words came out. He stuttered as if he'd been jabbed with a cattle prod. "I-I—"

"These are not mine. Who do these belong to?"

Junior stopped the car and turned in the seat. He looked as if he was searching for words but got lost in the search.

Virginia's eyes grew wide. "Let me out of this car right now. I don't want to go anywhere with you." She opened the door and reached into the back seat where she picked up Steve. "Come with me, Kenny. We're going back inside the house."

Junior backed from the driveway like a bank robber trying to escape the police. Virginia and the boys stood at the door and watched him spin gravel and disappear down the road. Tears careened down her cheeks unchecked. "You boys sit down on the couch and don't move. I'm going next door to use the telephone, and I'll be right back."

When she returned, she rushed around the house and gathered things, which she tossed on the bed. Kenny sat quietly and watched her stuff clothes inside a big suitcase.

Later, a car pulled into the driveway, and a stranger knocked lightly before he entered the house. He smiled at the boys before he looked at Virginia and shook his head. "Sorry this happened to you, Sis."

She swiped at the tears. "If we can just stay with you a few days until we get this worked out, I'll appreciate it. I didn't know who else to call. You've always been so nice to me and the boys."

"You've had it hard," he said and picked up her suitcase and took it out to his car. When he came back inside, the man approached the sofa and stuck out his hand. "Hi Kenny. You probably don't remember me, but I'm your Uncle Leon. You and your mom are going to stay with me and my family a few days. I have two boys your age, so you'll have a lot of fun."

Living at Leon's house was almost like living at Edna's house. There were no chores to do, no standing at attention waiting to attend to Junior's needs, and no whippings. Something happened inside Kenny's chest, which he could not understand. That happy feeling he had experienced at his Aunt Edna's home began returning. Life was normal—for a while. Jesus had answered his prayer and delivered him from Junior.

CHAPTER TWO

Satan had a plan, but God had a promise.

I will be with thee; ... when thou walkest through the fire, thou shalt not be burned; neither shall the flame kindle upon thee. Isaiah 43:2

THE HAPPY FEELINGS DID NOT LAST LONG, because it took only a few days until Virginia worked things out with Junior. She forgave him, and soon they were all back living in their old house with the big black scar on the living room carpet. Apparently, the few days away from Junior reminded Virginia of her former struggle and how financially difficult it was to survive with two young boys. Junior's extra-marital affair was never mentioned again.

From that point forward, Junior's go-to topic during conversation was about single women with children who lived off of government welfare, and how they were the outcasts of society. According to him, a woman could not make it on her own, and she should be grateful for a man to support her. If brainwashing really worked, then Junior's continual propaganda influenced Virginia, because never again did she seem inclined to escape her dysfunctional marriage.

Like a mistreated dog, Kenny remained quiet as possible and stayed out of Junior's sight unless his name was called.

His maternal grandfather often brought gifts for the boys. On two different occasions he brought them puppies. The last time he had visited, he brought both boys a big jungle-hunting outfit and left it under the tree for them to open Christmas day.

But on Christmas day, Kenny sat across the room and quietly watched Steve open his new jungle set. Inside was a plastic grenade, rifle, rubber knife, jungle hat and numerous other toys—a child's dream package.

Junior did not allow Kenny to open any of his Christmas gifts. According to Junior, Kenny had been bad and deserved to be punished. For several days, Kenny watched in silence as Steve played with his new toys, while his own Christmas gifts were stored unopened under the bed.

A couple weeks after Christmas, Kenny heard his mother call out his name. "Your Grandpa is here. You boys come in the living room."

December thirtieth was Kenny's birthday, and December thirty-first was Steve's birthday. Their grandfather always brought them birthday presents.

By the time Kenny got to the living room, Grandpa was down on the floor with Steve helping him open his birthday gifts. Grandpa grinned and gestured for Kenny to come over and give him a hug.

Kenny rushed into his grandfather's arms.

"I brought you present," he said.

Kenny glanced at Junior.

Grandfather pointed at two boxes on the floor and gestured for Kenny to open them.

Kenny looked at Junior and waited.

"Open it," Grandpa said.

Junior tipped his head. "Open it, boy."

Kenny knelt on the floor and tore into the packages. The first box contained a Tinker Toy set and the second contained a Lincoln Log set—the nineteen-sixties version of Legos®. No gift in the entire world could have made Kenny any happier. These two presents would become the creative outlet for his young imagination.

Grandpa helped him get the toys out of the boxes and Kenny played with them while the adults talked about frivolous things. Steve was soon bored and pulled out the big jungle box from where he kept it under the sofa. He began showing his grandfather all of his jungle weapons from inside the box.

Kenny worked to assemble pieces of the wooden Tinker Toy set. There were pieces of wood and dowel rods along with cardboard pieces to make windmills. Every few seconds he glanced at Junior to check his response and make certain he was not in trouble for playing with his toys. This was the best present he had ever received.

"Where's your jungle set?" Grandpa asked.

Kenny glanced at Junior again, but said nothing.

"Don't you play with it?" Grandpa asked.

Kenny looked at Junior.

"Bring it out here. Let's look at it," Grandpa said.

Kenny didn't move. He stared at Junior and waited for a response.

Junior canted his head toward the bedroom. "Go get it."

Kenny hurried to the bedroom and dragged out his unopened jungle set and carried it to the living room, a wide canoe-like grin on his face.

"You haven't even opened it?" Grandpa asked. "Don't you like it?"

"You haven't opened it, yet?" Junior echoed. "What's wrong with you child?"

Kenny didn't answer. Christmas had long past, but he knew he could not say anything about how Junior had not allow him to open his Christmas presents. But now as he opened the big box and looked at all the nice toys inside, a long sigh escaped his lips.

As soon as grandfather left, Junior sent Kenny and his toys back to the bedroom out of his sight. Kenny was not sure if he should play with his toys or put them away. Grandfather's visit had allowed him to open his gifts, but his peace did not last long.

"Kenneth Allen, get in here," Junior called.

Kenny hurried to the living room and stood waiting for direction.

Junior sat on the sofa. "Go out there and feed the dog."

A few days ago, Junior had brought home a full-grown German Shepherd named, King. They kept the big dog outside behind the house where he was tied to a tree with a heavy chain.

Kenny went to the cabinet and dipped out food from the big bag. Once outside, he dribbled food into the pan for the dog. King didn't like people to step into his territory, but he liked Kenny. The neighbors complained about the dog's aggressive nature, because their driveway passed alongside the backyard near the big German Shepherd. Each time the car passed, King went into a barking frenzy and lunged at his chain in an effort to chase the neighbor's car. Once he broke the big chain, but he never left the yard.

Junior followed Kenny outside. "Wait a minute." He sprinkled something over the dog's food.

"What is that?" Virginia asked. She carried Steve on her hip.

Junior grinned. "Gun powder. It'll make him more alert."

"You mean it'll make him mean," Virginia said. "Why in God's name do you want to make him mean? He's wild enough already." She rubbed the dog's ears and then went back inside the house.

Kenny took the dog's water bowl to the spigot where he rinse and filled it with fresh water. He liked King and didn't want anything to happen to him. He set the dog's water down and stepped back.

Junior slapped Kenny in the back of the head, and then kicked the water bowl over. "Clean that bowl out again. I've told you to always rinse it out good."

King growled and lunged toward Junior, but Junior was outside the reach of the dog's chain.

"I did rinse it," Kenny said.

"Don't talk back to me." Junior drew back his hand and glared. His eyes like burning glass.

King bared his teeth and growled again. The hairs on his neck stood on end.

Kenny backed closer to the dog. Trembling, he quickly picked up the water bowl and took it to the water spigot where he rinsed it numerous times before he filled it with fresh water.

Often, Junior lost his job and the family had to live on an unemployment fund. That meant he was home every day to torment Kenny. During the day while Virginia worked at the shirt factory, Junior's anger toward Kenny accelerated. In one way or another, he found different ways to torment Kenny.

One spring, finances became so tight the power company turned off the electricity to the house. This became a good thing for Kenny. With no lights, everyone went to bed earlier.

"What are we going to do about the milk and bologna we have left over from supper?" Virginia asked.

Junior was quiet a moment as he took a long draw on his cigarette. "Put them between the door and the screen door," he said. "It's cool enough outside that they'll keep."

"We got to have water to bathe."

Junior nodded. "Kenneth, get that bucket from under the sink and go knock on the neighbor's door. Ask them to fill it up for you."

"That's too far for him to carry a bucket of water," Virginia said. "He's only six."

Junior laughed and picked up his cigarette pack from the table. "He can cut across the field, and it'll be shorter. Besides, it'll make a man out of him." He snapped his fingers and pointed at Kenny. "Don't spill any of it either."

Kenny picked up the three-gallon pail and began to slip on his shoes.

"You don't need shoes," Junior said. "Quit stalling and do what I said."

Kenny left his shoes and went outside and started across the field between the two houses. Soon he had to stop. The ground was covered with cockleburs, and each step required him to search and find a spot with less of the prickly burs. It was nearly an impossible task, but Junior always insisted Kenny follow his exact instructions. Kenny learned long ago that any deviation from following Junior's instructions was always followed by punishment.

Finally, Kenny gave up, and with bucket in hand he walked back home and then walked along the edge of the road to the neighbor's house. The gravel at the edge of the road hurt his bare feet too, but it was not nearly as painful as the cockleburs.

The neighbor woman was nice, but inquisitive. "That bucket is a little big for you, young fellow. How old are you?" She set the bucket of water on the step.

"Almost seven."

"I didn't fill it full," she said.

"Thank you."

"How many of you live in that house?" she asked.

"Me, my brother, and Mom and Dad."

The woman shook her head. "With no electricity, and no water. Do you have food?"

Kenny nodded, "We're going to keep the milk and bologna between the doors at night." He picked up the bucket and started across the yard for the road.

"Why don't you wear your shoes, young man?"

Kenny looked down at his dirty feet. "My dad won't let me," he said softly.

When Kenny arrived with the water, Junior sat on the sofa puffing his cigarette "Looks like you spilled most of it even though I told you not to. Did you not hear what I said?"

Kenny placed the water bucket on the floor. "Yes sir."

"You'll just have to go back and get another bucket."

"That's enough for today," Virginia said. "He can go tomorrow."

"Don't argue with me." Junior raised his voice. "Take that other bucket and go back over there. Cut across the field this time. It's closer."

"But there's cockleburs in the field." Kenny said. "They hurt my feet."

Junior chuckled. "I don't care if they do. It's good for you."

Virginia picked up an empty bucket from under the kitchen sink and handed it to Kenny. "At least let him wear his shoes."

Junior arched one brow and pointed his index finger at Virginia. The room was silent for a long breath. "You heard what I said." His voice was soft and even.

A moment later, he turned back to Kenny. "Get over there and bring back a full bucket of water this time. If you don't, you'll have to keep going back until you get it right."

Crossing the field was a laborious and painful task. At times he had to stop and pick a cocklebur from between his toes. He wanted to cry, but tears would not come. When he arrived, the neighbor lady stood waiting on the concrete porch. "Why won't your dad let you wear shoes, honey?"

Kenny lifted a shoulder and didn't answer.

"Maybe I should carry this over there for you."

Kenny quickly shook his head. "I'll get in trouble. He said to fill it full this time."

"You can't carry a full buck. It'll be too heavy."

Kenny just stared down at his dirty feet and didn't answer, until the woman took the bucket and disappeared inside the house. "You want to come in and eat a cookie?" she called.

Kenny looked back at his house. From where Junior sat on the sofa, he could see Kenny through the window. "No, thank you."

A few minutes later, the woman brought the bucket of water outside. It was nearly full. "That's going to be too heavy for you."

Kenny thanked her and picked up the bucket. He had to walk slowly, because it was a lot heavier than before, and every few steps required him to stop to rest. Several times, he pulled the pointed cockleburs from his toes, but he did not spill much of the water this time.

Every day thereafter, Junior sent him across the field for water, and he always insisted Kenny go barefooted.

One evening a man came to the house in a big truck. Emmett was Kenny's maternal grandmother's boyfriend. From his parent's conversation, Kenny learned Emmett was already married to another woman. Bertha, his grandmother, knew Emmett was married, but she did not seem to mind.

Junior soon went to work for Emmett as a lineman for the electric power company. After a few days the electricity came back on in the house and Kenny was spared from making more trips across the cocklebur field. But Junior found other ways to vent his hatred for Kenny. Junior was an unhappy person, and Kenny become the source he used to vent his own internal anger.

*   *   *

FIRST GRADE WAS AMAZING. Kenny's teacher, Miss. Bell, was the most wonderful person in the world. Attending school was possibly the only thing that gave Kenny a glimpse of normality in life. For nearly eight hours a day, he was free from abuse and allowed to view the world from a different perspective.

Wetting the bed every night caused him more trouble than the devil himself. When he went to sleep, he always dropped into a deep pool of dreams in order to escape his real life, and he never regained consciousness until it was too late, and the bed was soaked with urine.

Junior insisted Kenny wet the bed on purpose and therefore deserved a whipping for each offense, which was nearly every night. He never showed grace or mercy, and his whippings always brought blood. Most of the time, Junior's instrument of punishment was a belt, but occasionally, it was an extension cord. Even so, no amount of punishment Junior inflicted could prevent Kenny from wetting in the bed.

"He likes to get whipped," Junior said.

"He does not." Virginia frowned.

"The kid's a masochist—he's one of those freaks who likes pain."

Virginia shook her head, but she learned to never interfere with Junior's punishment.

One day, Junior came up with his own special means of punishment. "You wear those wet pajamas to school today. Let the other kids see what you do. That'll teach you."

"Don't be silly," Virginia said.

"Do not argue with me."

"He can't go to school like that. He'll smell."

Junior's anger burst like a puffball underfoot. "Yes he can, and he will." He pounded his fist on the kitchen table for emphasis. "Once the other kids make fun of him, he'll stop his bed wetting. You watch and see if I ain't right."

Kenny stood horrified for a long moment. How would he explain himself to his teacher and his playmates? Miss Bell was nice to him, and he always got along with the other students, but now they would make fun of him and not like him. "I-I can't—"

Junior drew back his hand. "Don't you dare talk back to me."

Kenny's mouth was dry with tears. He'd rather die than wear wet pajamas to school. Miss Bell might even send him to the principal's office. Even so, he had no choice but to do exactly as Junior told him.

When he stepped on the school bus that morning, his pajamas were still damp and emitting the odor of urine. He could feel everyone watching him as he took his seat. Once seated, he closed his eyes, and prayed inside his mind. No one made any remarks about his smelly pajamas until he got to class and took his seat at his desk.

"It looks like you're wearing pajamas," a classmate said. "What happened to your clothes?"

Kenny lied. "These are new clothes my mom bought me. It's a new style."

"They look like pajamas," another classmate said. "They have bunny rabbits on them."

Kenny opened the lid of his desk to hide his flushed face. When he closed the desk top, Miss Bell stood over him. She didn't say anything, but the pitiful look she gave Kenny needed no words.

When the bus dropped him off at his house that afternoon, Kenny's day worsened. He went to the back of the house to feed King and found him lying on his side. His tongue hung out of the side of his mouth, his eyes glazed over. Kenny slowly backed away. He had never seen a dead dog before. The gunpowder had killed King.

Kenny liked school, and although weekends were a time of torment, he looked forward to Monday when he would get away from Junior. One day during a bathroom break before lunch one of the other first graders complained. "I'm sore today, because my dad whipped me last night."

"Yeah, my dad whips me all the time," another boy added. He pulled up his shirt. See I got a red mark where my dad hit me with a fly swatter."

Kenny turned away from the urinal and shook his head. "You guys don't even know what a bad whipping is like. I'll show you my marks." He raised his shirt and dropped is pants to show the bloody scabs on his legs and back. If wounds were something to brag about, then he would be a winner.

The boys suddenly grew silent. "Your dad did that to you?" one of the them asked.

"He does it all the time."

They quietly stared as if they were unable to move. Finally, one of the boys ran from of the rest room as if frightened. Seconds later, he returned with the principal. "Look," the boy said and pointed at Kenny who still stood with his pants down and shirt pulled up.

Principal Seville frowned. "Turn around, Kenny."

Kenny obeyed.

"Your father did this to you?"

Kenny nodded.

"Has he whipped you like this before?"

Kenny nodded again. "All the time."

"Are those marks from a belt?" Principal Seville asked.

Kenny shook his head. "Extension cord. But sometimes he uses a belt."

The principal blew out a puff of air and shook his head as if in disbelief. "Go on back to your class, Kenny. I'm calling your father to come in and have a talk with me."

Kenny did not realize what he had done until it was too late. Junior would be mad when the principal called him into the school. He might even give Kenny another whipping.

When Kenny got home from school that day, Junior had already met with the principal. Kenny stood at his bedroom door and listened to Junior explain to Virginia what had happened.

Junior laughed loudly for several seconds. "I pulled a fast one on him. I told that principal I'd let my temper get the best of me, but it was only one time. I promised him it would never happen again."

"Did he say anything about calling the police?" Virginia asked.

"Oh yeah. He was going to call the police right there during the meeting, but I saw he wore a Masonic ring. I gave him the Masonic Lodge handshake and told him us brothers had to stick together. The old man fell for it."

Virginia shook her head and looked down. "You're not even a Mason."

"I know. I just wear the masonic ring." He belly laughed again like a drunken man.

*   *   *

THE DAY WAS SOFT AND GRAY when Virginia loaded Kenny and his brother in the car. Kenny did not know where they were going, but Junior acted cheerful, and that was strange.

After they had driven a while, Junior turned into the long gravel driveway that led to an old farm house in the country. Not until they all went inside the house did Kenny discover it was his Aunt Edna's new house. She had moved from downtown Seymour to a rural area near Jonesville.

Virginia sent the boys outside in the backyard to play where Ronnie was chasing tame rabbits around the yard. Later, when Kenny came back inside the house, he discovered his mother and stepfather were already gone. A cardboard box full of their clothes sat on the dining room table.

Edna knelt on the floor in front of Kenny and explained how him and Steve would be living with her again. Kenny was glad, but he felt forsaken knowing his mother had left him again. He wandered around the house and finally went back outside where he stood behind the house and sobbed.

"I want my mommy," he said to Jesus. Tears flowed freely. He didn't understand his kaleidoscope of emotions, but he hurt inside. Freedom from Junior's oppression was a relief, but he felt alone and insecure without his mother.

"What are you doing out here?" Ronnie asked. "We've been looking for you. Come back inside the house with the rest of us. Your mom will come back to visit you. Don't you want to stay with us?"

Kenny nodded as he wiped his eyes and followed Ronnie inside the house where Edna sat on the floor entertaining Steve. Walter sat in the recliner watching a western.

"You boys want to get your bath and put your pajamas on so you're comfortable?" Edna asked.

Kenny lifted a shoulder. "Yes ma'am." A long sigh escaped his chest as reality set in that he was free from Junior's enslavement again. The fear in his chest seemed suddenly out of place, but he could not make it go away. How many days would he be free until Junior came back to get him this time? He did not want to know. For now, Jesus had answered his prayer, and that was good enough for him.

When Edna removed Steve's shirt, and pulled down the toddler's pants, she let out a laugh. "Where is your underwear Steve?" She looked at Kenny for an answer.

"We don't have underwear? Our dad says they cost too much money," Kenny said.

Edna wrinkled her brow as she shook her head. "Too much money?" You can't go without underwear." She stood and went to the other room. "Walter, did you hear that? These boys don't have underwear."

Walter shook his head. "I'm not surprised. We'll have to get them some."

Edna's farm house did not have inside water except for a pump on the kitchen sink. She produced a porcelain pan and let the boys wash up before bed, and then made a pallet on the sofa for them. Steve slept at one end and Kenny slept at the other.

The next morning Edna awakened them. "Get up boys, breakfast is ready."

Kenny sat straight up. Suddenly alert, his heart thumped against his chest. It took him several seconds to make sense of his surroundings. Like normal, he had wet the bed again. Now he was in trouble on the first day at his new home.

Edna stepped to the doorway, spatula in hand. A giant smile on her face. "You boys hungry?"

Kenny nodded and shook Steve until he sat up on the sofa beside him.

"What's wrong," Edna asked. "Are you scared of me?"

Kenny didn't answer. He stood and held the covers in front of his wet pajamas which clung to his skin.

Edna flipped on the overhead light. "Oh Lord. Did you wet the bed?"

Kenny nodded as tears rimmed his eyes.

Edna pulled the covers off the sofa and raked her hands along the sofa cushion. "Oh no," she groaned.

Kenny could not stop trembling.

"My couch is all wet," Edna said. "Steve, did you wet the bed too?"

Steve shook his head. "Kenny does it every night."

"Why didn't you tell me, and I would have put plastic under the covers. I thought you growed out of that."

Kenny stood stiff and stared, fearing the worst.

"You'll have to wash up before breakfast. I'll heat up some water and get you some dry clothes." She returned to the kitchen and pumped water into a pan and set it on the stove burner, all the while moaning in despair.

Kenny unbuttoned his pajamas. "Please Jesus, don't let me get a whipping today." He followed Steve into the kitchen where Edna had two plates on the table with two strips of bacon and an egg on each plate. Nearby, was a cup of milk for each boy.

"Walter's already gone to work," she said. "And Ronnie went to a friend's house, so it's just you boys and me today."

Kenny went to the back corner of the kitchen where Edna had set the pan of water for him to wash up. Why hadn't she said anything about whipping him? Would she wait and tell Junior?

As the months went by Kenny's bed wetting decreased, and he was never punished for his accidents. Even more importantly, Edna never made a big drama out of it.

"Those boys are not nearly as jumpy as they were when they first got here," Edna told Walter one evening. "Junior had them scared to death. Kenny's seven years old, and he acts like an adult. He's like an emotional cocoon. He won't hardly play with the other boys, and he keeps hiding. I never know where the child is unless I call his name, and then he comes running and stands at attention in front of me like some little servant boy."

Kenny stood outside by the porch window and listened to them talk.

"How much longer we keeping them?" Walter asked.

"Long as we can," Edna said. "Virginia never visits them and she hasn't called to check on them for months. I don't understand. It's not natural for a mother to forsake her children like that."

"I hope we can at least keep them until school's out. It wouldn't be good to move Kenny to a new school in the middle of the year," Walter said.

"Steve will start school in the fall, so I expect Virginia to want them back about that time," Edna said.

"Makes sense. She won't have to get a baby sitter with both boys in school."

Kenny walked around the house and entered through the back door. Edna was setting dinner plates on the table. "You boys come in and wash up. Supper's about ready."

On the table, Edna had catfish, fried potatoes and fresh vegetables from the garden. Everyone sat and waited until Walter said a prayer over the food. Ronnie was a teenager now, and he seemed to want to stir up competitiveness in everything he did. Soon he began arguing with Kenny over who was the tougher of the two.

Kenny knew he was no match for Ronnie, but he didn't want to admit it. He had found a straw of confidence since living with Edna, and it was difficult for him to succumb to Ronnie's dominance.

"Let's go outside and see who's tougher," Ronnie said as soon as supper was over.

Edna put the dishes in the sink. "You boys stop arguing."

Her words barely registered as Kenny followed Ronnie outside to the yard where they squared off ten steps apart. He didn't have a chance against his bigger cousin, but the words of his stepfather rang in his ears; "If you have to fight someone who's bigger than you, just pick up a club or something to make up the difference."

He spotted Ronnie's air rifle leaning against the corner post of the shed just within arm's reach. Kenny snatched it up and pointed it at Ronnie. "Come any closer and I'll shoot you."

Edna suddenly appeared at the door. "You boys stop that quarreling!" she shouted. "Kenny, you put that gun down right now."

Kenny shook his head. "No." He was already in trouble and might as well follow through with his threat.

"Kenny. Put that down right now and get in here."

He did not move.

"You boys should try to get along with each other," Edna shouted again.

Kenny hesitated, before he slowly lowered the air rifle and leaned it against the post and hung his head. "I'm sorry."

Ronnie was quiet a moment, and then he stepped forward and put his arm around Kenny's shoulder. "Don't worry, buddy. We're still friends." He ruffled Kenny's hair.

"You boys come back in the house. I got blackberry dumplings for dessert," Edna called.

Inside, things immediately went back to normal and Edna gave each boy a huge helping of blackberry dumplings with a large scoop of vanilla ice cream on top.

Living with Aunt Edna allowed Kenny to experience a side of life he barely knew existed. Ronnie guided Kenny around the old barn where they climbed into the loft and tried to catch chipmunks. When Aunt Edna was not watching, they played under the old apple tree where thousands of tin cans had been tossed through the years. Sometimes they even tormented the barn-yard goat, which the family kept for milk. And when they were bored they chased tame rabbits around in the back yard.

More importantly, every Sunday night Edna took the boys to the Columbus Apostolic Pentecostal church. A short, fiery preacher stood on the platform and waved his arms as he preached about God. Sometimes Edna allowed Kenny to go downstairs to the children's class at church where the teacher always had fun activities prepared.

On Saturday afternoons it was always Kenny and Ronnie's job to go into the chicken house and catch a big hen for Sunday dinner. The chickens were too wild to approach, but Ronnie taught Kenny how to bend a narrow hook on the end of a long stiff wire and hook a hen's leg. Once caught, the hen was taken to the back yard and executed.

The boys accomplished the execution by placing a broom handle across the hen's neck and standing on the wooden handle while at the same time pulling up on the hen's feet until her head popped free. The second boy stood nearby with a large galvanized tub ready to catch the headless hen and keep her from flopping around the yard and getting dirty. It was a nasty job, but at the time none of the boys seemed to know it.

Occasionally, the headless hen would get away and the boys had to chase her around the yard until they could trap her under the tub.

Ronnie also taught Kenny how to catch crayfish from mud puddles in the dirt road. Their only tool was a small scrap of board which they pushed down to the bottom of the mud puddle and held it there for a full minute. Once they let go of the board, it floated to the top and revealed dozens of crayfish scrambling to get back into the water.

Of all his childhood experiences, the one Kenny treasured the most was the overnight fishing trip on the home-made houseboat. He was only seven years old but Walter and the older men took him along and let him fish with them on the river. The memory became even more special when Kenny caught an eel on his fishing pole.

All of these experiences were like gifts of love from Edna, Ronnie, and Walter, and they left a tremendous impression of what life was really like. As he grew older, these experiences were always in the back of Kenny's memory, and they became a standard of how life should be lived. It gave him hope that someday his Cinderella life would end.

Late in the summer, on a sunny afternoon, Kenny was out in the field helping Walter clean out a fence row when Ronnie brought bad news. "Your Mom and Dad are here to pick you up, Kenny."

Dark shafts of fear shot through Kenny's chest and kept him parallelized. He was unable to move for a long time. "But ... I don't want to go home," he said quietly.

"You have to. They're waiting on you now," Ronnie said.

"No. I can't." Kenny could not move.

"They have your clothes already loaded in the car. I'm supposed to bring you back to the house. Come on or I'll get in trouble."

Kenny glanced at Walter who was working farther down the fence row. He wanted to cry and wail in complaint, but he knew it would do no good. Finally, he released a long sigh and dropped the grass whip he had been using. A lightning storm of images flashed through his mind as he followed Ronnie back to the house.

Virginia and Junior stood on the porch waiting for his arrival. They both wore wide smiles, which seemed out of place at the time. Kenny could not make himself smile in return. When he did not run up to his mother and hug her, she stepped from the concrete porch and hugged him. "I missed you boys. Are you ready to go back home?" she asked.

Kenny lifted a shoulder and looked at Edna. He felt as if he had swallowed some explosive mixture that was eating away at his insides. He had no choice in the matter. He understood that much.

Edna's family had been extremely good to Kenny and Steve, and he had hoped to live here with her family forever. As he left the house and walked to Junior's car, it seemed like a foggy bad dream, where he was marching to a the gallows to be hanged.

Inside the car, Junior's voice cut through the haze in Kenny's brain. "You boys glad to get away from this hillbilly, white trash?"

No one answered.

A slow tear worked its way down Kenny's cheek.

CHAPTER THREE

In heaven, God will not look us over for medals, but scars.

Fret not thyself because of evildoers, neither be thou envious against the workers of iniquity. For they shall soon be cut down like the grass, and wither as the green herb. Trust in the LORD, and do good; Psalms 37:1-3

BACK AT SEYMOUR, Junior pulled the car in front of a house I had never seen before. The house had been built close to the neighboring house, and the front porch was unusually small.

This is our new home," Mom said as we got out of the car. "This is Fifth Street and Riley Grade School is only a block and a half away. You'll be able to walk to school instead of riding the bus."

"It's got two front doors?" Steve said.

"It's a duplex," Mom said. "The house is divided into two parts. The people who own the house live in one half, and we live in the other half."

"It's a shotgun house," Junior said. "Each room is built behind the other."

We entered through the front door and stepped into the living room, but we could see straight through the house to the opposite end.

"Where we going to sleep?" Steve asked, once they were inside.

"You boys will sleep in the living room. The couch folds down into a bed." She demonstrated. "See how it works?"

We were never allowed to play outside, which resulted in us spending most evenings in front of the television. The sofa and chairs were seats for the adults. Us boys always sat on the floor, and often we fell asleep while watching television. Sleep was an escape for me, and I usually had difficulty coming back to the real world when I awakened.

"You boys get ready for bed," Junior said. "and Kenny, you lock the front door."

Steve shook me awake.

I stood and wobbled a moment as I stared at Junior. "What color do you want me to paint it?" I asked.

"I said to lock the door." Junior pointed at the door.

I nodded. "Okay. What color?" Frustration beat a heavy rhythm in my temple. This went on for a long minute or two while the family laughed at my confusion. Finally, I awakened enough to understand Junior's instructions. I locked the door and then stretched out on the floor where I immediately fell asleep again.

Without warning, my world instantly came alive again with me howling in pain. I jerked my legs up under me and curled up into the fetal position. Junior had burned the arch of my foot with his lit cigarette. Wide awake now, I cried and rubbed my blistered foot.

Junior leaned back in the chair and belly laughed almost uncontrollably.

Mom shook her head and turned off the television. "That's uncalled for. Why did you do that?"

"Don't get so alarmed," he said. "I didn't hurt him. I was just having a little fun."

She glared at him a moment as if deciding whether to argue with him or not. Finally, she cast a scolding sideways glance at him and disappeared into the bedroom.

This was the year I started third grade, and I loved Miss Keifer, my teacher. She was nice all the time. She not only made class fun and interesting, but she also walked across the street to the corner grocery and purchased Popsicles for the entire class during recess. It was a special treat for the class, but even more so for me, because we never had snacks or treats at home.

During recess at school, I kept to myself, because I was not good at making friends. While other children played board games in the classroom, I spent my time copying words from a novel onto a personal notebook. It was a long laborious project, but I kept at it, and Miss Keifer seemed pleased to see me so diligent in working on my penmanship. My intentions were to present the notebook to Miss Keifer once I finished writing out what I called my novel.

Each morning Miss Keifer had a special song time for the students. The class's favorite was the donkey song. While singing the song, the entire class would stand and demonstrate donkey actions.

I hated the donkey song.

In the middle of the song Miss Keifer taught us to stand and sing loudly; *this is the way a donkey talks, he-haw, he-haw, he-haw.* It was here the class raised their arms and drooped their hands like a begging dog, and at the same time squatted midway to the floor with each *he-haw*.

All of the other students liked acting out the song, but I was embarrassed to act like a donkey. Junior often called me a jackass, which let me know it was a demeaning term. I certainly wasn't about to act like one.

Miss Keifer called me aside. "Why don't you sing with us, Kenny? Don't you like that song?"

I looked down and didn't answer.

"I want you to sing with the rest of us, okay?"

I nodded and went back to my seat, emotionally wounded. I picked up my notebook where I had copied dozens of pages from the novel and tossed it all inside the metal trash can. The hours of work I had spent on the project didn't matter anymore. I gave up.

"Kenny? Why did you throw your book away?" Miss Keifer asked. "I wanted to read it when you were finished."

I didn't answer. I just sat in my seat and stared at the wall. This was the first indication of a pattern that stuck with me for many years. My method for dealing with frustration was to give up on things.

Nearly every day Junior told me how I was worthless and no good, and how I would never amount to anything. I tried my best to not believe him, but every time I faced a problem, I always remembered his words and give up.

Afternoons at school were the worst times for me. Foreboding always chased down my spine as I watched the clock approach three-twenty—the time when they dismissed school. It was then I had to go home and face Junior for the rest of the evening. Even later into adult life, a foreboding often settled in my chest as three-twenty in the afternoon grew near. I was like Pavlov's dog, only the school clock was the ringing bell.

Most evening, Junior and Mom sat long hours at the kitchen table where Junior dominated the conversation. Mom quietly listened to stories of his past conquests and victories at his work place. Usually, he sat around the house naked except for his white briefs. When he did wear a shirt, it was a handlebar T-shirt. Fortunately, neither parent drank alcohol, but Junior's chain smoking kept a haze of smoke hovering inside the house.

While I tried to stay in the shadows and be unobtrusive, Steve was quite different and spent his time as near the adults as possible. He played house and other imaginary games on the kitchen floor near our parents, and often he played under the kitchen table where they sat.

I always wore my shirt and pants when possible, but at times Junior made us boys parade around the house wearing only our underwear. He blatantly fondled my brother's bottom and talked nasty to him, but he never touched me in that way. No one in the family seemed to think there was anything abnormal about Junior's actions, because it had always been that way. Occasionally, Mom reprimanded Junior, but her scolding never changed anything.

School holidays were dreadful for me because I had to stay home with Junior. Those weeks when he was laid off from his construction job were even worse. When Junior had nothing to do, he turned his attention to tormenting me.

Profanity, the language of the ignorant, was always a large part of his vocabulary. He never spoke more than a sentence or two without using the most vulgar curse words possible. Not only did it make me feel uncomfortable, but at times Junior required me to use profanity, too. "I'm not raising no sissies," he would say.

Smoking cigarettes and chewing tobacco were not only acceptable habits in our house, but they were also Junior's preferred standard. I refused to even try smoking, and fortunately my mother took my side.

Our three-room apartment didn't allow many places for me to hide from Junior, because the bedroom was off limits most of the time. When my parents were in the kitchen, I found an excuse to stay in the living room and vice-versa. Usually, Junior kept me busy with chores, and eventually, I learned to volunteer to do extra chores, because it was better to control which chores I did rather than to wait for Junior to find something for me to do.

One afternoon during summer break, us boys were home alone with Junior, and we were hoping he would take a long nap. He was laid off from his job and Mom was at her job at the shirt factory. Junior announced it was time for his afternoon nap. I always prayed for God to make his nap times to start early and last long, because during these times I had a reprieve from his tormenting. Today was different.

"You boys come in here and take a nap with me," Junior said.

When I stepped into the bedroom, Junior was already in bed, completely naked, with only a sheet pulled partially over him.

"And take your clothes off," he ordered. His voice gruff and loud.

Steve removed all of his clothes and climbed into bed beside Junior. Something fell off the shelf inside my brain, and I hesitated. My first thought was to run out the door, down the street to the police station and plead for help. But I feared the police would not believe an eight-year old. Junior had always drilled into my mind that the police were against me, because I was such a bad boy.

I stalled as long as possible, but I finally had to remove my shirt and pants. I slowly approached the bedside, my legs trembling so much my knees nearly knocked together.

"What do you have them underwear on for?" Junior snapped. His voice hateful. "You don't have to wear underwear every time you go to bed. Get them off."

I trembled as I obeyed and quietly slid under the sheet next to my naked stepfather. I prayed inside my mind as I had never prayed before. Many times, praying to Jesus had saved me from trouble, and now prayer was my only source of help.

Within seconds Junior began snoring. He had fallen asleep almost instantly. Jesus answered my prayer that day and possibly altered my life. I released a pent up sigh and could not stop thanking Jesus for his help. It was a day I never forgot.

Years later, I learned that the landlord and his wife who lived in the other half of the duplex attended an Apostolic Pentecostal church. Perhaps their prayers were also instrumental in my deliverance.

*   *   *

JUNIOR WAS GONE SEVERAL DAYS of the week on his new job, which was like a vacation for me. Even Mom seemed to enjoy the evenings better without Junior. But the good times did not last long. Soon his job relocated him where he could be home every night. Apparently, his new job also included a pay increase, because he moved the family from the old duplex to a nice Bedford-stone apartment on Carter Boulevard.

Since he was always angry with me, I never saw a difference between his good moods and bad moods. But Saturday was go-to-town day for both parents, which resulted in a few hours of reprieve for me.

Junior called me to the table where he sat drinking coffee. "I want you to get a bucket of soap and water and start scrubbing the walls," his tone sharp. "Start there in the hallway, you hear me?"

"Yes sir."

"Don't just stand there, get moving."

I grabbed a bucket from under the kitchen sink, filled it with warm water, and carried it to the hall where I sprinkled in a heavy dose of cleanser. I dipped the scrub brush inside the bucket of water and began scrubbing the wall like Junior had instructed me.

Soon he was hovering over me like an angry Marine sergeant. "Scrub it all the way up to the ceiling."

"I can't reach it."

He boxed me on my right ear. "Use your head and get a chair to stand on, you idiot."

Mom came into the hall. "We're going to town. You boys be good while we're gone."

"Let's take Steve with us," Junior said.

The wings of my heart lifted, knowing I'd soon be alone for a couple hours. I kept scrubbing the wall until I heard the door click shut behind them. When I heard the car doors close and the car engine start, I released a long sigh and began to pray intensely for God's help. "I haven't done anything wrong, God. Why are they mad at me? Help me do better. Make them not mad at me. Please."

I went to the refrigerator to find something to eat. Normally, I wasn't allowed to eat like the rest of the family. Usually, I had to wait until Junior was finished eating and moved from the kitchen table to the living-room chair, because in his words, "I don't want to see your ugly face while I'm eating."

Powdered doughnuts were Mom's favorite, but us boys weren't allowed to eat them. Any candy in the house was usually meant for Steve unless I managed to sneak a stash for myself. I finally settled on bologna and crackers. I took only one slice of bologna and returned the package exactly as it had been placed in the refrigerator to prevent Junior from noticing it had been moved.

Later, when the family returned, I was still scrubbing the same wall, and it didn't look any cleaner than it did before I began scrubbing. The intensity of Junior's anger increased without reason, and he began to curse and ridicule me, accentuated by an occasional slap in the face.

Steve sat on the sofa opening a new toy Junior purchased for him. Mom stood removing tags from a new outfit they had purchased for Steve. They wanted to take him back to town and parade him around the downtown streets in his new sailor outfit.

When they returned, most of their conversation that day was about how people had made over Steve and how cute he was in his new sailor outfit. I held no animosity against Steve. He was my baby brother and I loved him. But I knew my birthday was coming up soon, and although Mom never made a big deal out of our birthdays, she usually baked us a cake and purchased some trivial present for us.

The following week I was arguing with Steve while our parents were at work when he ran into the bedroom and shut and locked the door.

"Let me in," I shouted and kicked the door. "Let me in right now or

I'll break this door down."

Steve taunted me. "Leave me alone. I'm not letting you in"

"Come on, let me in." I kicked the door again, harder this time. When I did, the toe of my shoe went through the door. I stared in shock a moment. My pulse beat fast in my veins. I knew Junior would not only give me a whipping when he got home, but his intense anger would last several days.

"Steve. Open the door. I'm in trouble."

"Why?"

'I just kicked a hole in the door."

"You're lying."

"I'm not lying. Open the door."

After a moment of silence, Steve slowly opened the door, not sure if I was trying to trick him or not. "Oh no," he said slowly. "Dad will be mad."

"Oh God, help me," I pleaded aloud. "Please God. I am sorry for all the things I did wrong." I went to the kitchen and grabbed a butter knife and tried to pry the broken pieces back into place, but nothing I did made the hole in the door look any better. There was no hiding my sin either, because our bedroom door faced the bathroom, which meant Junior would notice it right away. I was doomed.

As soon as Mom walked through the door that evening, I confessed what I had done and showed her the hole in the door. She shook her head and arched one brow. "You're going to get a whipping for this young man. That door will cost us a lot of money to replace." Her eyes flashed anger. "Why can't you be good? You're always doing something. What am I'm going to do with you?"

I was quiet the rest of the evening, and prayed inside my head while I did my chores. Only God could help me now. Notwithstanding, I knew I deserved punishment. I was guilty, and this was not an isolated incident. I often did things that deserved punishment, but thankfully, I got by many times without getting caught.

When Junior came home, I stood at the kitchen stove frying potatoes and praying as I waited for the best moment to tell him what I had done. Junior was predictable. Every night he went through the same sequence without fail.

First, he removed his hat and handed it to me, then he sat in the kitchen chair while I unlaced his work boots and removed his shoes and socks. Finally, he would take off his shirt and pants and I would remove the belt and wallet and place them in the proper spot on the corner of the counter.

After I had put the pants and shirt in the laundry, I said one last prayer and approached the kitchen table where he sat. "I have something to talk to you about," I said in a straightforward adult manner.

He shot me a sideways glance. "What is it?"

"I kicked a hole in the bedroom door today."

He glanced at Mom and then back at me as he lit a cigarette and squinted his eyes. "How'd that happen?"

"Steve locked me out of the bedroom and I was trying to get inside." I sucked in a deep breath and continued. "It was my fault. I'm sorry, and I know what I did was wrong. I deserve a whipping for what I done, and I'm ready for it right now." I could hardly keep from trembling, knowing what was coming.

God answered my prayer, and my straightforwardness took him by surprise. The makings of a grin passed over his face for an instant and then quickly disappeared. He stood and walked to the bedroom to examine the door, and then returned to his seat. "Don't you have chores to do?" he said in his usual gruff tone.

I turned and began washing dirty pans in the sink, not really sure what had just happened. Apparently, my adult-like manner surprised him so much he wasn't able to administer the punishment I deserved. Once again, I prayed my way out of trouble, and he never mentioned anything about punishment for the hole in the door.

"We got a call from your fourth-grade teacher," Mom said.

My heart flipped in my chest. I was aware of a long list of things I had done at school.

"He wants us to meet with him. What did you do at school that got you in trouble?"

I shook my head. "Nothing. I didn't do anything." Both parents quizzed me about the meeting, but I had no idea what the meeting was about. Not that I had a clean slate. Quite, the contrary. But I was not about to give up information for something I had done and then the teacher inform them of a different sin I had committed.

My main worry was that he'd tell them I was leaving school each day. I was supposed to eat lunch at school in the cafeteria, but I always left the school during lunch hour. Since the school was only three blocks away, I told my teacher I was walking home to have lunch with my mother. I never went home.

Instead, I used my lunch money to buy a pint of ice-cream, which I took to a wooded lot near our house and ate it. The entire pint of ice-cream would be gone before I went back to school. Two days of ice-cream used up all of my lunch money for the entire week, but it was worth it.

That evening, I stayed home while my parents attended the meeting with my teacher, Mr. Lane. When they returned home, Junior called me to the kitchen table and made me stand within arm's reach while he began a long reprimand. "You're a thief and a liar."

I kept silent.

"You stole erasers from the other student's desks."

I shook my head. "I did not." I had stolen a few times; once from my grandmother's pocketbook and another time from the grocery store, but I had never stolen anything from school.

"What did you do with the erasers," Junior asked.

I wagged my head in defense. "I don't know anything about it." It would have been easier to give up the stolen erasers if I had them, but this was one time I was innocent.

The reprimand went on for several minutes until finally, Junior sent me to bed without dinner. I was hungry, but going to bed was a relief. I prayed for God to help me, and finally I drifted off to sleep.

Every day Junior treated me roughly and chided me, usually with comments like; *You'll never amount to anything. You're ugly just like your father, and you'll be in prison before your sixteen years old.* His demeaning talk was usually accompanied by long strings of cursing and name calling and punctuated with him backhanding and slapping me. In addition, he required me to always maintain eye contact when he spoke to me. Eye contact seemed very important to him.

That night, I barely slept, because my skin itched all over. When I awoke the next morning, little red bumps covered my body, and I could not stop scratching. My body felt like it was covered with an army of stinging ants. I examined myself in the mirror, and discovered my face was covered with the little red bumps, too.

Mom nodded when she examined me. "You've got chicken pox. It's going around. You'll be okay after three or four days."

I didn't feel okay. My body felt miserable. But even though I was sick, my parents never allowed me to have any relief from doing my chores, nor was I allowed to spend any extra time in bed. In all fairness to them, keeping me busy was possibly their strategy to keep me out of trouble.

School was out for Christmas break, which prevented me from miss-ing school over the chickenpox. The little red blisters drove me to tears as it took more than a week to heal.

A few days later, Steve woke up with the same condition. Like me, his back, chest, and face were covered with the red blisters. "He's got them bad," Virginia told Junior. "I think we should take him to the doctor."

Junior agreed and they loaded Steve in the car and left. A couple hours later they arrived back home, where they gave Steve his medication and put him to bed.

Life at home would not have affected my mind so much if my parents had shown me an occasional time of love and affection to counter balance the hatred. But there were no such times. In spite of the hateful world around me, I somehow learned that Jesus was my friend, and I always looked to him for help to rescue me from the evil I faced each day.

Although, I did not deserve his help, he often came through in a miraculous way. There were times when I accidentally broke something and knew I would be punished, but neither parent discovered my mistake. Many times, I simply stood in the living room and begged God to make my parents afternoon nap last for hours. Often, my prayers worked, and God granted me a short reprieve.

*　　*　　*

I KNEW IT WAS WRONG TO STEAL, but at nine-years old I discovered stealing along with lying were survival tools. Soda bottles were worth three cents at the grocery, and a frozen cream pie was only thirty-three cents. I worked hard at collecting soda bottles to return to the store, and it became a profitable way to make personal spending money for candy.

Often while running grocery errands for my mother, I found soda bottles tossed carelessly in the ditch along the road, and I collected and turned them into the grocer for a bottle deposit refund. Another time, I cut through an alley in town and discovered a hoard of bottles on a home owners back patio. I stole some of them and sold them at the grocer. I knew it was wrong, and although I did it only twice, the sin never left my mind.

A few times, I collected enough soda bottles to buy an entire case of candy bars. I took the candy home and hid the box in the garage where I could nibble on it every day.

We typically never had ice-cream or snacks at home, and one day when I had no money I mustered enough courage to steal an ice-cream bar from the neighborhood grocery. After making certain the man in the deli department was not looking down the aisle in my direction, I raised the cooler lid and quickly tucked a sprinkle-coated strawberry ice-cream bar inside my waist band. I pulled my shirttail over it and headed to the counter where I paid for the items Mom had sent me to purchase.

Outside the store, I straddled my bicycle to go home with the strawberry-sprinkled ice-cream bar on my mind.

"Don't you think you should pay for that ice-cream, young man?"

My heart skipped a beat as I gripped my bicycle's handlebar and turned toward the voice. "What?"

The man filling the soda machine outside the store was balding and wore a white apron heavily stained from use. "That ice-cream bar you stole, don't you think you should pay for it?"

I swallowed hard. How had the man known? "I-I'll go back inside and pay for it."

"Not so fast, young man. What's your name?"

"Kenny Noble. I'm sorry. I shouldn't have done it."

"What's your phone number?"

I told him before I realized I could have easily given him a false number.

"You can go to jail for stealing, you know."

"Yes sir. I should not have done it."

"You think your parents are going to be happy about what you've done when I call them?"

Fear wrapped itself around my heart like steel bands. "Please don't call my parents, sir. I'll never do it again, I promise. Please." Tears ran freely down my face.

"I'm obligated to call them. I wouldn't be doing the right thing if I let this go."

"Please mister, please. I have a stepfather who hates me, and he'll kill me if you call him. I mean really, he will kill me. He tells me all the time he wishes I were dead." I was not exaggerating, because I honestly believed Junior wanted to kill me.

The man closed the soda machine and locked it. "I doubt if he'll kill you, but you have done a bad thing."

I interrupted him. "I won't ever do it again, I promise. I'm begging you, please don't tell on me."

"Wish I could believe you." He fisted his hands on his hips and stared at me for a long moment. "I'll think on what you've done and decide whether to call your parents or not, but you better never steal from anywhere again. Can you promise me that?"

I nodded as I wiped tears and then raised my right hand. "I swear to God, I will never do it again."

The man let me go, and all the way home I began praying like a revival preacher. For several days, each time the phone rang, I feared it was the grocer calling to tell my parents what I had done. But the call never came, and I avoided going back to the little grocery as long as possible.

October brought a special freshness in the air for me. At nearly ten-years old I decided my life would be much better if I lived by myself in the forest rather than with Junior. The thought lingered in my mind for several days, and the more I thought about it, the more I liked the idea. I was confident I could take care of myself. After all, I was already doing most of the cooking, and laundry for the family at home, so I could certainly survive living on my own.

Once I made the decision to leave, the wings of my heart soared like never before. Freedom from Junior was always the utmost goal of my life. I was not exactly sure where I would go, but I planned to hide out on the river bank for a few days, and then jump on a passing train and ride away to another state where I could live uninhibited in the mountains until I was an adult.

On the day I left home, Junior gave me money to go to the post office and purchase a six-dollar money order. He had to pay alimony every month from his first marriage, and at that time six dollars was approximately a half-day's pay. Since I would never have to give account to Junior again, I decided I would enjoy a new toy of my own before I left home.

Downtown, I took the six dollars to the hardware store and purchased an army-type play gun and brought it home. It made a popping noise when shot and had its own grenade launcher. I played with it a only few minutes before I began packing my clothes to leave. Junior would be fighting mad, and I cringed to think of his anger. But this was one time he would not be able to punish me. Even worse, I had not done any of my chores that day.

Finally, I picked up my bag of clothes and told Steve goodbye for the last time. I had thirty minutes before Mom came home from work, and even though Steve was only seven-years old, I was confident he would be fine by himself for a few minutes. As soon as I walked out the door, a tremendous joy swelled inside my chest.

* * *

I WAS SUDDENLY LIVING A NEW LIFE, and I laughed loudly "Free. Free." No more reprimands from Junior. No more name calling. No more bloody whippings. I was officially on my own, and I would never see my family again. My insides vibrated with excitement.

Darkness was only two hours away, and I had to get as far from the house as I possible. October nights were cold, but I had brought along plenty of clothes with me. I walked down the side streets of town and headed for the railroad tracks.

I knew Junior would not go to the trouble to walk to any great lengths to look for me. He had often told me how much joy he would have when I was no longer around, and he would not have to look at my face.

At nine years old, I didn't know much about the roads, but I knew the railroad tracks would take me west, and that was where I wanted to go. By the time it was dark, I had walked from south-west side of town to Hangman's Crossing, which was three or more miles from our house. I began getting tired. My clothes-filled pillowcase was heavy, but I hooked it over my shoulder and continued walking the railroad tracks even though my steps were growing much slower.

I did not remember dropping my bag of clothes, and I did not remember curling up and laying down in the middle of the railroad tracks and closing my eyes. How long I slept, I could not be certain, but I was awakened from a deep sleep by the sound of a blaring train horn. When I opened my eyes, the train's single spot light glared down on me from only a few feet away. The rumble of the train was deafening.

The horn sounded again, sending adrenalin rushing through my veins. I leapt to my feet and ran wildly away from the blaring horn just as the train sped by me. The breeze from the passing train let me know just how close I came to death.

As I ran wildly away from the train, I crossed the road and stepped into the path of oncoming traffic. A driver honked his car horn and swerved on the road. Fortunately, I escaped the impact of the car and cheated death twice that night. I would never again take a chance of falling asleep on the railroad tracks.

The train destroyed my bag of clothes, but I was alive. Frightened and tired, I abandoned the idea of walking on the railroad tracks to get out of state. While the train rumbled by, I hid in a nearby field along a fence row as my heartbeat returned to normal. Raindrops began falling, lightly at first and then increasing in intensity. I desperately needed a shelter for the night.

A used car lot was nearby, and after checking several cars, I found one with unlocked doors. The rain came down harder, and by the time I climbed into the backseat of the car my clothes were already soaked. I didn't mind, because I took comfort in the idea that at least I had a safe shelter for the night.

After removing my shoes and socks, I stretched out on the back seat. I was homeless now, and I would have to improvise. My clothes and the food I had packed and brought with me were gone, but I was not discouraged. I could get by.

Sleep was fitful that night, because I worried I might sleep too late into the morning and get caught inside the car. Every time I closed my eyes, I dreamed about Junior jerking the car door open and yanking me out of the back seat. I locked the car doors, but numerous times during the night I awoke, sat up, and looked outside to check my surroundings.

The car windows steamed up, and I worried it might give me away. Finally, dawn arrived, and at first light I left the car and began walking again.

My new plan was to go to Aunt Edna's house in hope she would hide me and take care of me. Even if she would not hide me, then I knew she would certainly help me. By now my parents would have the police searching for me, which meant I could not walk on the roads. Junior often warned me how the police were not my friends, and many times he threatened to call the police and have me put in jail to punish me for my childish wrong doings. Sadly, I believed him.

Aunt Edna lived beyond the Jonesville area which was at least fifteen miles away from the car lot at Hangman's Crossing. The trip took me all day and by sundown I barely made it to Jonesville. I used the same strategy I'd used the night before and slipped inside someone's car for the night. Once again, I left the car at first light for fear of getting caught.

My feet were swelled from walking so much, and my stomach growled for something to eat. I had not eaten for nearly thirty-six hours and after several miles of walking, I was extremely hungry and thirsty. Worst of all, I was emotionally distraught.

Even though it was October, the sun warmed me enough that I had to remove my jacket and carry it under my arm. All the while I walked, I kept a constant dialogue of prayer for God's help. I had no other source.

As I walked the country roads, praying and sometimes crying, I suddenly came upon a fully wrapped candy bar someone had tossed out the window. Although the grass was wet with dew, the wrapper was clean and dry. Even more amazing, it was one of my favorite candy; a maple-cluster nut bar. I ate it and thanked God for what I considered a miracle. As soon as I devoured the candy bar, I found a second and then a third one alongside the road. At nine-years old, even I understood this was an act of God.

The day grew arm, and eventually, thirst became so great I succumbed to kneeling on the gravel road and drinking water straight from a mud puddle. I didn't know anything about fungus and germs. I only knew I might collapse if I did not drink something soon. The temptation to walk up to someone's door and ask for a glass of water was great, but I knew there would be questions.

Outside of Jonesville, I walked downhill on a gravel road and passed a telephone repairman who stood working on one of the gray metal boxes mounted on a telephone pole. When I was within earshot, the man turned and spoke. "Hi, I'll bet your name is Kenny Noble, isn't it?"

A knot of panic formed in my stomach as I adamantly shook my head. "No, I'm George Claycamp."

The man grinned and went back to his work.

I increased my pace, and had gone only a few steps when I heard the telephone man shut his van door and start the engine. The vehicle passed me on the road and pulled into the next farm-house driveway. He knocked on the door and soon stood alongside the homeowner staring my direction.

The police were likely on their way, which prompted me to begin praying more intensely. As soon as I walked down the hill and was out of sight from the homeowner, I left the road and ran into the woods. Eventually, the woods ended into a large grassy field full of grazing cattle. I climbed the fence to cross the field with the idea of staying close to the road in order to keep my bearings.

But I was less than half way across the field when out from among the group of cows emerged a big black bull with a giant set of horns. The big guy trotted straight toward me with his head held high sniffing the air. Fear got the best of me, and I turned and high-tailed it back to the fence. As soon as I was safe on the other side, I looked back to discover the black bull had been close on my heels. I altered my route and traveled the long way through the thick woods and circled the pasture.

The sun set and my steps became very slow. I was so tired and sore that I considered giving up, knocking on a door, and asking the homeowner to call the police to come and arrest me. My thirst became so great I was desperate to do anything for a drink of water. Just before dusk, I came to a cluster of houses on a country road where I hurried to the back of the first house hoping to find a water spigot. There were none, so I knocked on the back door intending to ask for a glass of water. No one answered.

Near the back door stoop was picnic table with a porcelain pan of water. Inside the small pan were a half dozen combs. I did not hesitate. After I removed the combs I drank the entire pan of water. I knew I was drinking germs, but I was so thirsty that germs were a minor concern at the time.

Back on the road, a carload of teens stopped and offered me a ride, but I refused. They would ask questions and want to know where I was from, and I decided nothing good could come of it, so I declined their offer and continued walking in the direction I hoped was Aunt Edna's house.

Finally, as the last light of the day faded, I came to the long lane that led to her house. Joy filled my heart, and my fatigue seemed to lessen as I approached the farm house. The long trip had worn me out, but I loved Aunt Edna and it was worth it. She was the only person who had ever shown me unconditional love. I tried to imagine what she would say when she saw me, as I slowly walked up the long lane to the house.

* * *

I COULD HARDLY STOP GRINNING as I stepped onto the front porch. There were no cars in the drive, but Edna had never had her license. I knocked and waited. When no one answered, I walked around the house and tried several windows until I found one that was unlocked.

Flakes of paint pealed from the old window as I raised it enough to slip inside the house. Once inside, I smelled the memories from years past. It was and emotional rush.

Much of the furniture was missing, and the lights would not come on. Edna had moved. The only things left in the house were the big pieces of furniture.

I dropped onto the sofa and unlaced my tennis shoes. My feet were so tender and swollen I could barely get my socks off my feet. In the darkness, I fumbled around the kitchen and discovered a pan of leftover oatmeal on the stove. Except for the three candy bars I'd picked up alongside the road, I had not eaten for nearly three days.

The left over oatmeal was another miracle from God. Never had anything tasted so good.

Once I finished off the oatmeal, I slowly limped back to the living room. My feet were quickly swelling, and I considered dropping to my knees and crawling to the sofa. Instead, I slowly scooted along until I could stretched out on the soft cushions. I gently propped up my tender feet and began to relax. A lot had happened in the last three days, but I was too tired to process my next move. The world around me quickly faded as I dropped off into a deep sleep.

Someone came through the door and awakened me. Instinctively, I sat up on the sofa and tried to stand, but the pain from my swollen feet immediately forced me to collapse back on the sofa. It was daylight outside, which meant I had slept completely through the night.

"There he is. I had a feeling he'd be here." Edna stepped into the room and set her huge black pocketbook on dining-room table. "Kenny, Oh my boy, Kenny." Here voice rose an octave.

I swallowed and cleared my throat.

"We have been looking all over for you. Are you okay, honey?" She rushed up and wrapped her arms around me.

I didn't speak for a long minute as I tried to evaluate my situation. Since Edna didn't drive, I knew she would not be alone. If Junior was with her, then I was trapped, because my swollen feet would not allow me to run. Georgie, Edna's eldest daughter, came through the door and greeted me, but no one else was in sight. I let out a sigh of relief.

Edna wore her signature black dress with her hair in one of those old-fashioned buns behind her head. She always talked loudly as if she was hard hearing, but she never went without a smile.

"I'm okay." I repositioned myself on the sofa.

"Your mom and dad are looking for you. You know that?" she asked.

My growling stomach let me know I was still hungry. Hopefully, Edna would not be angry when she found out I had come into her house through the window.

"Why'd you run away, honey?"

"Mom. Do you really have to ask that question?" Georgie asked. "You know how Junior treats those boys. And he's never kept it a secret how much he despises Kenny."

I wiped my eyes. Their understanding meant so much to me right then. "He's mean to me all the time," I said. "He whips me until my legs and back bleed. He tells me every day how much he hates me and that he hopes I die.

Edna wagged her head.

"I had to get away from him. I had to. I didn't know where else to go." Sobs interrupted my speech.

Edna sat beside me on the sofa. "You poor child. I wish there was something I could do." She shook her head. "Oh God help us. Help us Lord Jesus, help us." She closed her eyes a moment and shook her head.

Georgie went to the other room and made a phone call. I assumed she was calling the police and my mother.

I was too tired and sore to run any more. Junior would be so mad, but what choice did I have? If Edna didn't help me, then I had nowhere else to go.

Edna looked around the room. "We moved to Columbus, honey. After Walter died, I didn't want to stay out here in the country by myself. You had anything to eat?"

I nodded. "I ate that oatmeal left on the stove."

"What? That wasn't oatmeal. That was slop for the animals. I forgot to throw it out. Oh Lord. You poor things. You look pitiful. How long have you been here?"

"I just got here at dark last night." I pointed to the window. "The window was unlocked, so I didn't think you'd care if I stayed here for the night."

"Of course not, child. Where have you been sleeping?"

I lifted a shoulder. "Anywhere I could. I slept on the ground some, and in someone's car a couple times. Are my parents coming to get me?"

The front door opened and in walked my maternal grandfather, Dick. He wore bib overalls with a pencil protruding from the vest. A pocket watch with a silver chain hung from his waist. He made eye contact and grinned. "You knew where to go, didn't you boy? Are you all right?"

I nodded again.

"He doesn't want to go home, Dick. What are we going to do?" Edna asked.

Georgie stepped into the room. "I called their house, but there was no answer. They must be out looking for him. I should go find them and tell them he's here."

"No!" I shouted. "Please. Don't tell them."

Everyone looked at me a long moment. Edna broke the silence. "We have to tell them, Kenny. They'll put us in jail if we don't tell them you're here." She shook her head a moment and looked me up and down. "Look at his feet, Dick. Look how their swelled."

"I'll just run away again," I said. "I'll have to. My step father says he wants to kill me."

"What does your mother say?" Edna asked. "Doesn't she stop him from hurting you?"

I shook my head. "She never says nothing."

Edna took me by the hand. "Honey, if you don't want to go back home, you just tell your mother you don't want to go home. You hear? Stand up for yourself."

I looked down at the floor as I fought back tears. They didn't understand. There was no standing up for myself with Junior. He overpowered everyone around him. Not only was I never allowed to talk back or express my feelings, but I was usually not allowed to talk except in reply to Junior's questions.

Before I had time to sort out what to do, the dreadful moment came. The sound of tires on gravel sent my pulse into overdrive. From the sofa, I watched my mother get out of the car, walk up the sidewalk and come inside the house. She looked directly at me and broke into a huge smile. "Are you okay?"

I did not believe the smile was real for one moment, but I nodded as I watched the door for Junior to enter. My first thought was Junior had refused to help search for me.

"We were all worried sick about him," Edna said.

My mother sat on the other side of me and rested her hand on my leg. "I've been worried about you, too. You sure you're all right, honey?"

I looked down at the floor. "Yes."

She took me by the hand. "Let's go in the back room and talk a minute." She stood and led me away from the safety of the others.

Silence hung in the room like a damp fog. As I limped along beside her, I looked over my shoulder, in time to see the pitiful expressions of the others staring at me. They looked as if they were watching a man go to his execution.

In the back bedroom, my mother sat on the edge of the bed alongside me. She was quiet for several breaths. "You know, a long time ago I had a little girl and they took her away from me. I haven't seen her in years. All I've got left are you two boys, and I don't want to lose either one of you."

I wasn't accustomed to affection and immediately began sobbing uncontrollably.

She put her arm around me and hugged me. "I couldn't stand to lose another child." She kissed me on the head. "You know mommy loves you, don't you?"

I nodded as the sobs and heaves became more intense.

"I want you to go back home with me and we'll get things straightened out. Okay?"

I swallowed hard, knowing I did not have a choice. Tears ran down my cheeks as I thought of Edna's words; *Stand up for yourself. Tell her you don't want to go home with her.* But I knew that no matter what I said, in the end, I would have to go back home.

What I wanted would not matter. Resistance would not help me. If I refused, she would simply go out to the car and bring Junior inside. He would enforce her wish easy enough.

"It's going to be all right." Mom took me by the hand and led me to the front door. "He's going home with me," she announced.

No one spoke a word. The other three adults remained speechless as she led me out the door and down the sidewalk to the parked car. Junior sat in the driver's seat, a stream of cigarette smoke rolling from the open window.

I did not know it, but years later, my grandfather confessed he had put a handgun in his pocket and walked out to the car where Junior waited. He had the intention to kill him, but before he got to the car, he decided he could not do such a terrible thing as to commit murder. He turned around and came back inside the house with the others while Mom talked to me in the back bedroom.

Mom opened the car door, and I climbed into the back seat beside Steve while my heart pounded like a baby kicking under a blanket. As we drove away, I looked over my shoulder and watched the house grow distant behind us. Edna, Georgie, and Grandfather Dick stood watching from the porch. Finally, the trees along the driveway blocked my view of the house. The reprimands would begin soon, and I immediately began praying for God's help to give me the right words to say in defense.

*   *   *

INSTEAD OF GOING HOME, Junior turned the car into a parking spot in front of the police station. A spark of hope rose up inside me as I imagined them putting me in a jail cell instead of taking me home.

Once inside the police station, and elderly man introduced himself. "Hi, I'm Detective Martin. We talked on the phone," he said.

Junior shook hands with him, and the two talked a moment.

Finally, Detective Martin turned his attention toward me. "Kenny, would you come back to my office a few minutes? I'd like to talk to you a bit."

Inside his office, I sat on the opposite side of the table facing Detective Martin. I was not sure what was going to happen to me, but I was hoped Junior would turn me over to the police and wash his hands of me.

"Talk to me son," Martin said. "What's going on? Why did you run away from home?"

I looked down and lifted a shoulder. "I don't know. I just did it."

The Detective shook his head. "I'm not buying that. Something's wrong. Listen, you can trust me. I'm here to help you. You don't have to be afraid of me. Tell me the truth."

A ray of sunlight peaked through the office blinds and warmed my skin as I cleared the tears from my throat and began, "My step-dad hates me. He tells me so every day. He whips me with an extension cord, and he makes me work all the time when I'm home. Sometimes I'm even scared to go to sleep at night, because he threatens to kill me."

The detective nodded. "What else?"

"He won't let me have any friends. He never lets let me go outside and play like other kids." I looked down and lowered my voice. "And he always tells me I'm ugly and stupid."

The detective stared at the table and nodded as if in thought. "Do you think you're stupid?"

"No."

"You like your stepfather?"

I shook my head. "Not much. And he don't want me to like him, either."

"How old were you when your mother married your stepfather?"

I lifted a shoulder again. "Four, I guess. I don't remember it."

Martin slid his chair back, crossed his arms, and stared at me a long moment. Finally, he nodded. "Wait here. I'll be right back."

He was gone several minutes. When he returned, Junior was with him. The two men sat down at the table, one on each side of me. Detective Martin arched his brow and looked at me. "Now Kenny, what I'd like for you to do is tell your stepfather exactly what you just told me a few minutes ago."

My heart plummeted. There was no way I would do that. I would likely have to go back home with Junior, and if so, I would be punished for anything I said to make him look bad.

"Go on. Tell him exactly what you told me," the detective repeated.

I knew of only one way to get out of this. "I lied," I said quietly. "I made it up."

Junior grinned and gave Martin an *I-told-you-so*, look. "See what I put up with? The kid's off in the head."

Martin wrinkled his brow. "Why did you lie to me, Kenny?"

I lowered my eyes and lifted my shoulders.

No one spoke for a long minute. Finally, Martin stood and extended his hand to Junior. "I guess that wraps this up. We'll arrange for some psychiatric testing and see if we can get you some help. A working man doesn't need this kind of problems in his life."

Junior nodded. "No one knows what I've had to put up with on this one. It's a daily battle. His brother is completely opposite."

The two men talked while I continued to stare at the floor. Finally, Junior snapped his fingers in my direction—a signal I was to follow him. Without a word, the family all walked to the car and rode silently to the house.

Once inside the house, Mom immediately sent me to my room, which was probably an act of kindness to save me from Junior's wrath. As I sat on the bed and prayed, I promised God I would do anything he wanted if he would only help me through this. I knew so little about God and religion, but was from experience, I knew when I asked him for help, he often helped me. As a result, my *go-to* solution for hard times was to pray to God.

Life was different the next few days. Junior hardly spoke a word to me, and there was no mention of me doing any chores. No one reprimanded me, and when Junior came home from work each night, I stayed hidden in my bedroom. He never called my name, and I considered it an answer to prayer. Usually, Mom would come to me room after he had gone to bed and tell me to come out and eat my supper.

It was not until the following Saturday when I learned the secret to Junior's new behavior. He loaded the family in the car and drove a long time. Everyone was silent most of the way. Finally, Junior turned the car into the parking lot in front of a modern brick office building.

We all went inside where Mom stopped at the receptionist's desk. "We have an appointment for testing for our child."

A strange man in a white shirt and tie appeared and immediately took me into a back room where he asked me a lot of questions. I answered his as honestly as I could and hoped I said the right things. Next, the man gave me several written exams, which took a long time to complete.

After the exams were over, he leaned back in the chair and crossed his arms over his chest. "Kenny, I want you to tell me about yourself. Tell me what your life is like from the time you get up each morning until you go to bed at night." He waited.

At first I was hesitant, but the man nodded and encouraged me along. I explained how I kept the alarm set for four-forty five each morning so

I would be the first person out of bed. At the sound of the alarm, I was expected to be on my feet. A snooze button was never allowed.

I looked down at the table as I talked. "I start doing chores as soon as I get up. I make coffee and wake my stepfather first, and then I stand at attention near the table until he's ready for me to refill his cup. A half hour later, I wake my mother and brother. I fix breakfast for my brother and then begin making beds and start dusting."

As I explained my Cinderella life, I tried to choose the right words that would not get me in trouble in case Junior was listening in the other room. Several minutes later, I looked up at the psychologist only to discover he had fallen asleep, his eyes closed, his head tilted forward.

I stopped talking and waited. When the silence wakened him, he nodded and stood. "I'll be back in a few minutes." He picked up the exams and left the room for a long time.

Finally, the door opened. "I think we're done here, Kenny," the psychologist said. "Let's go have a talk with your parents."

In a larger room, the man gathered the family around a big conference table. He shuffled his papers and cleared his throat before he began. "After significant testing, my staff and myself have concluded that Kenny is a normal nine-year old. We find no abnormalities of any kind."

I lost focus on the man's words as I watched Junior's countenance change. He was not happy. My guess was that he expected the psychologist would find some type of mental problem that would result in my getting admitted to the institution.

Suddenly, it all made sense to me. For the last several days, the conversation at the dinner table had been how the mental institution was the best place for some people. My parents had told each other stories that they had heard from coworkers and family about mental patients and their success after admitted to an institution. I had not understood they were prepping me for what lay ahead.

All the way home, Junior and Virginia were unusually quiet again. Junior was visibly disappointed, and appeared to be brooding for several days thereafter. These were glorious days for me. Not only did I receive a reprieve from his torment, but I was also elated to learn I was normal. This was completely opposite of what Junior had been telling me most of my life. I wanted so badly to point that out to Junior, but of course, I was smart enough not to mention it.

* * *

BOTH PARENTS WERE UNUSUALLY NICE TO ME. I knew it was a facade, but I did not know why. No one mentioned my chores, and no one asked why I had ran away. Once again, their secret came out a few days later when a stranger arrived at our house.

Mom gathered the family into the living room as soon as the stranger arrived. When we had company, I was always told to sit on the sofa. We all sat quietly and waited for the man to speak.

"Hi Kenny. I'm George Armstrong, your probation officer." He was a big man with bushy caterpillar eyebrows and a square jaw. "I've come to discuss some thing with you and your family, and hopefully get this worked out for everyone."

He first began to question me about general things; was I glad to be back home, and would I be glad to get back to school? I answered the questions carefully and always noted Junior's response. He sat quietly in the rocking chair across the room.

Finally, Mr. Armstrong asked the question, I knew was coming. "Why did you run away from home?"

I lifted a shoulder and looked down at the carpet. I wanted to tell him what life was really like, but I was learning more and more not to trust anyone in authority. My experience with Detective Martin had taught me that authority would betray my confidence; therefore, I carefully chose my response to every question.

Although, I held a grudge against the detective for several years, later in life I realized he was likely not trained to handle child-abuse families. In addition, the staff at the police station may have been short handed and as often is the case, he may have been stepping in to do someone else's job.

Mr. Armstrong slid forward on the edge of his seat. "Kenny, when you took Junior's money and purchased that army toy. Didn't you know it was just a toy?"

Of course I knew. I just wanted to have a little fun, even if it was short-lived. But I played the dumb card and arched my brow. "They showed on television that it was just like a real gun."

George was silent a moment. "Do you get enough food to eat here?"

I glanced at Junior before I nodded.

"Do you and your brother get along?"

"Yes," I gave a truthful nod.

"You know your parents love you, don't you?"

I hesitated. The answer I was expected to give was not the one I wanted to give. Junior made no secret to me or anyone in the extended family about his dislike for me. Even his own mother blatantly reprimanded him.

"Junior, you are going to answer to God Almighty for the way you treat that child," she would say. He always laughed it off.

"Yes," I answered.

"Then why would did you run away?" he asked.

I did not have an answer that I could give and still feel safe. If I told the truth, I would be punished severely once the probation officer left, and if I believed my stepfather's words—I might possibly lose my life. So I lifted my shoulders again and gave my go-to answer. "I don't know."

Junior seemed amused by the conversation. He reminded me of a grinning cat—the smile seemed so out of place.

Finally, Mr. Armstrong stood to leave and announced that he was required to come back and check with the family every a few weeks. Junior followed him outside where they talked in private a long time. As soon as Mom closed the entry door, she sent me to my room.

Now that the visit from the probation officer was over, life immediately returned to the way it had always been. Junior not only made certain I kept up with my chores, he also gave me additional work to do. I ate dinner alone at the kitchen table once everyone else was finished eating, and then I was sent to bed early while the rest of the family sat in the living room and watched television.

December thirtieth arrived and I waited patiently all day expecting someone to mention my birthday. I assumed that before the day was over my mother would bring out a small present or at the very least give me a hug and tell me happy birthday.

I was wrong. That night I quietly crawled into bed without so much as a birthday wish from anyone in the world. On my tenth birthday, I cried myself to sleep.

December thirty-first was my brother's birthday and the family celebrated in style. Mom purchased Steve a store-bought cake with fancy decorations and his name on it. Until then, I had never seen a store-decorated cake before.

Steve blew out the candles and Mom sang happy birthday to him as she took pictures with her new Polaroid instant camera. Steve opened his gifts as I stood quietly in the next room and watched from a distance.

Perhaps it was the sad forlorn look of self-pity I wore or maybe it was her guilt, but Mom finally looked across the room at me and smiled. "Oh. Yesterday was your birthday, wasn't it honey?"

I nodded and wiped at the tears.

"Happy birthday to you too," she said, and went back to taking pictures of Steve as he opened his gifts.

That was it. My tenth birthday passed with only a belated birthday wish from my mother. I went to my bedroom and cried until I couldn't cry any more.

It never crossed my mind that I should be envious of Steve. We were close. Through the years we had been together even though our parents had forsaken us. In some ways I felt as if Steve was my son more than he was my brother, because I had always taken care of him.

After my birthday, I made up my mind to run away from home again just as soon as good weather arrived. Only this time I had experience and I would be more prepared. I was ten-years old now, and I could live in the woods alone where no one would be mean to me again. I didn't mind living alone, because in many ways I was already isolated.

At every possible opportunity, I shut myself in my bedroom and played Elvis Presley records or read fiction books. Music lifted my spirits like nothing else in the world, and reading books became an escape for me.

Junior moved the family to a new house every year where each new dwelling was a slight improvement over the last. Each move also meant attending a new school. Because of this, I never learned the concept of making friends at a new school. I usually kept to myself during every recess.

My social skills were very immature for my age, because Junior never allowed us boys to play outside with neighbor children or to socialize with other people in any way. He kept the family isolated. We never attended church, and we were never a part of any sport organization. Fortunately, we had a three-month span where we were allowed to go to the Boy's Club after school for a couple hours. Even so, we never quite fit in with the others and most of our time there was spent watching television or playing board games.

I was nearly eleven-years old when Junior moved the family to a house he rented on King Avenue in Seymour. Our new home had three bedrooms and a garage, something the family had never had before.

My growth spurt came early, and by this time I was nearly six-feet tall. Junior seemed to hate me even more as I grew older. Every time one of the grandparents said, "Kenny's going to be a big man," it seemed to antagonize Junior even further.

In private, he often reminded me how much I looked like my real father. "You're big and ugly, just like your father," he would say.

I took it in stride, because it didn't take a New York lawyer to understand he was jealous of my mother and her past relationships. Yet, often I dreamed about meeting my real father. I never saw his photo until I was forty-years old, so I had to imagine how he looked.

I also laid in bed at night and imagined him finding me and rescuing me from my stepfather. Mom never talked about my real father or my sister, Diane, but at the top of my childhood fantasy list was the goal to meet them both.

Each morning, there were two times I dreaded. The first was helping Junior get dressed. I had to put his belt through his pant belt loops and then hold out his pants for him as he stepped into them. Next, I would hand him his T-shirt I had just freshly ironed. After that, I dropped to my knees and propped his foot on my leg in order to put his socks on each foot, followed by his boots. If I did not get his boots laced the way he liked them, the go-to punishment was a quick backhand on my face or a box on my ears.

After he was dressed, I packed his lunch, started his car and warmed it, then hand him his wallet and hat.

The other dreadful time of each morning was when Junior would turn to Steve at the breakfast table and tell him to go check and see if I had wet the bed. If so, then a whipping was promised for that evening. Unfortunately, Junior never forgot or missed a whipping he promised.

Sadly, I wet the bed about every other night, but many times I was able to hide my sin in one way or another. Sometimes I took extra clean sheets to my room the day before and hid them. As soon as I woke up in the morning, I would get up and change them. Other times, I would sleep on the floor to keep from getting the bed wet.

It should go without saying I tried every trick a child could come up with to stop my bed wetting. I refused to drink any fluids except the bare minimum. I tried gadgets such as rubber bands, balloons, soda bottles, and even any medication I could confiscate. Nothing helped. When I fell asleep, it was like diving off into a dark pool and the present world became so distant that nothing disturbed me until that alarm went off the next morning.

Junior seemed to take pleasure in prolonging my inevitable punishment when a whipping was due. He would never whip me and get it over with; instead, he would prolong it to the evening and sometimes for a day later, which made the suffering even worse. All day my heart felt as if it had a weight pushing against it knowing I'd get a whipping that night.

When he come home for the evening, he would sit down to the kitchen table and remind me that after supper we would *talk turkey*—his term for punishment. Once supper was over and I washed the dishes, he would go the living room where he would call out, "We're going to talk turkey as soon as you get them dishes done.

When the moment arrived, he usually sent me outside to cut a willow whip that always grew along the fence row. "Be sure you get a big switch," he said. "Because if you don't, then I'll go out and cut a bigger one myself. As much as I disliked cutting my own switch, I took care to get one to satisfy Junior's standards. I feared to do otherwise. The main requirement was the switch had to be six feet tall and stout.

"You can't believe he wets the bed on purpose," Virginia said.

Junior laughed. "He's a masochist. The boy likes pain. That's why he does it. He wants me to whip him. He's messed up in the head."

In reality, I believed it was Junior who had mental problems. He seemed to enjoy inflicting pain and acted as if taunting me before a whipping was foreplay to some sexual act. He always put on his pants and followed me to the back bedroom where he would make me strip naked.

He would then grab me by the wrist and whip me across the backside and legs until there was nothing left of the switch but a stub. All the while, his face contorted as if he was in a frenzy while he followed me around the room and cursed as I danced in a circle.

I always cried and begged for mercy, but mercy never came. When it was over, he always tossed the remaining foot-long piece of stubble on the floor. "Get your clothes on and get to bed," he'd say and leave me cringing in pain. Large whelps immediately appeared on my legs and back. Most of them bled and soon scabbed over.

There was never a discussion of why I was getting punished or that it was his job as a parent. Instead, it was; "You're going to learn that I'm the boss, and what I say goes. I'll beat that stubbornness out of you if it's the last thing I do."

More than once, I took the risk of cutting notches in the switch so it would break more easily. He never knew what I'd done, but for some reason the pain did not seem any less. Only once did I get caught when I cut the notches too deep and Mom swung the switch through the air to practice. When she did the switch fell to the floor in pieces and I was busted.

It was during the summer of my eleventh year, I experienced an answer to prayer that I have never forgotten. My brother Steve and I were home alone, and like most young boys we often scuffled with each other. That day Steve chased me through the house, and as we both laughed I circled the kitchen table where he could not catch me.

He grabbed a large butcher knife from the table and chuckled as he chased me around the table, faster, and faster until he cut the corner too sharp and slipped and fell. Immediate cries of pain sent a shaft of fear through me as I hurried around the table and knelt beside him where he was curled up on the floor screaming. Blood flowed freely down his head, and I realized he was not faking. Fortunately, the butcher knife did inflict any damage.

At the sight of blood running his head and neck, I grew frightened. He finally held still long enough for me to examine his wound, and I discovered an inch or longer split in his ear from where his head had hit the sharp edge of the kitchen table.

Something this serious required me to call Mom from work, and I knew that would not turn out well. But I had no choice, because he was a bloody mess and would need stitches. I was frightened, but poor Steve was nearly hysterical. He was only ten-years old and this was the most he had bled in his entire life.

"Steve, let's pray," I said out of desperation. I did not know what else to do. No one had taught me how to pray for someone, but I instinctively put my hand on his head. "Jesus, we need you right now. Help us Jesus. Stop the bleeding and help us, please."

"Jesus! Help me," Steve cried. "Jesus! Help me."

After a full minute or two, we both stopped praying and I took my hand away from his head. The bleeding had not only stopped, but there was not even a scar where the wound had been. Not only did he not need stitches—he did not even need a bandage. God had heard his cry for help and healed him instantly. We cleaned up the blood and Mom never knew about it.

So many people underestimate the spiritual connection of little children; yet, Jesus heard the simple cry of a frightened ten-year old child and healed him.

CHAPTER FOUR

God takes care of what we go through.
It is up to us to take care of how we go through it.

The LORD is my light and my salvation; whom shall I fear? the LORD is
the strength of my life; of whom shall I be afraid? Psalms 27

JUNIOR SENT ME OUTSIDE to mow the yard. I started the push
mower and made several laps around the backyard when suddenly a
loud noise like a gun-shot sounded behind me. I jumped and turned to
look behind me, not sure what to expect. Junior and Steve stood at the
edge of the patio laughing at how they startled me with the cherry bomb.
I kept pushing the mower.

Mom came outside and stood next to Junior until I finished mowing.
"We just got a phone call from my Grandma Ross," she said to Junior
as soon as I shut off the mower. "She wants to come and live with us a
few weeks until she finds an apartment. I told her I'd have to talk to you.
She's says she'll pay us."

Junior put his hands inside his pant pockets and stared down at the
patio a moment. "If she pays rent, we'll try it for a while. I guess I can put
up with her for a few weeks."

Mom nodded. "She promised it would only be for a month at the
most. She's waiting for a vacancy at the apartment complex where she's
trying to get in."

I quietly pushed the mower back into the garage, but inside my head,
I was doing handstands and jumping around in the yard. My great-grandmother's presence would subdue Junior's harassment as long as she was
with us.

Mom walked over to where I was sweeping grass from the driveway.
"Kenny, I want you to run to the store for me as soon as your finished."
She handed me her list along with the money, and then hurried back
inside to call her grandmother and tell her the news.

I finished sweeping the drive before I hopped on my bike and left.

I loved to run errands and get away from the house, but I had to pass a vacant lot where several older teenagers played baseball. If they saw me coming down the road, then they would often run out to the center of the road and block me from passing in order to bully me for a while. Mostly, it was one high-school boy who led the others in taunting me.

The boy was too big for me to fight, because I knew I could never hold my own against him. Most of the time, I got away before the gang could get to the road and block my path; but occasionally, the entire gang picked up dirt clods and pelted me with them as I rode by the lot. It not only humiliated me, but it also made me angry.

That evening, as soon as I left the house to run the errand for my mother, it suddenly began raining. It was a warm summer evening and I did not mind getting wet, but I worried about getting passed the vacant lot without trouble. I pedaled hard, and just for fun when I came to a chuckhole I pulled up hard on the handlebars and popped a wheelie.

Too late, I realized my predicament. When I pulled the front end of the bicycle up in the air, the front wheel stayed on the blacktop and rolled off the road into the ditch. Instantly, fear surged through me as I tightly gripped the handlebars and went down onto the pavement face first. Pain shot through my neck and down my spine. For several seconds, I could move. All the while the rain pelted my skin like tiny stinging bees.

When I sat up, I spit white gravel from my mouth and wiped blood from my face. I rubbed my finger across my front teeth. It was not gravel, it was my broken teeth I had spit out. Only two jagged fangs remained. Turmoil erupted inside me. How much more was I supposed to endure in life?

I stood and dragged my bicycle over to the side of the road as I cried, not from physical pain, but from the emotional wound. I could not fathom going through life with my two front teeth missing.

After several minutes, I finally found my tire in the ditch and with my bicycle under one arm and the tire under my other arm, I walked back home. The dam of tears would not stop flowing as I cried out in desperate prayer to for God's help.

My clothes were soaked when I arrived home. I set my bike next to the house and entered through the kitchen door. Mom shut the refrigerator door and turned to face me. "You got back fast." Her countenance changed immediately. "What happened to you?"

I could not speak for a moment.

Her eyes widened. "Did you get in a fight?"

My face crinkled up. "I broke my front teeth out." Sobs choked off my words as I hurried to the bathroom mirror. My reflection was like a knife in my heart. Two jagged fangs were all that remained of my front teeth. Just like my stepfather had always told me; I was ugly, and now I looked like a monster.

Mom came into the bathroom and stood alongside me. "Let me see." She put her hand on my chin and examined my broken teeth. "It doesn't look that bad."

I knew she was lying. "Yes it does." I bent over the sink and cried like a baby.

Junior remained in the living room chair where he sat reading the newspaper and did not say a word.

Mom stood quietly a moment as if trying to find the right words to say. Finally, she let out a long sigh and walked back to the kitchen.

I went to my room and changed out of my wet clothes and then plopped onto the bed. All of my peers at school would laugh and call me a freak. I cried until sleep overtook me.

* * *

MY BROTHER AND I LIKED TO SNEAK OUT of the house on occasion and go to the city park while our parents were at work. Since we did not have friends, we stayed to ourselves and roamed around the park. No one ever bothered us except a bully named Russel who often tried to pick a fight with me. Russell was three years older than me, but he was not quite as tall as I was. He went out of his way to bully me every time we crossed paths whether it was on the street, at the store, or at school.

The first confrontation was at the city park on a hot summer day. Steve and I were drinking from the public water fountain when Russel approached us. "What's in your pocket?" he asked.

I ignored him and took a long drink of water from the fountain, hoping he would go away. I had brought a baseball along in hope that Steve and I could play catch.

"I said, what is in your pocket, punk." Russell repeated as he stepped closer.

"None of your business," I said and turned to walk away.

"I'm making it my business, you punk."

Steve had been hiding behind me but suddenly stepped out and walked closer to Russel. "You better leave my big brother alone. He'll punch you in the nose."

Russell lifted his chin and locked onto my gaze. "Let me see what's in your pocket or I'm going to knock you out right now."

"I'm not afraid of you." I lied.

"Good then let's settle this. Right here, right now."

"I got to go home. Some other time, fruitcake," I said.

"Okay punk, then meet me here tonight at six, and I'll show you what's right."

"All right, I will. And pack your lunch, 'cause it may be an all day job." I turned to Steve. "Come on, let's go home."

We always made certain to arrive home in plenty of time to complete our chores before Mom came home from work. If she knew we had gone to the park without permission, we would have been punished.

A couple weeks later I left the house during the day while Mom was at work and rode my bicycle to visit a girl I had met at school. She was babysitting during the day for a family on the south-west side of town near the Glen-Lawn church.

For the first time in my life I began to develop friendships with some of the teens in that neighborhood. The house where she was babysitting became a teen hangout during the day, and everyone treated me nice and made me feel welcome.

One day I was in the house sitting on the sofa as numerous teens moved through the house. One of the girls passed through the living room where I sat. "Kenny, I want to introduce you to a friend of ours."

When I looked up, there stood Russell. I had been a no-show for our scheduled fight a few weeks earlier and now I had to face him. I was busted. Even worse, I was busted in the presence of my new friends.

"You didn't show up. What happened to you?" Russell asked.

"I showed up. You're the one who didn't show up." Lying had become my go-to solution to get out of trouble. Russel and I argued a few minutes until he offered a challenge I did not want to hear. "Let's go out to the back yard and settle this right here and now."

I did not know how to get out of the predicament, and I did not want to back down in front of my new friends. In my mind, I had no choice but to fight him. Even worse, I knew I had no chance of winning. Everyone in the room followed Russell and me single file down the hallway and out the back door into the yard.

If there was any one time in my life that God interceded at a crucial time, it was that day. As we went out the back door, I pulled out my stepfathers German Boker pocketknife from my pocket. Russel was one step in front of me as we zigzagged through the shotgun house. I was embarrassed and I hurt inside.

I opened the blade of the big pocket knife and a surge of adrenalin went through my entire body as I drew my hand back to stab Russell in the kidney. For three seconds my heart fought against my brain.

It was one of those times when I responded the way Junior had taught me. He had often told us boys that when they were in a fight and the other person was too big to whip, then to use something as a weapon to make up the difference. That time had arrived.

My rush of adrenalin subsided without incident. I could not stab him. I folded the knife and put it back inside my pocket. If God had not interceded in that three seconds, then my future and ultimately my eternity would have been very different than what it is today.

In the back yard, I squared off to face Russel with about ten steps between us. The news of the fight spread like wildfire in the neighborhood, and dozens of teens gathered around to watch. I knew I was about to get whipped and humiliated even further.

My new social life was the most important thing in the world to me at that time. Home life was miserable, and now I was about to lose the only friends I had ever made.

Suddenly, I produced the big pocketknife again. "Okay, now I'm ready. Come on in and get it." I waved the knife back and forth in front of me.

Russell stood up straight. "No way. I'm not fighting you with a knife. Put that away."

I was in way over my head and I knew it. In the back of my mind, I worried that I might not make it home before my mother arrived home from work. Fortunately, no one called the police and after several minutes of arguing with Russel, my anger subsided to tears. I cursed Russell with long lines of profanity.

Finally, a man walked over to my corner of the yard. "Kenny, you don't want to do this, trust me." His tone was quiet and friendly.

I glanced his way and gripped the knife tighter. "Russel started this, and I'm going to finish it, one way or another," I shouted.

The man nodded. "I know how Russell is. But don't let him do this to you. Give me the knife, and we'll do this another day when you're not so angry."

I looked around at the crowd that circled the yard. Everyone stared at me like I was an animal at the zoo. Some looked frightened, while others wore an expression of amusement. "I'll meet you at the park at six thirty." I pointed the pocket knife at Russel. "Don't back out on me this time."

I folded the big pocket knife, dropped it back inside my pocket, and walked away, refusing to make eye contact with those around me. No one spoke as I got on my bicycle and rode away.

Now my new friends would call me a coward and make fun of me. Even worse, I still had to fight Russell. The incident had only prolonged my defeat.

More time had elapsed than I realized, and when I arrived home my mother stood over the stove frying potatoes. When I walked through the kitchen door, she gave me a laser beam glare that would light a candle at a hundred feet.

I tried to smile, but it would not stick.

"Where you been, young man?"

I had no answer. The ordeal had me so emotionally upset that I had not been able to think of a single excuse on my way home. I opened my mouth, but only stuttered.

"You're supposed to have supper ready, and here it is time for your father to get home." She put the lid on the iron skillet.

I stood motionless searching my brain for a lie to get me out of trouble, but nothing came to mind. The experience I had just suffered was bad enough, but now I also had to face the wrath of my stepfather.

Mom turned her full attention on me, her fisted hands on her hips. "I ask you a question; where have you been?"

I swallowed hard. The only thing I could think of was the truth. "I got into a fight and couldn't get away."

She frowned. "You were fighting?"

I nodded. Heat rushed up my neck and warmed my cheeks.

"You're lying. Let me see your stomach."

I raised my shirt, uncertain what she expected to see on my stomach.

"Your stomach's not red." Her brow rose. "You haven't been fighting. I want to know the truth." She folded her arms and glanced at the clock. "What were you fighting about."

"A girl." I lied.

"You are such a liar. I don't believe a word you're saying. You don't even know how to tell the truth."

I decided if I raised my voice and became adamant about my story, then she might believe me. "We're supposed to meet again at the park and finish the fight. If you don't believe me, you can come and watch." As soon as the words came out I was sorry, but I could not call the words back.

"When?" she asked.

"Six-thirty. At the park."

When Junior came home, Mom explained what had happened. "He's such a liar," she said again. "I don't believe him for one minute."

Junior nodded as he dipped out a generous helping of fried potatoes onto his plate. "We'll find out at six-thirty." He arched one brow and glanced at me. "Because I'm going to drive you there myself, and if you're lying then you're getting a whipping from me. Understand?"

"Yes sir." I gulped down my food in hope I could get away from the table before either of them asked more questions. There was no way out of this dilemma. If I showed up at the park, then Russell would beat me up, but if I lied and told my parents I had made up the story, then Junior would punish me.

Just before six-thirty, Junior loaded the family into the car and drove us to Shields Park. Over a hundred people had already gathered near the fountain, waiting to watch the fight. Junior parked the car near the street curb where he could watch. Once he cut the ignition, he turned around in the seat to face me. "I want to tell you one thing." He paused for emphases. "If you don't whip this kid tonight, then I'm going to whip you when you get home. Understood?"

I nodded and opened the car door. There was no way I could whip Russell. Not only was he several years older than me, but he also had more fighting experience. Russell was known as a fighter, and it was obvious he enjoyed his reputation. On the other hand, I was not the least bit interested in making a reputation for myself.

As I walked up the sidewalk toward the crowd someone spotted me and the crowd split and formed a circle with me and Russell in the middle. Russell pulled off his T-shirt. "You ready?"

I nodded and lifted my fist knowing I was doomed. Without hesitation, Russell rushed in, knocked me down, and began to pound my face like a wild man. My fall to the ground gave Russell the advantage. Immediately, he straddled my chest and planted one knee on each of my arms. Once he had me securely pinned to the ground, he continued pounding my face like I was a punching bag.

Somewhere in the scuffle, I got one lucky punch or two at Russell's face, which left his nose dripping blood like a slow running faucet. As he knelt over me, his blood dripped onto my face. When he tired of punching me, he rolled over and pinned me in a painful scissor lock and squeezed until I cried out in pain.

"I give up. Stop."

He squeezed the scissor hold a little longer than necessary before he released me. I rolled out of his grip and stood but did not speak. Blood still dripped from Russell's nose, and someone offered him a tissue.

My first thought was to attack him again, in hope I might get lucky, but my bleeding lips told me it was a terrible idea. It had been humiliating to leave the car without family support and then walk up the sidewalk where the crowd had gathered to watch me get beat up.

But now it was even more humiliating to walk away from the silent crowd and head down the sidewalk toward the car where Junior waited to give me another whipping.

With my head hung low, I tried to fabricate a believable story as I slowly walked back to the car. I hoped the crowd had blocked Junior's view. When I opened the car door and dropped into the back seat, Junior turned around to face me. A giant grin plastered on his face. "He beat your tail off, didn't he?"

"No, I beat him. I got him in a scissor hold and he cried uncle," I said.

Junior laughed and shook his head. "I saw him on top of you. He messed you over good."

Mom turned in the seat to face me. "What did he hit you with? You got blood all over you."

Only then did I realize the blood covering my face made me look gruesome. In truth, I was more humiliated than physically hurt, but my mother's concern was rewarding. Junior didn't mention anything about giving me the whipping like he had promised, and from the worried look on Mom's face, she would not allow it anyway.

Some good did come out of the fight, because it was the last time in all my school years that Russell tried to bully me. That one punch to his nose apparently encouraged him to find another victim and leave me alone.

* * *

THE SUMMER AFTER MY TWELFTH BIRTHDAY, Junior was laid off from his construction job and stayed home every day to make my life miserable. I had no rest from him from daylight to dark. As soon as Mom left for work in the morning he turned his attention to tormenting me all day.

"You get your rear in there and dust every table in the living room," he said. "Dust every what-not and picture frame."

He would never allow Mom to set out photos of me. Occasionally, she would try, but he would make her put them face down on the end table, or put them away in the drawer. He did not want anything to remind him of my presence in the house.

"Dust the legs of every piece of furniture, too. You hear me?"

"Yes sir." I quickly retrieved the dust rag and polish from under the kitchen sink and hurried to the living room. Fortunately, Junior's favorite spot at the kitchen table placed him with his back to the living room where he could not see me.

I removed every item from each piece of furniture, and then poured few drops of Old English furniture oil on it and wiped it clean. All the while, I silently prayed for God's intervention.

"Come in here, Kenneth Allan."

I dropped my rag and hurried to the kitchen. "Yes sir?"

"Go outside and cut me a long willow switch."

When I completed the task and came back inside, he took the switch and propped it against the table within arm's reach. "Now get back to your dusting."

After a couple minutes in the living room he called out for me to go to the other room. "You've been in there long enough. Go dust in the bedroom."

I stopped what I was doing and picked up the rag and bottle of furniture polish and headed for the bedroom. To get to the hallway, I had no choice but to pass him. When I did so, he whacked me hard across the back with the willow switch.

I cried out and hurried to the master bedroom where I prayed for God's help. A few minutes later, Junior repeated the process. "Kenneth Allan, get back in here where I can keep an eye on you."

With rag in hand, I hurried past Junior knowing what was coming. I had no choice but to walk passed him. He swung the switch and hit me across the legs, often followed by a low guttural chuckle. "What do you think of that Stevie? I think we're going to teach that boy a thing or two today."

Steve sat at the kitchen table with Junior, his coloring books and crayons spread out on the table. "Yep," Steve said.

"Come in here, Kenneth Allan."

I stood at arm's length from Junior knowing things were about to worsen.

"Look me in the eye."

I locked onto his gaze.

"You are the ugliest person I've ever seen. You know that? You're going to be just like your dad, big, ugly, and you will never amount to a hill of beans. You hear me?"

"Yes."

"What did I just say?"

"That I'm ugly and like my dad, and won't amount to much."

"You believe that?"

"Yes sir." I knew what I was expected to say, but inside my mind I reasoned that my future was not up to him—it was up to me and Jesus.

He turned in his seat, clenched his fist, and gritted his teeth a moment as if he had difficulty controlling himself. "I ought to knock your head off your shoulders."

I maintained eye contact and remained quiet.

"I'll be so glad when you're sixteen, because the day you turn sixteen, you're out of this house and on your own. I don't care if you have to sleep in the street. You understand what I'm saying?"

"Yes sir."

Every day, the same scenario repeated itself. The only variations were the different chores he assigned me to do. God did answer my prayers, because Junior seemed bored at times and would leave the house to go downtown. All the while he was gone, I spent most of my time in prayer. My prayers worked too, because often his trips downtown lasted several hours.

Relief came when my maternal great-grandmother finally moved in with us for several weeks. Junior toned down his punishment when she was around, which was most of the time. They gave her my bedroom and stored her belongings in Steve's bedroom. That left no place for us boys to sleep except on a pallet on the living-room floor. Later, that proved to be a benefit for me.

One Saturday morning, my parents came home from town and opened the door and called Steve outside. From the expression Junior wore, he had a surprise. Steve dropped what he was doing and hurried outside.

I dried the dish water from my hands and stood in the doorway. There on the driveway sat a brand new string-ray bicycle. It was sparkle purple with a long banana-type seat and high-rise handlebars.

"Wow. It's a five speed," Steve said as he straddled the new bicycle. He pedaled it to the end of the driveway and back. "Thanks Dad." He parked the bicycle, gave Junior a long hug, and then gave Mom a hug and kiss, too.

I waited.

"Let's go back inside the house," Junior said. "You can ride it later." He turned to me. "See what you get when you're good and don't cause trouble?"

I was hurt, but not surprised. Several weeks later, at Mom's prompting he purchased a new bicycle for me, but instead of a cool sporty bicycle he brought home a granny-style cruiser for me. It was rust brown with a grocery basket on the front, and I was embarrassed to ride it.

Fall arrived, and I was ready to run away again in order to escape my tormented life. I was twelve years old and confident I could pass as a six-teen- year and maybe get a job in another town. If not, I would not mind living alone in the woods until I did turn sixteen.

Running away from home had become my go-to solution when things got difficult. Most of the time I stayed hidden in the woods for three days, but eventually I became so hungry and tired, I gave myself up. Now that I was older, I intended to plan my escape better.

When I was home alone, I went through the house and searched for anything I might need when I escaped. I arranged each item in the cabinet where I could pick it up quietly in the dark without making noise. A pillowcase became my knapsack, which I hid inside a lower cabinet door we never used. If Mom found it, I planned to deny I knew anything about it. Either way, I was willing to take the risk.

I determined I would go farther away than I had ever gone before and never come back. This time, I wrote a letter of farewell.

BY THE TIME YOU FIND THIS LETTER, I WILL BE LONG GONE. DON'T BOTHER LOOKING FOR ME, BECAUSE I AM GOING A LONG WAY OFF. I ONLY REGRET I MIGHT CAUSE PAIN TO MY BELOVED MOTHER WHO REALLY CARES FOR ME.

Once everyone went to bed that night, I stretched out on the pallet in the living room and waited until I was sure everyone was asleep. If Junior caught me, I planned to rush out the door empty handed. Fortunately, since my great-grandmother was living with us he kept his bedroom door shut and the air conditioner running.

I stayed awake until two am as I imagined my new life and how great life would be when I got away from my parents. Finally, I decided every-one must be sound asleep and I tossed back the covers. I moved through the house like an experienced burglar and slowly removed the items I needed from the cabinets; a knife, pan, drinking glass, coffee, frozen food, oatmeal, and sugar.

A few minutes later, the bed in my great-grandmother's room began to creak. I quickly stopped what I was doing, hid my pillowcase full of supplies under the kitchen table, and went back to the pallet where I pretended I was sound asleep.

Grandma shuffled into the living room. She was a large woman and labored with every step. After staring quietly a moment, she finally spoke. "You are not asleep. What are you boys doing to make so much noise?"

My heart beat hard against my chest, but I did not respond.

"Talk to me, or I'm waking up your father," she said.

I opened my eyes and tried to feign sleepiness. "What?"

"Are you running away again?"

"No!" I lied.

She shook her head, her thick jowls jiggling. "I don't believe you. I'm waking up Junior."

"No. I'm okay. I'll be quiet."

She locked onto my gaze a long moment before she turned and shuffled back to her bedroom. A moment later, I heard the bed creak again.

I remained motionless for nearly an hour. Finally, I got up and put on the clothes I had hidden. Once dressed, I placed the letter I'd written on the table and slowly opened the kitchen door. My pulse thumped heavily in my ears as I stepped outside with my stuffed pillowcase in hand. There was no turning back now. If Junior caught me, I had no choice but to run.

I quickly got Steve's new bicycle out of the garage, wrapped the top of the pillowcase around the right grip on the handlebar, and pedaled away. My heart beat like a woodpecker for fear the house door would open any second and Junior would come after me. The weight of the loaded pillowcase made it difficult to steer the bicycle, but after the first mile or so, I began to get the hang of it.

There wasn't much traffic at four o'clock in the morning and I feared a policeman would stop me and question why a twelve-year old was out on the road so early in the morning. I pedaled into town and turned right on Highway 11, which led me out of town to the river. Just before I reached the bridge I stopped and walked the bicycle down the steep embankment and hid it.

Freedom was a good feeling. It was still dark, and I didn't have a flashlight, but the moon peeped in and out of the clouds, and I managed to feel my way around in the darkness. I hooked the pillowcase over my shoulder and worked my way along the ditch line toward the river. Every sound in the darkness made my pulse spike, but praying to Jesus made me feel as if I was not alone.

There were cows in the field nearby, but my destination was a strip of woods along the river where Edna's family kept a homemade houseboat tied to the bank. The boat would be my new home for the next few days.

Once deep into the woods, I pulled out the bed cover from my pillowcase, folded it in half and crawled between the two layers. Noises in the darkness frightened me. Animals were all around me, some calling, some rustling leaves. Somewhere out in the river, fish were splashing along with frogs who kept a steady croaking rhythm in the night. I pulled the covers over my head and tried to ignore the sounds. With every breath, I prayed to Jesus until sleep finally overtook me.

* * *

SINGING BIRDS AWAKENED ME after daylight the next norming. I peeked out from under the blanket to find a thick fog had settled over the wooded area. Nearby, a woodpecker pounded out a fast drumbeat. The forest was alive. From where I was curled up on the ground I could see cars passing over the iron bridge downstream of the river.

I thanked God for my new freedom. My chest seemed to swell with excitement as I listened to the birds sing. The sun peaked over the horizon and warmed the earth. In the distance, a siren sounded which reminded me that the police would be looking for me.

My first project was to build a fire and fix breakfast. Later, I planned to board the houseboat and hopefully find a way to get inside out of the elements. It was unlikely anyone would think of looking for me inside the boat, and I would not burn any lanterns at night to give myself away.

Smoked sausage links were on the menu for breakfast, but starting a fire turned out to be more difficult than I had imagined. I had plenty of matches, but the heavy dew made it impossible to find anything dry enough to burn. After several failed attempts, I finally gave up on the idea of cooking sausage for breakfast and settled for a peanut butter sandwich instead.

By now my parents knew I was gone, and they had likely called the police. I cringed when I imagined Junior's anger at me not being there to fix his coffee and serve him. He would have to lace his own boots and pack his own lunch. I was afraid to laugh about it, but I did take comfort knowing this would be one time I would have a better day than he would. Thinking about it made me feel good.

At the river's edge, I examined the houseboat. The river's current had pulled it away from the bank, where it tugged hard against the giant log chain that bound it to a tree. I grabbed onto the chain and tried to pull the boat closer to the bank, but I was not strong enough to move it.

The only possibility for me to board the boat was to make a long running jump from the bank to the boat and hope I did not fall short. I knelt and inched my way to the edge of the river bank. The brown water below me churned and swirled next to the bank. If I jumped and did not make it to the boat, the roiling water would likely suck me under, and I would drown.

Uncle Walter had always said, rivers were deeper near the banks than they were in the middle. Finally, my fear won out, and I decided it was too dangerous to try the jump and gave up. Today was not the day for me to die. There were other options instead of living on a river houseboat. My independence allowed me to easily change my plans and go live somewhere else.

I went back to my blanket where I fixed another peanut butter sandwich and ate it. My Uncle Morris had always been kind to me and I hoped maybe I could stay with him and his family. His wife, who was also named Edna, was a very jolly person. They had four boys of their own, and I could not imagine one more boy would be a burden to them. Of course, I was thinking like a child and not an adult.

My only problem was getting to their house. They lived at least fifteen miles south of Seymour near Uniontown, and I was five miles north of town. That meant I faced a twenty-mile walk.

All that day, I walked along country roads and through fields. At night I slept in a homeowner's car and began my journey at first light the next morning.

Late the second evening, I arrived at my Uncle Morris' house on U.S. 31 near Uniontown. Darkness had fallen, and the night sky twinkled with a million stars, making the heavens glitter. It looked as if everyone was inside the house for the night when I slipped inside the old barn near their house. No dogs were around, for which I was grateful. I climbed up into the loft and used pieces of thick house insulation to make a bed for the night.

When morning came, I peeked through the cracks between the boards and watched the different family members leave. Morris left in his pickup truck first, and then the four boys all met the school bus.

I lay back and rested while I imagined them adopting me and letting me live with their family. My greatest hope was to never see Junior again. If I worked around their house to earn my keep, then maybe they would let me stay.

Of course, I would have to go to school, but I would not mind that. In my mind, there was no reason for Junior and Mom to prevent me from staying here. It was obvious they did not want me.

My body was too tired to run any farther anyway. The long walk had taken a toll on me. I prayed for God to be my helper and make a way for me until I fell asleep.

I slept most of the day until late in the afternoon, the school bus stopped at the house and dropped off my cousins. The four boys were a loud bunch, hollering, chasing each other, and laughing. Excitement rose up in me, and I wanted to show myself right away, but I feared how things might turn out and hesitated. Finally, I could not stand it any longer. After they were in the house a few minutes, I came out of the barn and walked up to the house.

"Does your mom know where you are?" Edna asked.

I grinned and shook my head. "I ran away from home."

"You know I have to call her and tell her you're here, don't you?"

That was not what I wanted to hear. "I could just stay here with you—a few days," I suggested.

"Has your dad been mean to you," she asked.

I looked away. "He hates me, and he tells me so every day. I wish I could stay here."

"I wish you could too," she said. "But I don't think your mom would allow that."

"Why not?"

Edna did not answer as she turned and went inside the house.

My parents came to pick me up right away. I was out in the yard with my cousins when I saw their car pull into the driveway. A dark lump formed inside my chest, and I wanted to run again, but I was just too tired. This was my fourth time to run away, and based on past experiences, when I returned home things were going to go badly for me.

Both of my parents were friendly to Edna and Morris, but they did not say anything to me one way or the other. I stayed outside with the other boys while the adults went inside the house and talked. All the while I waited, I hoped and prayed they were working something out where I would not have to go back home.

*   *   *

MY DREAM WAS SHORT LIVED. Within a few minutes, Mom came outside the house and called my name. "Come on Kenny, it's time to go home."

Once inside the car, Junior went into a rampage. "That letter you left for your mother was a slam against me. You were trying to hurt me, weren't you?"

I did not answer. Nothing I said would matter.

"You said you loved her and didn't want to hurt her, but how do you think it makes me look to the police and neighbors?"

I kept quiet. My mind focused on other things. I imagined a different life of freedom. Four more years and I would be sixteen. I could join the army with my parent's signature, and they would surely be glad to get me off their hands.

Junior continued his diatribe. "The police have been out looking for you. We have to pay them for that. You think we have extra money to pay the police? See how much trouble you've caused? And what did you do with Steve's bike?"

"It's in the weeds by the river," I said.

Junior looked at Mom and began to shake his head. "You never rode all the way to the river bridge. That's at least five miles. Did your Aunt Edna come and pick you up?"

I wagged my head. "I rode the bike all the way."

Both parents were quiet a long moment. "You're a liar," Junior said. "I don't believe you."

I kept quiet. Answering would not do any good.

Steve sat beside me in the back seat busying himself with a notepad and a coloring book.

When we arrived back at Seymour, Junior drove passed the turn-off road to our house and headed out of town toward the river. "I want you to show me where you left that bicycle," he said.

When we arrived near the river, I spoke up. "It's down there below the first guardrail."

Junior quickly swung off the road. "Get down there and get it, right now. And hurry up." He opened the car door, got out, and stood near the car while I went down the embankment and retrieved the bicycle.

"You did not ride that thing all the way out here. Edna helped you, didn't she?" Junior asked again.

I shook my head. "No."

"You lie to me one more time, and I'm going to—" He doubled his fist and shivered as if he was having difficulty controlling himself. After he stared directly into my eyes for a long minute, he tipped his head toward town. "Get going."

"Aren't you going to put it in the trunk?" Mom asked.

Junior released a string of invectives. "Not on your life. He's going to ride it all the way back to town. We'll see how soon he wears out riding this far from home."

I stood waiting on the shoulder of the road holding the bicycle. Now, I wished I had kept on running instead of stopping at Uncle Morris's house. It would have been much easier to sleep on the ground tonight than to subject myself to Junior's wrath. I considered jumping from the bicycle and running into the woods, but I knew they would call the police and get the police dogs after me. If that happened, then I would have to face Junior anyway.

"Go!" he shouted, and brought me out of my thoughts. "Get on that bike and ride. I want to see how far you can go."

I straddled the bicycle and began pedaling back to town. I knew I could ride back to town easy enough. In fact, I was certain I could ride to home and back to the river a dozen times. As I rode I begged God to help me. Junior was more angry than I had ever seen him before, and I knew only God could help me now.

Junior turned on the car's emergency flashers and drove on the side of the rode behind me, always staying close to the back wheel of the bicycle. A few minutes later, he rolled down the car window, stuck his head out and shouted. "Pedal faster." Every sentence was sandwiched with curse words and name calling. "Hurry up you lowlife, you're not pedaling as fast as you can. You're not fooling me."

When we arrived inside the city limits and were about to make a left turn onto fourth street road, I made the mistake of standing up to pedal in order to get across the highway and beat the oncoming traffic. Junior suddenly realized I could pedal faster standing up, and he pulled the car up alongside me. "You stand up and pedal that bike all the time. No more sitting down. You hear me?"

"Yes sir." But after a few seconds of standing and pedaling I was in excruciating pain. I tried to relax a few seconds as I dropped onto the bicycle seat, but Junior honked the car horn, stuck his arm out the window and shook his fist at me.

The pain in my legs became so great my legs began to cramp and hurt until I could not stand it. Each time I dropped to the seat for a few seconds Junior honked at me. Tears from the pain ran down my cheeks as I prayed for God's mercy.

As I approached the vacant lot near our house, I spotted the bullies out in the field playing ball. My muscles tensed. "God, don't let this happen. Please God. I'm already in enough trouble."

The group of boys saw me coming and began running toward the road to head me off. I pedaled faster. If my parents witnessed them bullying me, then I would have to explain, and Junior would take delight in knowing someone else hated me too.

When the bullies realized they were too late to block the road and stop me, they picked up dirt clods and began pelting me as I rode by the empty lot. Some of the dirt clods found their mark. They hurt, but the real pain came from the humiliation in front of my family.

To my surprise, Junior saw the situation differently than I expected. Immediately, he skidded the car to a stop, got out and began yelling curse words at the group of teens. "You boys are going to get a good beating from me, if you ever do that again."

One of the boys replied with a wise-crack remark, which only fueled Junior's anger. Junior shook his fist and cursed even louder.

I took advantage of the situation and kept pedaling toward home. When I looked over my shoulder, Junior was still arguing with them. It was rather humorous that none of the bullies wanted to confront him.

I arrived home and parked the bicycle in the garage before Junior caught up with me. Inside the house, I stood in front of the kitchen sink and waited for my punishment to begin. "God, I'll do anything you want if you'll just protect me tonight. I know I've done wrong to run away, but if you don't help me, I may not survive this night."

*   *   *

I CRINGED WHEN JUNIOR SLAMMED THE ENTRY DOOR. "I can't take any more of that kid. We have to do something with him." He pulled off his shirt and took a seat at the kitchen table. Steve went to the living room and turned on the television.

Mom sat across from Junior at the table. "Why were those boys throwing dirt clods at you," she asked.

I lifted a shoulder. "They don't like me."

"Why? What did you do to them?"

"I didn't do anything. They just like to pick on me every time I ride by their house."

Junior slid his chair a few inches back from the table. "Get over here and stand in front of me where I can look you in the eyes." He pointed to a spot on the floor within arm's reach.

I obeyed, knowing what was coming. I had been in this same situation many times before. I had learned long ago to never talk back to Junior, and to reply with a simple "yes sir," and otherwise keep my mouth shut. Most important of all, I had to maintain constant eye contact when he spoke to me.

As usual, he began demeaning me with angry comments about my potential, my ugliness, and how I was destined for a worthless life because I had the blood line in me of a no-good father.

My mother never spoke up or took my defense. She always appeared distracted with a magazine or a newspaper. After a few minutes, she interrupted Junior's ranting. "I'll make a phone call tomorrow," she said. "One of the women at work said her family had a son they finally put in a Christian boy's home. They said it done wonders for him."

Junior gave her a sideways glance as he considered it a moment. Then he turned his attention back to me. "I should rip your head off your shoulders, for all the problems you've caused your mother and me. Is that what you want?"

"No." My voice was weak.

"I talked to a man at work the other day, and he told me for fifty-dollars he could get rid of you permanently. Permanently. You understand what I'm saying?"

"Yes."

"Look at me when I talk to you."

I stood motionless and stared dead center at his pupils. It was an ordeal I had been through many times, and it always followed the same progression. So I was not surprised when Junior backhanded me across the face. "Answer me. Do you understand what I'm telling you boy?"

"Yes," I repeated, louder this time.

"You'll never know where nor when."

I swallowed hard.

He kept locked onto my gaze, his black eyes never blinking. Suddenly, he flinched as if he was going to hit me.

I jumped back.

He did not laugh. "You may be on your way home from school when someone drives by and blows your brains out of your head." He paused a moment and then let out a laugh that sounded like the laugh of a devil. "And I'll never have anything to do with it."

On the outside, I stared motionless and passive at Junior. But inside my head, I prayed for God's help. I knew enough about God to know he was all powerful, and it did not take a theologian to understand that an all powerful God could read a person's thoughts and even alter those thoughts if he wanted to do so. Because of that, I hoped and believed in the possibility that God had more control over my future than Junior.

Junior's tirade continued for nearly an hour before he finally stopped. "You go to your room and stay there unless me or your mother call your name. You understand?"

I nodded and hurried to my room, glad to be alone. No one asked me if I was hungry, but I did not care. I would eat after they went to work in the morning.

No one mentioned it, but in the three days I had been gone, my great-grandmother had moved out of the house. The tension in our home was probably too much for an eighty-year old woman.

As soon as I shut the door to my room, I thanked God it was over—at least for the day. Someday life would be different, and I would be old enough to live on my own and be free of his torment. Until then, I would depend on God to help me.

My thoughts were interrupted by Mom's loud telephone voice. I quietly cracked open the door to my room and listened. From the one-sided conversation it was evident she was talking to my probation officer. I held my breath in order to hear every word she spoke.

She hung up the phone. "He's in town and said he can stop by right now," she said to Junior.

"I hope to God he can help us." Junior stood and put on his shirt. "Better get that brat out here and talk to him about this."

"Kenneth Allan? Get in here," she called.

I hurried into the kitchen as if I did not know what was going on.

"The probation officer is coming by to talk about finding you a place in a Methodist orphanage. I want you to act as if you like the opportunity. Tell him it's what you want to do," she said. "You hear me?"

I nodded. "Yes ma'am."

"Go comb your hair and put some good clothes on."

It had been several days since I had taken a shower, but I put on clean clothes and combed my hair like she said. After I was ready, I stalled until I heard the knock on the front door.

"Kenny?" she called, her voice sweet and soft.

I hurried to the living room, where she pointed to the best chair in the living room. "Sit up straight," she whispered just before she opened the door and greeted Mr. Armstrong.

After pleasantries were exchanged, Mom explained how someone had told her about a Christian orphanage that took troubled boys in and raised them. "Is there any way they would accept Kenny? she asked, her tone pleading.

The probation officer nodded. "Yes, it is possible, but I'll have to check on availability and get back to you."

Mom released a long sigh. "Kenny is a good boy, and I think this might be better for him."

Junior had been sitting quietly as if he was sulking, but he immediately brightened when he heard the probation officers response. His demeanor changed as if someone flipped a switch inside his brain. "We've done all we can. I don't know what else to do." He shook his head and chuckled as he shifted in his seat. "The kid's stubborn—I can't break him."

The probation officer stood to leave. "It'll take some time, but I'll let you know something in a couple weeks."

As soon as he left, everyone's attitude toward me changed dramatically. They even told me to sit in the living room and watch television with them the rest of the evening. It was odd, but I obeyed. In reality, I preferred the comfort of my own room where I would not be subject to Junior's menacing stare.

At first, I did not understand what had just happened, because the following two weeks were possibly the best two weeks I had experienced at home with my parents. Junior stopped cursing me, stopped slapping me, and stopped demeaning me. There was no mention of extra chores, and Mom took over the family cooking. I got the impression they wanted my last days with them to be a good memory.

They even encouraged me to go outside in the backyard during the evenings. I took advantage, but once outside, I did not know what to do with myself. I just walked around the yard like a lost man.

At the dinner table, the conversation always turned to excited talk of how they would come and visit me at my new home, and how the new life was going to be so much better for me in the long run.

"And we'll send you money from time to time," Junior added.

My own excitement wanted to build and grow, but I was skeptical. They made it sound as if I was going to a Christian prison. I did not want to go to prison, but even so, prison would be a great improvement over my current life. I continued to pray and to thank God every day that this was working out for me.

After two weeks passed and the probation officer had not contacted my parents, I began to worry. But Junior seemed to worry more than I did. Finally, he suggested Mom contact the probation officer to make certain the ball was rolling the right direction. He was obviously eager to get me moved out and into my new home.

"I'll call him right now," she said. We all waited until she got off the phone. She wore a worried look. "He's coming by the house tomorrow evening."

Although I enjoyed my new freedom at home, I would certainly have no remorse when I left this family behind. In bed at night, I imagined coming back at eighteen to visit my brother and mother. As an adult, Junior would not have any power over me. It was a good dream.

During the two and half weeks we waited for the probation officer's news, Junior had seemed like a child waiting to leave for Disney World. He talked kindly to me, and he even kept his pants on until bed time as if he expected the probation officer to arrive unannounced.

When the probation officer finally arrived, the entire family sat in the living room listening intently to his announcement. But the news was not what they expected. The probation officer hesitated and worked his jaw a moment. "After a lot of thought, I've come to the conclusion that Kenny is too good of a boy to be put in one of those homes."

"Oh?" Mom said softly.

"He'll be much better off in the long run right here with his own family."

A dark lump formed in my stomach. I wanted to run over to the sofa and grab onto the probation officers legs and beg; "Please, please don't leave me here. They don't want me. Any place will be better for me than here." Instead, I sat quietly like a worm waiting to be squashed.

Junior made more small talk until the probation officer stood to leave and then Junior followed him all the way out to the car as if they were old friends.

As soon as she closed the front door, Mom turned and stabbed her finger in my direction. "You better go to bed right now, young man. I don't want to hear another peep from you tonight." Her eyes flashed fire as if she was angry for something I had done.

Dumbfounded, I turned and hurried to my room, unsure what I had done wrong. I was just as disappointed as they were.

From my room, I listened as Junior enter the house. He let out a loud string of curse words, punctuated by a deep groan. "Why? Why can't we get a break? Am I going to have to put up with him until he's grown?" More cursing.

I did not understand the change in their attitude toward me or why they suddenly treated me so roughly, especially since I had done nothing wrong. Jesus had become my nearest and only friend, and I spent most of the night begging him for help and protection. Junior hated me, and for no reason. The hope that sustained me was that someday would be different. Someday, I would be free from him.

*   *   *

JUNIOR'S CONTEMPT FOR ME WORSENED. He quickly gave me extra chores to keep me busy, and he ridiculed and harassed me from daylight until dark. Nothing I did suited him. To make matters worse, he continually demeaned me with negative jargon. According to him, I would be a loser the rest of my life, and the world would be better off without me.

I was beat down so much, I dared not utter a word in defense, but in my mind I would think; *It isn't up to you if I am a success in life or not. Those things are up to me and Jesus.*

It never occurred to me to open the little white Bible that mother kept on the bedroom dresser. If I had done so and found any of the Scriptures of hope and promise, then I would have gained the direction and strength which I desperately needed. But no one told me there was value in reading the Bible, and all I knew about God was that prayer offered unlimited possibilities.

Even so, I often beat myself up mentally for my daily mistakes which Junior pointed out. "Why can't I do anything right?" I'd ask God.

One thread of hope I carried with me through childhood was a note Mrs. Hamilton, my sixth grade teacher, scribbled on the top of an assignment I turned in; "With every rising of the sun, think of your life as just begun." Those words never left me, and no matter how many times I failed and did wrong things, her words always came back to me and reminded me that I had a fresh start each and every day.

As I helped Junior get dressed each morning, he always found a reason to slap me numerous times. If I did not get his boots laced tight enough, he would slap me. If I missed a loop while putting his belt through his pant loops, he would slap me. All he needed was some small error on my part, and he went into a slapping frenzy.

Strangely, I bore no desire for revenge. I only wanted to get away from him and be set free from the Cinderella life he forced upon me. That idea became the subject of my dreams each day and night. My go-to phrase in my mind was always; *someday it will be different.*

My bedroom was next to the bathroom, and normally I slept straight through the night. But one night I was awakened by Junior calling out in desperation to God. "Please, God, help me. Have mercy," his tone was pitiful, and he did not seem to care who heard him.

Suddenly I was wide awake as I wondered if he was really dying.

Mom stepped to the bathroom door. "Anything I can do?"

"Yeah." He groaned as if it was his last breath.

"You want to go to the hospital?" she asked.

He cursed. "You can tell that boy of yours to stop poisoning me."

Mom released a long sigh. "He wouldn't do that."

"He's trying to kill me. He's put poison in something I ate. I know he did. Oh God, please help me."

I remained perfectly still, and expected Mom to come into my room and question me, but she didn't, and eventually I fell asleep again. When I got up that morning, Junior had already left to go to work and Mom was at the kitchen table drinking her morning coffee, a worried look on her face.

"Where's Dad," I asked. I did not like to call him dad, but I was not given a choice in the matter.

"He's already gone to work. He's sick."

I played dumb. "What's wrong with him?"

Mom met my gaze. "He thinks you poisoned him. Did you?"

I shook my head and frowned. "No." Actually, it had never occurred to me to poison him or try to punish him in any way. I was top frightened to attempt retaliation.

Mom seemed to believe me and never brought the subject up again. Nothing more was said about it, and Junior became quiet and reserved for a couple days. But as soon as he began to feel better, his hatred for me seemed to worsen even further.

As usual, bed wetting always provided the excuse he needed to vent his anger on me. Although I truly tried everything I could think of to prevent my bed wetting, I never stopped as long as I was under Junior's care.

One day he came up with a more severe method of punishment. "From now on, every time you get a whipping, I'm going to add a switch to it. So tonight you get whipped with two switches, and the next time it'll be three." He sat at the kitchen table in his handle bar T-shirt smoking a cigarette, his work pants unbuttoned, his belt hanging loose.

Mom sat looking over the evening paper, but said nothing.

"Get a knife out of the drawer and go out and cut me two of those willow shoots from the fence row," he said.

I did not move.

"I want whips as tall as you are. And if you don't cut them big enough, I'm going out there and cut them myself, so you better bring in two good-sized switches."

Trembling, I fought back my fear and turned to obey. Fortunately, I had fooled him on my last whipping when I cut several small notches in the side of the big switch to make it break more easily. The trick worked, but for some reason it did not seem as if the pain was any less severe. The thought of getting whipped on my naked body with two of these willow whips was more than I wanted to endure. I went outside and stood barefoot in the yard praying and crying, not sure what to do.

I cut the two large willow whips and prayed. "Jesus, I can't stand to be whipped with two of these. He never stops until there's nothing left but the stub. What am I going to do? Help me, Jesus. Please."

Finally, I made my decision, tossed the knife point-down into the ground, and then turned and ran across the back yard. When I came to the end of the back yard, I made a high jump over the neighbor's fence. Unfortunately, the barbed wire on top of the fence caught my pant leg, and I went face down in the dirt. My get-away was not turning out well.

Excruciating pain went up my spine. I was not certain if I blacked out or not, but when I had my senses back, I pulled myself loose, stood, and ran across the neighbor's field, through the woods and onto the road. I wore only pants and a white T-shirt—no shoes or socks.

Instead of following the road, I cut across the farm field and entered the woods. I knew Junior might drive along the road and look for me, but he would never go to the trouble of searching for me in the woods.

I had no plan in mind, other than escape the double whipping, and it was nearly dark. Already, I was cold and since it was nearly dark, I worked my way back out into the plowed field where I could see where I was walking. The ground was soft and muddy from the rain earlier that day, and every step I took my feet sank in the mud above my ankles.

I walked westward most of the night with the idea that I might walk to my Grandfather Dick's house in Medora. It was at least thirty miles away, but I had no other option. I didn't like the idea of sleeping outside, in the cold October night, but I had no choice and kept walking along the west-bound railroad tracks until past midnight.

Finally, I came upon a house with a small barn near the tracks. I quietly made my way to the barn and went inside. A small dog on a leash in the yard began barking as soon as I entered the homeowners property.

Inside the barn, was a horse in a stall and to the far side were several bails of straw. I fell to my knees and raked up the loose straw into a pile to make a bed. It was much warmer inside the barn where I was out of the wind, and the smell of the old barn was comforting.

The dog continued to bark for several minutes until the homeowner came to the back door and turned on the outside light. "Shut up, Blackie. There's nothing out here."

The dog kept barking.

I quietly sat up and watched through the cracks between the boards. The homeowner stepped out onto the back-porch stoop. My heart raced like a horse out of the starting gate, because if the man found me, he'd likely call the police.

I whispered a prayer. "God I'm not bothering anything. I just need a warm place to sleep for the night.

"Shut up!" the homeowner shouted again to the dog. "Or I'm going to smack you." He turned off the light, went back inside, and closed the door.

A long sigh of relief escaped my lips as I lay back down. The dog continued to bark for a long time, and I got up and left at the first sign of daylight.

I continued to walk along the railroad tracks toward Brownstown. I had already walked several miles, and since I had not eaten dinner last evening, I became extremely hungry.

Fortunately, it was late in the fall and the farmers had left dozens of small watermelons behind in the fields when they picked their crop. I helped myself to several of them. Without a knife, I had to improvise and bust the watermelons open. Like a primitive cave man, I ate the red flesh with my fingers. Watermelon was not my favorite food, but at that point I was grateful for anything to eat. Once I was full, I continued westward to Brownstown, always keeping a constant dialogue of prayer as I walked.

By the time I arrived at Brownstown it began to rain, and I took shelter on a wooded hillside just outside of town near Bob Thomas Auto Sales. After walking close to fifteen miles in the last few hours, I was tired and sleepy, but my body was too cold and miserable to sleep. I stretched out on the ground under the tree and folded my arms across my chest to retain warmth, but it was nearly impossible to sleep with rain dripping on my face.

As I lay flat on my back with my eyes closed, I imagined how life would change one day. If only my parents would only give up looking for me, and I could get a job and take care of myself. I didn't care where I lived. It could be the smallest room in a garage somewhere. Just to be free would be my greatest joy.

The police were likely looking for me, so I avoided walking on the road. The county sheriff's office was only two blocks from main street in Brownstown, and a nice warm jail cell seemed tempting compared to the miserable cold I was experiencing.

Hungry, cold, and wet, I finally walked out of the woods and onto the road. I had not walked long when a car pulled up alongside me and rolled down the passenger window. It was a policeman. "What's your name?" he asked.

"George Claycamp," I lied again.

The officer laughed. "George, get in the car with me a minute."

I turned and looked at the field behind me. I could easily climb the fence and outrun the policeman. My wet T-shirt clung to my skin, and a gust of wind reminded me that I was cold and exhausted. After a moment's hesitation, I dropped into in the front seat of the cruiser beside the officer.

He picked up his radio microphone and talked in code I could not understand. The dispatcher on the other end laughed when the officer said George Claycamp.

"Don't you know, you should not run away from home?" the officer said. "You should come to us for help. We're your friends. We want to help you."

I nodded my understanding, but I did not believe him. I had heard that promise before, but I always had a tough time trusting anyone. Especially, after the Detective betrayed me a few years ago. Every authority figure in my life had betrayed me. Even the psychologist could not stay awake long enough to listen to my problems. The only friend I had ever been able to count on was Jesus, and I believed he was the only one I could trust.

The officer took me to the county jail where I assumed they would summon my parents. Instead, they locked me in a large cell with another teen several years older than me. I was grateful to be warm again, and the TV dinner they served tasted great. But after several days passed and my parents didn't show up, I began to seriously wonder what was going to happen to me.

Junior often insisted I would be in boy's school before I was sixteen-years old, and now I worried his words might be true. Even so, from what I had heard, life in boys' school would be better than living with Junior.

My cell mate was soon moved to another facility and the county jail became lonesome, but at least I was warm. During my six-week incarceration, I had no visitors and only an occasional cell mate. Breakfast was always two yeast dough-nuts and a cup of black coffee. Lunch and dinner was always a warmed TV dinner in an aluminum pan.

The secretary at the county jail office showed me kindness by sending up a soda and a couple candy bars. I never met her, and I never learned her name, but I have never forgotten her kindness.

The juvenile section of the County Jail had four bunks and a metal picnic table inside the cell. Everything was painted green except the gray floors. The juvenile section was separated from the adult prisoners, which meant most days I was alone. For several weeks the only person I saw was the man who brought my daily meals, and I never tried to engage in conversation with him.

Days of solitude allowed plenty of time for reflection and prayer. But even though I was lonely and bored not once did I regret my decision to run away from my parents. I was as much a prisoner at home as I was in a jail cell.

I often prayed and promised God I would live right and be a good person if he helped me. No one had taught me exactly what *living right* really meant, but I assumed the basic items on the list were; no killing and no stealing.

One afternoon after I had been in the jail for several weeks, an older gentleman wandered upstairs and stopped near my cell where he looked me over intensely. He didn't say anything at first, but I began to feel conspicuous. After a moment, he turned his attention to the cell bars as if he was a contractor considering a bid on painting the bars or something. I got the impression he had never seen the inside of a jail before. Of course, this was my first time inside a jail, also.

I put down the magazine I'd been reading and nodded a greeting.

The portly man looked as if he was near retirement age. His white hair was thin and disarrayed, his shirttail hung partially outside his pants. I guessed him at five-foot eight inches or shorter. He had a doughy belly that battled against the buttons of his dress shirt as if they might pop at any moment.

With his hands plunged deep into his pockets, the jingle of change broke the silence. Once again, he turned his attention back to me and looked me up and down a long minute. "What are you in for, Bud?" he finally asked.

I was glad to hear him finally speak. "Running away from home."

He frowned. "Why'd you do that?"

I lifted my shoulders. "Jail's better than home, I guess."

"You're missing school while you're in here. Don't you like school?"

I nodded. "As much as anybody."

"It's the principal of the thing that bothers you, huh?" He laughed at his own joke, and then examined the cell bars again as if in thought. Finally, he turned and left without saying another word.

*　　*　　*

THE TURNKEY UNLOCKED MY CELL. "Someone wants to talk to you downstairs." He led me downstairs to a small office in the corner of the building. Inside the room, my probation officer sat behind a cluttered desk talking with the same portly man who had just visited me.

They immediately grew quiet as I entered the room. Mr. Armstrong, my probation officer, gestured for me to take a seat in the vacant chair. "Kenny, this is Earl Nossett. He's a pastor who lives outside of town in the Acme community."

Earl stood and offered his hand. "Glad to meet you, Kenny."

I shook his hand before I dropped into the vacant chair, anxious to hear why I was summoned to this office. At first I assumed they were about to reprimand me for missing so much school—even though I was in jail and had no choice in the matter.

Since Earl was a pastor I considered he might be here to talk to me about God. He continued to look me over, his brow slightly furrowed.

George stared at the manila file in his hand. "Kenny, what do you think about getting out of jail and going to stay with Reverend Nossett for the weekend?"

The wings of my heart lifted. All I heard was *get out of jail.* Did he think I was brain dead? I wanted to say, No thank you, I'll stay in my green cell for a few more weeks and eat doughnuts and TV dinners. But I had never seen my probation officer smile, and I feared he might not have a sense of humor.

At that point, I was so lonely I was on board for anything they offered. "I'd really like that," I said quietly.

The two men talked softly a moment longer before Earl stood. "Kenny, let's go to my house and have a talk."

I quickly stood and followed him outside to his white El Camino, half-car and half-truck. Once we were outside of town, he seemed pleased to demonstrate his skill at steering the car with his belly. "We'll have to get your clothes from your parents," he said.

During the twenty-minute drive to his house, Earl filled me in on his own life. "I pastor two country churches and my wife, Louise, works as a cook at the Cortland school."

I looked straight ahead and nodded. Conversation was not my thing, and I knew the less I spoke, the less likely I was to give away my inabilities.

He pointed to a cluster of white boxes in a field as we drove along the country road. "Those boxes are my beehives. I raise honey. Hope you like honey, because at my house you can have all you want."

"I like honey and peanut butter."

"I'll let you help me work with the bees sometime. I have to extract it from the comb and put it jars and then the local grocers sell it for me. You got any hobbies?" he asked as he rolled down the window.

I shook my head, embarrassed that he had to roll down the window. I had not taken a shower since I'd left home and that was over two weeks earlier.

Once we were at his house, the first thing he showed me was his room full of pendulum clocks. Three walls inside the room were lined with shelves, all full of clocks.

"I'm a retired jeweler. Kept all my equipment so I can clean watches and rings. Sometimes I do minor repairs for people." He gestured to the clocks on the shelves. "In my free time, I refurbished old pendulum clocks. It all keeps me busy."

I nodded and tried to appear interested. Inside, I wondered if this was really happening to me or if it was a dream. I feared I might awaken and suddenly be back home with Junior. It didn't take a brain surgeon to understand how quickly my visit here could be quickly terminated if Mr. Nossett did not like me.

The first clock struck twelve o'clock and began to chime twelve times, before it finished another clock joined in and then another. Soon the entire room was ding-donging in beat and out of beat. It was very cool in a retro sort of way.

Earl's wife, Louise, came in from work and introduced herself. She was a short, frail grandmotherly type who could not seem to keep still. She smiled and made small talk before she led me to the room adjacent to the clock room. "This is where you'll be sleeping. It was my son, Danny's room, but—." Her voice cracked.

A small phonograph player and a stack of forty-five vinyl records sat on the bedside table. "Who do all the records belong to?" I asked.

"They were Danny's. He liked his music." She covered her mouth and stepped into the other room a minute.

"Our son Danny, was killed in a train wreck last year," Earl said. "He was only fifteen. We really miss him."

I did not know what to say, so I said nothing.

"The house is so empty without him." Earl cleared his throat. "But this is where you'll sleep, and you're welcome to treat this room like it's your own."

I understood the things that were not spoken; this kind couple was willing to help a troubled juvenile in hope of filling the empty space in their hearts. Occasionally, they mistakenly called me Danny, but it was minor nuisance compared to the new life they offered me.

That first night with Earl and Louise was the best of times and the worst of times. I was both ecstatic and tortured at the same time. Until then I had not been aware of just how much I feared being in the company of people. For most of my life, I had never been around people enough to realize I had this fear.

I liked people, but I suddenly felt as if the waters were closing above my head, and I was going to drown. I did not know what to do or say around strangers. The only place my parents ever took us was to visit Junior's mother or my maternal grandfather.

As soon as we arrived at the grandparent's house, my stepfather would always snap his fingers once and point to a chair. "Sit there and don't get up until you're told." Children never engaged in conversation, and were never allowed to play at our grandparent's house.

That first night, dozens of the parishioners stopped to visit the pastor. At first, I assumed it was the normal routine in a pastor's home, but eventually, one of the visitors explained, "This is not normal, Kenny. We're all curious to see the new person in our pastor's family, and of course we want to welcome you to our community."

They kept coming late into the evening, and even past bedtime; the elderly, the young, and everyone in between arrived at the pastor's house to get a peek at the new guy in the neighborhood.

I planted myself on the sofa in front of the television and pretended I was engrossed in a cowboy movie. In the back of my mind, I still worried this might be a trick. Junior could suddenly walk into the house and take me back home with him. But when the woman explained how the entire rural community was curious to meet the pastor's new son, it was then I understood that I was not on a weekend visit.

This precious elderly couple was going to be my first official foster parents. Junior was not coming to get me, and my dream had finally come true. Jesus had truly answered my prayers, and I was finally free from Junior—at least physically. It would be years later before I was free emotionally.

In my mind, I struggled to take on a new perspective in my world view. I had never experienced this type of life before, and I had no clue how to manage this new freedom along with all the kindness that suddenly came my way. I had no clear reference point of what normal life was supposed to be like, and I soon discovered it was impossible to simply turn off the emotions and attitudes that had taken years to develop inside my head. I was deeply flawed, but I did not know it yet.

A dark fear lived inside my chest most of my life, and it would not leave. Even though I no longer needed to have a fear of Junior, the fear remained. Until now, there had been no room in my life for any fear other than the fear I had of my stepfather. Right away, I subconsciously began to substitute other things to fear in place of Junior.

At the top of the list was the fear of people. Suddenly, I was thrust into meeting new people who expected me to converse with them and mingle.

While living with my parents, I had absolutely no social involvement except for school. Now, I was surrounded by strangers, and I did not know how to interact with them. When I did try to interact with others, my words often came out wrong, which made me feel even more awkward.

Of course, I had developed a serious speech impediment as a result of my missing front teeth. I had a lisp, and I could not articulate some sounds clearly. Often people could not understand me when I spoke. This was mostly because I talked extremely fast, while I held my hand over my mouth.

While around people, I became self-conscious of my hands, and developed the habit of jamming them deep inside my pants pockets. That created another problem since I had already trained myself to talk only when my hand covered my mouth. To resolve this bad habit, I learned to face away from people as I talked in order to prevent them from seeing my broken teeth.

As a result, I lost the ability to make eye contact. When I looked away from the person I was talking to, they would look away too, as if something else had my attention.

To help my problem, I cleverly developed the skill of talking without moving my upper lip. Often I even pressed my index finger against my upper lip to hide my broken teeth as I talked.

People told me I mumbled, and they were right. I did mumble, but I was self-conscious and I refused to change. I wanted to be normal and fit in, but my bad habits compounded my problems. I refused to talk, and I refused to smile.

Without question, I was an emotional wreck, even though I was not aware of it yet. My thirteenth birthday was approaching and like most teenagers I craved a social life with other teens. But I was stuck in this love-hate attitude, because I wanted to be alone where I felt safe; yet, at the same time I needed the company of my peers.

As soon as I moved in with Earl and Louise, I immediately gravitated to my new bedroom where I played music on the little record player. Music inspired me like nothing else I had ever experienced. It was like a drug for me. I sat on the bed looking through the big stack of those forty-five singles. At home I had only two albums of Elvis Presley and one single of the Beetles—Hard Day's Night. From the stack of forty-five singles, I chose my new favorite; a Petula Clark single, titled *Down Town*.

When you're alone and life is making you lonely, you can always go— downtown. When you got worries, all the noise and the hurry seems to help, I know—downtown. Just listen to the music of the traffic in the city. Linger on the sidewalk where the neon signs are pretty.

"You can't hide in your room all the time." Earl's voice broke into my thoughts. He stood in doorway behind me. "Why don't you come in the living room and watch television with Louise and me."

I nodded and lifted the needle from the record player and shut it off. Only rarely had I sat with the adults at home to watch television, and then I wasn't permitted to talk. Now, my new foster parents wanted me to converse with them, but I had no skill at dialogue.

"You want something to eat?" Louise asked as soon as I dropped beside her onto the sofa.

I shook my head. "No thanks." Truthfully, I was very hungry.

Earl began to question me. "Kenny, I am having a difficult time believing you're only twelve years old."

Almost thirteen, I thought, but I said nothing.

"I talked to your probation officer today, and he said your father and mother both were big people. You ever met your real father?"

I wagged my head. "Not yet."

"I went to the hospital today and had them look up your birth certificate. Not many twelve-year olds are six-foot tall, but the hospital records don't lie."

"What about my clothes," I asked.

"Your probation officer contacted your parents and asked for your clothes and bicycle, but they won't let us have anything of yours. Don't worry. We'll get you some clothes."

Earl and Louise seemed pleased as a new mother to have me in their home. They went above and beyond any kindness I had ever experienced and treated me like their own family. In a strange way, my good fortune was difficult to accept. As a result, I always kept my distance from people and refused to trust anyone. Earl called me out on it several times, but distrust was the only way I knew to survive.

According to Earl, I was like a wild-eyed animal who had just been released from a cage and uncertain which way to run. The elderly couple had no way of knowing all the baggage I brought with me when they took me into their home.

I had been set on a path to destruction years before, and a few kind words would not break through the shell I had built around myself. To my shame, I stopped praying. Life was going so well, I did not have the need to pray. Even so, God continued to reach out to me, but I had difficulty recognizing his call to me.

CHAPTER FIVE

God holds us responsible, not for what we have, but for what we could have. Not for what we are, but for what we might be.

When my father and my mother forsake me,
then the LORD will take me up. Psalm 27:10

THE FIRST WEEK SEEMED LIKE HEAVEN to me. I soon learned the little rural community was very close-knit. Numerous teens from A three to five mile radius around often stopped at the house to play basketball and hang out. I assumed their parents insisted they befriend the new guy, and I was grateful. But my self-image was so low, I could not comprehend the idea that other people might actually like me or that they sincerely wanted to be my friend.

Suddenly, I had more freedom than I had ever experienced before. Freedom the other young people took for granted. For example, the country grocery was only a quarter of a mile away, and I was allowed to walk up the hill to the store anytime I wanted. All I had to do was ask permission or leave a note stating where I was going and when I'd be back.

The little country grocery was the social watering hole for the teenagers in the area. At the end of the day, several teens gravitated to the store's gravel parking lot to play basketball or just hang out. Inside the store several chairs were positioned in the center of the room near a kerosene stove.

At first, it seemed strange for people to come into the store and sit and talk for no particular reason. Later, I realized that hanging out in the store and socializing was one of the elements that bound the community together.

My life changed dramatically overnight, and something unexpected happened as soon as I moved in with Earl and Louise. My bed wetting stopped almost immediately. When I did have an accident, Louise and Earl never made a big deal out of it, and unlike my stepfather, they never mentioned it to anyone outside the family.

I volunteered to work around the house and do chores like mowing the yard, and even changing the flat tire on Louise's car. Earl and Louise always complemented my work, and that was a new concept to me.

Neighbors even called the house and ask if I would come and work for them. Mostly, it was farmers who called and wanted me to help them put up hay. Stacking hay on the wagon and in the barn loft was hard work, but fifty-cents an hour was more money than I had earned in my life. At that time, the minimum wage was a dollar-sixty an hour, so I considered myself making good money for a young teenager.

Although I was grateful for this new life, I continued to struggle in order to adjust. At home I was accustomed to lying, and keeping secrets in order to survive. Every authority in my life had always been the enemy as far as I was concerned, and changing that mindset was difficult.

I had developed that attitude as a survival method, and I could not turn it off in my brain and readjust at will. I had never trusted anyone, and even though my external world changed, I was still the same person inside. Earl and Louise wanted me to be honest and open, but I continued to revert to lying and deceptiveness.

Often, I went places that were off limits, and I lied about the company I was with. In addition, I got into things that were off limits for me. For example, one day while I was home alone, I took Earl's rifle outside and did some target practicing in the back yard. That was not something an inexperienced thirteen-year old should have done; especially, since it was my first time to shoot a firearm.

I avoided eating at the table with others. My stepfather criticized my eating manners, and made me feel uncomfortable when I did eat at the dinner table. Yet, I had no reservations about raiding the refrigerator when Earl and Louise were in another room.

Peanut butter was my main food source during that time, and I could not get enough of it. Earl prompted me to mix peanut butter with fresh honey, and I was immediately hooked. Louise purchased giant half-gallon jars of peanut butter just to keep me happy. She always cooked for the family, but I loved peanut butter.

As the weeks passed, Earl and Louise were always careful to prevent me from having alone-time with girls. At thirteen-years old, I could not comprehend they were trying to protect me. But like most teenagers with determination, I found numerous ways to deceive and manipulate situations in order to spend time with girls anyway.

In contrast, while in public I was always transparent to a fault. No one had ever taught me how to behave in public, or how to shake hands, or how to be polite to others. The few times my mother and stepfather did visit relatives, my instructions were always the same; "Sit in that chair. Don't get up, and don't open your mouth."

Suddenly, I was free, but I did not know how to manage my new freedom. I was six feet tall, and big for my age, but I was immature below my years.

As a new guy in the close-knit community, everyone extended a lot of grace to me, but at the time, I was completely oblivious to their kindness. I always acted the way I felt. Filtering or monitoring my words and actions seemed an alien concept to me. The lack of a filter got me in trouble on numerous occasions, not only with adults, but also with my new peers. Simply put, I was wild, uncouth, and sometimes even frightening to those around me.

Junior had shaped my life more than I realized, and whether I liked it or not, I was developing into a mirror image of him. Deception seemed like the normal way to live, and telling lies to boost my self image had advantages, from my point of view.

I soon learned that in the teenage world the *bad boy* was not only accepted but even respected by other teenagers. My early growth spurt turned out to be an asset after all.

Fortunately, my first day at junior high school taught me a valuable life lesson about the flip side of the bad-boy life. Outside the junior high school, I stood waiting for the school bus to arrive when three upper class men came around the corner of the building, and turned their attention on me.

"Hey smiley, what would you do if I hit you in the stomach—smile?" the leader of the three asked.

I wasn't certain how to respond, but in an attempt at humor, I said "Probably." Humor seemed to win people over and I considered myself pretty funny at times.

Bam!

The largest boy hit me in the stomach without warning. His two friends laughed and patted him on the back. "Nice going," they said.

Cold sweat instantly broke out on my face, as I dropped my books and bent over to suck in deep gulps of air. For a moment it seemed I might pass out. After several deep breaths, I finally gained my composure enough to speak again. I cursed the ruffian and his ancestry with every foul word I had learned from Junior—some I used twice.

The three teenagers laughed and turned to walk away, until suddenly the leader of the three realized I was blatantly cursing him. He stepped within arm's reach. "What did you say to me, punk?

Before I had time to answer, a teacher appeared around the corner. "What's going on here boys? Do we have a problem?"

"No sir, nothing is wrong," the three said in unison and hurried away.

The teacher looked me over a moment before he went inside the school without saying a word.

For several weeks after the incident, I avoided Chad, the leader of the three ruffians. If I didn't Chad would taunt me each time he found me in the hallway or cafeteria. On many occasions, I changed my direction when I saw Chad coming my way. I even skipped eating lunch in the school cafeteria in order to evade Chad's torment.

But there was no hiding from Chad in the evening as I waited for the school bus to arrive. He took advantage of the situation and humiliated me many evenings. With other students watching, he would threaten me and try provoke me into a fight. It was easier to avoid him and not answer his taunting. I was accustomed to Junior's bullying, and I knew exactly how to accept it.

"You don't have to take that from Chad," other students told me. "You can take him, easy."

After several students encouraged me to stand up to Chad, I finally summoned the confidence I needed. One day during lunch break I found Chad outside with his circle of friends. I walked up to him and stood my full height, my heart pounding loudly against my chest.

"I'm ready to take you up on that offer to fight," I said. "We can meet across the street after school tonight.

"You sure that's what you want to do?" he asked. "It won't end well for you."

Chad and I were the same size, but he was a couple years older. His hesitation to fight fueled my confidence and determination rose up in me as I swallowed hard and nodded. "I do." I would not hide-out from Chad any longer.

Immediately after school, I dropped my books off at the locker and hurried to the scheduled meeting spot. To my surprise more than two hundred students had already gathered in the alley across the street from the school. Adrenalin raced through my veins like fast moving water as I pushed my way through the crowd. Chad stood in the middle of the crowd where he seemed to enjoy the attention he was getting.

No preliminaries were needed. Both of us squared off facing each other. Chad spit on his fist. "This is going to be easy," he said. He threw the first punch, which glanced off my arm.

I punched back, and soon we were a flurry of wailing arms, dancing in a circle like two young roosters. When I realized I was holding my own against Chad, it fueled my confidence even further. We fought only a minute or two when suddenly, a firm hand grasped me by the shoulder and pulled me back away from Chad. It was a teacher.

"You boys come to the principal's office right now." He gripped Chad by the neck and squeezed so hard that Chad cried out in pain. The teacher guided him back to the school property and took us both to the office.

In the end, the principal punished Chad, because he was an upperclassman and had been in trouble before. It was my first offence, so the principal reprimanded me and let me go. "You were just a victim of a juvenile delinquent," he said. "Chad has been in trouble before."

I worried the principal might call my foster parents, but he never did. I had not wanted to fight Chad, but once I did, he not only left me alone, but he also became friendly.

As a result of the fight, I suddenly became popular at junior high. Students whom I did not know began speaking to me, and even the upper-class girls smiled at me in the school halls. It was a good feeling, because the rumor was out that I had whipped an upperclassman.

I was the upcoming bad boy of junior high school. Sadly, fighting gained me respect among my peers, and I got into numerous fist fights from that point onward.

To emphasize the bad boy look, I carried a pack of cigarettes with me even though I did not smoke. Smoking was a stupid habit as far as I was concerned. My stepfather had tried to make me smoke on numerous occasions, but I always refused. Fortunately, my mother took up for me.

I also began using profanity, because I thought it made me appear older and more mature. Junior had always encouraged me to curse and swear and at times he even forced me to use profanity. Like smoking, I thought cursing was also stupid—the language of the ignorant. Yet, I was desperate to fit in with my peers, and I was willing to do whatever it took to reach that goal—even if it meant doing things I really did not want to do.

In my case, I always had to think about what curse words I was going to say before I spoke. Curse words never flowed out of me like it did my peers. So many of my peers cursed like a musician who played by ear and could play anything without thinking about it. I was like the musician who only played by note; I had to think about it before I cursed.

A VISITING EVANGELIST stayed with Earl and Louise while he preached revival services at the little church where Earl pastored. I attended every church service, but I knew next to nothing about God or the Bible, and I did not seem to grasp the Gospel message that came from the pulpit.

At the end of the last revival service, the congregation sang a heart-warming tune; *Why do you wait, dear brother? Oh, why do you tarry so long? Your Savior is waiting to give you, a place in his sanctified throng.*

The Spirit of the Lord swept through the little country church and several young people hurried to the altar. That night was my first time to experience conviction from God, but I did not know what it was or what to do about it. Down at the altar, I wedged myself in among the other praying teenagers and bowed my head.

Tears flowed down my cheeks, but I did not understand why I was crying or even what I was supposed to be praying about at the altar. The evangelist knelt on the floor in front of Rita, the young girl next to me. "Why are you here at the altar, Rita?" he asked.

"I just want to be closer to Jesus." Her voice cracked with emotion.

He nodded, prayed for her, and moved down the line of teenagers until he came to me. "Kenny, why are you here at the altar tonight?"

With no answer in mind, I repeated Rita's answer, "I just want to be closer."

The evangelist nodded, prayed for me, and moved to the next young person at the altar.

If only someone had taken the time and interest to teach me God's plan of salvation it would have saved me a lot of frustration and pain in the following years. It was not until years later that I learned what it meant to be saved.

I had sent a lot of prayers up to God, and I was confident he had answered many of those prayers. But since I had not been taught anything about God, I made the assumption that everything was okay between God and me as long as I did not murder or rob anyone. Jesus was reaching for my heart, but I did not distinguish his voice.

Earl gave me a Bible and encouraged me to read it every day. It seemed boring to me, but I made an effort. One day I sat on the edge of my bed reading the Gospels when suddenly it dawned on me that Matthew, Mark, Luke, and John were the same story by different authors. That bit of knowledge was a milestone in my life, because it was the first thing I learned from the Bible.

Earl also encouraged me to enjoy outdoor sports. He purchased a new fishing rod and reel for me and encouraged me to use it. I spent several evening fishing in the old ponds hidden behind the house and up in the woods around Persimmon Lake.

One hot summer day I decided to go swimming in one of the old ponds instead of fishing. A small raft seemed like a lot of fun, so I gathered two empty five-gallon buckets with lids attached and an old wooden pallet from a junk pile in the woods. At the house, I found a roll of wire which I used to attach the buckets to the bottom of the wooden pallet.

Once I was satisfied with my creation, I slid the homemade raft down the bank, pushed it out onto the water, and then climbed on top of it. It floated, but it would not set level in the water, and soon the buckets I wired to the bottom of the pallet slipped out.

I tossed the buckets up on the bank and began swimming around the floating pallet. I did not own a swim suit, but my jeans and T-shirt worked just fine. As I swam under the water and opened my eyes, I spotted the two large loops of wire hanging down under the pallet. The challenge of swimming through the wire hoops seemed like a good idea at the time.

I swam halfway through the first hoop when the wire loop snagged on my jeans and would not break free. I jerked and wiggled, but I only became more tangled with the weight of the pallet on my back. Panic rose up in me, and I began to flail and thrash around under the water. But no matter how much I tried, I could not get myself free from the wooden pallet stuck on my back.

After what seemed like a three full minutes, I could not hold my breath any longer and realized I was going to drown. As one last resort, I stopped thrashing and calmly forced myself to methodically untangle the wire. It took a long time, and I was near the limit of holding my breath when I finally broke free and resurfaced.

I sucked in giant gulps of air and thanked God for sparing my life. From that day forward, I never swam alone.

When autumn arrived, Earl wanted to take me on my first hunting experience. "I have never even held a shotgun in my hands before," I said.

"No better time to learn." Earl took me out to the backyard where he placed a can on the fence post and let me shoot his shotgun at it a several times.

"It kicks pretty hard," I said. "But it's fun to shoot."

Back inside the house, Earl pulled another shotgun from the closet and handed it to me. "You take this 870 Remington, and we'll go hunt rabbit a few hours. I bought this for Danny just before his accident."

"Wow. This is a nice gun," I said.

Earl made certain the gun was unloaded. "Just keep the muzzle pointed up at all times, and never point it at anything you don't intend to shoot. Now let's go to the woods and have some fun."

Once we were inside the woods, Earl loaded my gun, and we walked up and down hillsides for nearly an hour without seeing anything. Finally, we were about to give up when a large covey of quail flushed. As the quail rose up in front of us, I turned to Earl. "Aren't those quail?"

He nodded. "Take a shot. Hurry."

I mounted the gun to my shoulder and pulled the trigger. The first quail dropped. More quail flushed and I ratcheted another shell in the chamber and fired again. To my surprise a second bird dropped to the ground.

"Wow, you're a natural." Earl bent and picked up the dead birds. "Let's try that again." He handed me a handful of shells. "Load up and we'll kick those birds up one more time."

We walked in the direction where we had last seen the birds disappear and flushed them several more times. Sadly, I could not connect again.

"It's called beginners luck," Earl said. "But you'll get better with practice. I'll walk along the bottom of the ridge and you walk along the top. Maybe if we spread out, we'll kick up a rabbit or two."

I obeyed, but a few minutes later, I slipped and fell down the hill. After examining the shotgun I discovered it was unharmed, but the fall had jammed mud inside the barrel.

Earl did not see me fall, and I did not say anything. It was a nice shotgun and I knew he would not be happy if he discovered I had jammed the barrel of his nice shotgun full of mud.

A few minutes later, we gave up hunting and headed back to the house. On the way back, he picked up a tin can. "See if you can hit this when I toss it up." He stepped to my left side and tossed the can high into the air.

I mounted the shotgun and fired. The can fell to the ground unharmed. "Missed again," I said and glanced at the end of the barrel to see if the mud was all gone. "Oh no!"

Earl was already a few steps ahead of me. He stopped and turned. "What's wrong?"

"The shotgun. It blew a hole out the side." A long strip of metal about a foot long had torn away from the left side of the barrel.

Earl's brow wrinkled. "Don't shoot it anymore. You've gotten mud in the barrel and stopped it up. That gun is ruined."

"Sorry," I said, and waited for him to berate me as I unloaded the gun. "I didn't know it would do that."

Earl just shook his head. He did not seem angry with me. "God sure looked out for me, because I'm just lucky to be alive," he said. "That barrel exploded on the same side where I was standing, and it could have easily killed me—and you both." The incident obviously bothered him, but he did not reprimand me. I realized that once again Jesus had protected me from danger.

*　　*　　*

TEN MONTHS WAS ALL the longer Earl and Louise could take. I wore them down. It was a good time for me, but the trouble I caused the two elderly people turned our relationship from one of friendship and guidance to one that was more like a police relationship. I was always in trouble for something, and they learned they had to monitor me to prevent me from worse trouble.

Because of my wild personality and attitude, I caused a disruption everywhere I went. Like a typical teenager, I pushed every situation to the limit, almost as if I needed to test my new boundaries.

I skipped school several times, passed ornery notes among my peers, and did my best to spend time with older girls. Although, my fights at school were many, most fighting was a result of upperclassmen bullying me. I was big for my age, and it seemed older guys wanted to put a notch in their reputation for whipping the big guy at school.

Earl and Louise were near retirement age, and the constant problems I caused were more than the kindly couple could handle. Every time my probation officer visited, Earl updated him. "He's a lot to handle. Louise and me are just simple people. We can't take the drama this boy brings."

George, stared at me a moment. "I understand, but after what he's been through, it would be unnatural if the boy was any different than what he is now."

Earl tried to mentor me and help me grow. He also tried to teach me a good work ethic. One day he gave me a job that seemed overwhelming to me.

"I want you to clean and scrape the inside of these wooden hive boxes." He picked up a section of the hive and demonstrated. "You just scrape off all the honeycomb until the sides are smooth. Once you get this stack done, there's another stack in the back yard." He handed me the scraper. "Don't stop until you get them all clean." His tone betrayed his sour mood.

Earl had never been grumpy to me before then. I scraped the insides of the hives in the garage and then moved to the stack in the back yard. The hot sun had dried the honeycomb, which made it difficult to get the dried honeycomb off of the boxes. I scraped each one until I thought it was appropriate and worked my way through the stack.

I sat on one of the boxes deep in thought when Earl joined me in the back yard. "Since we're going on vacation next week, you should go across the road and collect your money from the neighbor.

My heart sank. The farmer across the road had hired me numerous times to help with chores, but each time he offered to pay me, I promised to collect later. For some reason I was embarrassed to ask for the money even though it was owed to me. "I don't need any money," I said.

"What do you mean?" His voice escalated. "Of course you need money. We're about to go on vacation, and you've got at least a week's pay coming to you"

We argued a moment until I began crying. "Don't make me do that. I don't want the money. He can just keep what he owes me."

Earl's eyes widened. "What is wrong with you, son? It's your money, and he doesn't mind paying it to you. You worked for it. Now go over there and get it."

I wagged my head. "I'm not doing it. I don't care what you do to me."

Earl was silent a long minute. Finally, he turned and headed back toward the garage. "I'll go get it for you this time, but I don't understand what's wrong with you." He scratched his head. "I can't take much more of this," he mumbled.

He took a few steps and then turned around and walked back to where I sat scraping the boxes. He examined the boxes I had cleaned. "You have to do a better job than that. You see this?" He pointed to the honeycomb on the inside of one of the boxes. "All that has to come off."

"I can't get it off," I said. "It's too hard."

"It is not too hard. You are just lazy and don't want to do this." He put his hands on his hips. "Louise and me are trying to help you, son. But you've got to help yourself. And so far I haven't seen any indication you even want to help yourself."

I shook my head. "I'm trying to be good."

"And while we're talking, I've been getting some bad reports about you. I hear you've been getting in fights at school. Is that true?"

I looked down at the scraper in my hand and did not answer. Guilty as charged.

"And I've also had a couple mother's call me and saying you won't leave their daughters alone. You can't understand it now, but some of these mothers don't want their daughters going steady with a juvenile delinquent. Just because a girl likes you doesn't mean her fam—" He stopped and let out a long breath before he shook his head and walked away.

The Lord had good timing, because Earl's eight-year pastorate term ended that year and instead of renewing their term, the Methodist headquarters transferred Earl and Louise to a new pastorate in a distant town.

"It's not right to move you away from your family and the community where you were born," Earl said. "I'm going to find another family to take you in."

In truth, moving away was probably the excuse Earl needed to get out of his commitment of caring for me. He was a good man, but we fought a lot of battles, and even though I had turned thirteen, I did not mature any during the year I spent with Earl and Louise. The Lord handed me a great opportunity, but I did not recognize the gift I was given. Without knowing it, I abused a wonderful blessing God gave me.

Earl and Louise had treated me like I was their own child, but sadly, they had gotten the worst end of the bargain. I constantly caused them trouble; skipping school, fighting with other teens in the community, and sometimes saying things in public not becoming to a pastor's son. Even worse, on numerous occasions, I caused this local pastor embarrassment with his parishioners and the community he was trying to serve.

Earl shopped me around among the local farm families, but no one wanted to take over the project of mentoring a wild teenager. Going back home to my parents was definitely not something I wanted to do again, but the way it appeared there was no other option. Fortunately, my parents did not want me.

* * *

THE PRAYERS OF EARL AND LOUISE WERE ANSWERED when a farmer and his family agreed to take me into their home. The Trueblood family had three children of their own and I was only a year older than their oldest son. Their small dairy farm with a few pigs, and two ponies was only a half-mile away from Earl and Louise.

Bud Trueblood was short and stocky, worked hard, and never said much. Betty made up for Bud's quiet nature. The red-headed Catholic was personable and liked by all who knew her.

Their two girls were three and four years younger than me, but the family immediately welcomed me like I was the prodigal son returning home.

Even so, I was frightened to start over again with a new family. As a teenager I did not understand the financial sacrifices my foster parents made for me in order to give me such things as clothes, school supplies, and other expenses a teenager incurs. Mike shared his room with me as well as his teenage toys, like bicycles and go carts.

Shelley and Stacey were so kind to put up with my immature teasing and treated me as if I was a real brother. I turned fourteen-years old while I lived with the Trueblood family, and they too had no idea how much baggage I was bringing into their home.

Bud worked hard on the farm every day while Betty took care of the family, kept the house in top shape, and also worked full time as a government inspector at the local egg farm down the road. Like most farms, each family member had specific chores to do each day in order to keep the farm working properly. Mike and I helped feed and milk the cows, and we often drove the farm tractors when there was plowing or discing to be done in the fields.

Mike seemed elated to have one of the school's bad boys as his best friend. When he had trouble with bullies, I quickly took care of the problem for him. But Mike was a congenial guy and got along with nearly everyone, so he rarely needed help from his new big brother.

Living at the Trueblood farm was an amazing experience. It was here I rode my first pony and learned to milk cows. We made a homemade go-cart, and refurbished a broken down minibike. In the summer months, the backyard pond provided fun times of swimming and fishing. In many ways, I lived in a teenagers heaven.

Although Betty was a devout Catholic, she made certain all four of us children were involved with the youth at the community church where Earl had pastored. The church was only a few hundred yards from our mailbox, and we walked to the church where Earl had pastored for Sunday School and Youth Service.

One of the first hardships I brought to the Trueblood family happened on the school bus. One morning, I took it upon myself to intercede for a younger teen who was getting bullied by an older and bigger student. After I ping-ponged my way to the back of the bus, I got in the big guy's face. "Leave the wimpy kid alone, fat boy," I said.

Before our conversation went any further, the bus driver looked up in his giant rear-view mirror and thought I was bullying the big student. "Noble, sit down," he yelled.

"But I'm just trying to help th—"

"Three days, Noble. You're kicked off the bus for three days."

I took my seat and glared at the bully. "You got me in trouble."

The bully refused to look at me.

I sighed, knowing I would be in serious trouble. Betty would have to drive me ten miles into school, which would be a big nuisance for her, and now I was an embarrassment to her family. I moved closer to the front of the bus. "Don't anyone get off the bus until fat boy gets off," I said to the students around me. "I am going to get even with him for causing me to get kicked off the bus."

As soon as the bus driver opened the door, I was the first one off. I placed my books on the ground, and waited. No one else moved. The bus driver didn't seem to know what was going on, but finally a few students stepped off the bus. When the bully stepped from the bus to the school grounds, I pushed him down and punched him in the face three times— one for each day.

Calmly, I picked up my books and went directly to the vice-principal's office where I told him what I had just done and why. "I know it was wrong, but I am not sorry," I told him.

"It's even worse because it was premeditated," Mr. Pitman said. "You didn't hit the boy in anger. You thought about it ahead of time and planned it."

"And if I get in a lot of trouble," I raided my voice. "then I'm going out there and hit him again—one for each day of detention I get."

Mr. Pitman shook his head and left the room to check on the boy I had hit. "Have someone call the boy's parents," he said.

I was angry, but I had the idea things could not get any worse, so I decided to hold nothing back.

"That kid, Noble, is dangerous." The bus driver was in the other room talking to the principal. "I don't want him on my bus at all. He's dangerous to me, and he's dangerous to the other kids. You never know what he's going to do."

When Mr. Pitman returned to the little office where I sat, I expected him to get harsh and hateful; but instead, he spoke softly and firmly as he told me I would have to be punished and that proper steps would be taken according to the school's policy.

I became emotionally distraught. This was new territory for me. In my mind, I was a good person, and the world around me was spiraling out of control. Pressure from home along with school life pushed me over the top. I jumped up from my seat, kicked the principal's desk as hard as I could and began yelling at him. "Shut up and listen to me …."

Teachers came running down the hallways like bugs converging toward one destination. A male teacher shut the office door to prevent the other students from hearing my rampage. My tirade was short-lived and I sat back in my seat and waited.

After he counseled me, Mr. Pitman made an appointment for me to come back later. "I'm not going to paddle you right now, because I am angry," he said. "You come back later today and we'll discuss this further."

I did not understand his principle of waiting until his emotions subsided, but later Mr. Pitman paddled me, which was only one of several I received during those school years. The paddlings always stung, but they were minor compared to Junior's punishment. Sadly, one of the results of a paddling was that it always moved me up a notch on the bad-boy list. My peers seemed to respect me more, and some of the girls seemed to like bad boys.

Bud and Betty were devastated over what I had done, because they felt responsible for my actions. When they told me the bully I hit was spending the night in the hospital, I was shocked. At first, I assumed his parents were exaggerating and making a big deal out of nothing, but apparently the boy's eyes had swollen shut and he needed medication. My first thought was how Junior would have been so proud of me for what I had done.

It was then I realized how wrong I had been. The world around me seemed to come to a screeching halt as I got a glimpse of the kind of person I was becoming—just like Junior.

I went to the boy's house and apologized. I was sincere, but in my mind, fights were just a guy thing where testosterone was leveled out between men. I felt certain everyone was making too much of a big deal out of this. However, I completely understood that the boy's trip to the hospital was a serious infraction on my part.

The boy's father talked badly to me, and I could not blame him. It was his son I had beat up. Fortunately, this became my last fight while in public school.

A few weeks earlier, I had punched a boy and knocked his front teeth completely out. The fight was over a deceitful girl we both liked. I walked away free and clear from that fight, because the student had refused to give up my name to the school authorities.

Soon afterward, while attending a mid-week youth meeting at the church in Acme, I heard about Pentecostals. During a group-led discussion on different religious experiences, one of the young ladies told of her visit to a Pentecostal church when she went camping at Lake Mon. The youth group all laughed when she described the Pentecostal's demonstration of the Spirit with their hand clapping and aisle walking.

About the same time, I received news that my Grandmother Bertha had cancer and was not doing well. A few weeks later, my mother called and wanted me to go with them to the family Christmas gathering at my grandmother's house. I had not seen my mother since the night I ran away from home about two years earlier, but I agreed to go with her since I would not be alone with Junior.

At the Christmas gathering my Grandmother Bertha was bedfast from debilitating cancer, and the family moved her bed to the middle of the living room where she could watch the children and witness the activities of the day.

Junior was civil to me the entire evening, and when he dropped me back off at the Trueblood house he handed me a fifty-dollar bill as a gift. Not only was that more money than I had ever held in my entire life, it was also the first time Junior had ever shown me any thread of kindness.

A few weeks later, my mother called again and made arrangements to pick me up and take me to my grandmother's funeral. That funeral was possibly the single-most important element of my life, because it triggered a series of events that altered my mother's life and ultimately my own.

Before her death, Grandmother Bertha had insisted the family call the Pentecostal minister to pray for her during her sickness. She also made it clear, she wanted the same Pentecostal minister to preach her funeral. That contact with the church resulted in drastic changes in my mother and Junior's life.

At the funeral, Junior appeared friendly and even respectful during the few hours we were together. From my point of view my parents had indeed changed since attending church. But it had been more than two years since God had delivered me from Junior, and a lot had happened in my own life, too. I was approaching my fifteenth birthday, and I considered myself a young adult. In reality I was no more mature than a ten-year old.

At the Trueblood farm, Bud taught me how to handle the milking machines and I was able to help him in the evenings and on some mornings. He had taken a new job working at a factory in order to help the family finances, and us boys had the responsibility to lighten some of his work load. Sadly, I was too young and immature to understand the financial stress the family was suffering at the time.

One evening during the milk run, I looked out through the big milk-house window and saw Bud walking up the gravel driveway toward me. His steps were slow, his head was down, and his expression bleak.

Inside the milk-room he stood quietly and waited until I cycled the three cows from their milking stations and back out into the pasture before he stopped me. "You called my daughter a whore?" he asked.

I frowned and searched my mind for a way to respond. "What?"

"You called my daughter a whore," he repeated. "Shelly asked her mother about the definition of a whore, because she thought it was a female boar. She was only asking because you called her a whore."

I swallowed hard, knowing I was guilty as charged. Like most brothers and sisters, we often had mild quarrels. We called each other names, and then blackmailed one another with threats to tell Bud and Betty about our name calling.

At first, Bud appeared to struggle to control himself. If he hit me, I could not complain because I certainly deserved it.

Those words to Shelly had slipped off my tongue in an argument over some trivial thing. Neither Shelley or myself had even been seriously angry at the time. I nodded. "I did that, but I didn't mean anything by it."

"You didn't mean anything buy it?" he raised his voice. "Do you know how angry that makes me?"

I looked down at the floor.

"We've taken you in and given you a home when no one else wanted you," he said. "We put up with your baggage because we want to help you. And now you do this to us? That's my daughter you slandered—my flesh and blood."

The dam of emotion burst open as tears rolled down my cheeks. "I am sorry. I know I don't handle myself right sometimes. But I don't know *how* to act. Everywhere I go, I don't fit in. I'm not even sure what I'm doing in life or why I'm even alive."

I wiped at my tears with my sleeve. "It always bothers me that I've never had a father, and I've always wanted to meet my real dad, because I just feel so lost and all alone."

My sobbing grew uncontrollable and I could hardly talk. It was the first time I had ever emotionally opened up to anyone. The speech was not planned speech, it just came out.

The confession immediately washed Bud's anger away. He put his arms around me and began to weep and sob along with me.

I felt even more awkward with Bud hugging me and bawling on my shoulder. Our chests heaved in unison for a long minute, I just stood there without returning his affection. Never in my life had a man hugged me or even shown me affection. Finally, I wrapped my arms around him and we both wept like two babies.

We were still hugging and crying when Betty walked into the milk parlor. Apparently, she came to make certain Bud was keeping his temper under control. She stood quietly as if she was unsure what was happening.

Finally, Bud stood back and wiped his eyes. "I know how you feel, because I didn't have a father, either. I was raised by my aunt. My own father came to this area and visited the rest of the family a few weeks ago, but even though he was within five miles of my house he never bothered to come by and see me."

The emotional experience should have been a milestone in my life. It could have been a demarcation for emotional healing and growth, but I was too immature to understand the significance of this emotional encounter, and my wounds were so deep that the one-time connection had little effect on my wounded soul. Either way, I did not know how to process this connection with Bud.

People often told me I was in a shell. They were right of course, but at the time I could not comprehend what they meant. In areas like working and getting things done, I was mature beyond my years, because Junior had trained me to be responsible. Yet, my social abilities and interactions were more like a five to ten-year old in a fifteen-year old body.

Even worse, it did not appear that my social skills were growing. I seemed frozen in my ability to interact with others in any healthy way.

In so many ways I was developing into a mirror image of Junior and did not know it. As I got older, I came to understand Junior suffered from some of the same insecurities as I did; yet, they manifested themselves differently in him than they did in me.

After living with the Trueblood family for a year, I heard rumors that Junior and my mother were attending an Apostolic Pentecostal church, and that their lives had changed dramatically. Imagining them attending any type of church was difficult to process. If my mother and step father were Christians, then it was definitely a drastic change and very near a miracle.

Occasionally, I wondered what it would be like to be part of a real family who loved and cared for me. The Trueblood family tried so much to show me love, but I had no emotional ability to accept it. They went above and beyond anything anyone could expect of a foster parent, but they were almost too late. I was untouchable.

At times, I made attempts to step out of my shell, but as soon as problems arose I always rushed back inside. The shell was my security—my way of surviving.

For nearly three years I had lived in foster care, and like most teenagers, I wanted to identify with something. Had there been gangs at the school I would have been deep in the middle of them.

After a year and a half, I wore the Trueblood family down too. I realized I had exhausted their mercy and grace, and I wanted to find a way out before they gave up on me. I began thinking life with my mother and stepfather might not be so bad since they had become Christians. They had treated me so well the last two times I had been with them that I became infatuated about a fairy-tail home life.

I secretly wrote a letter to my mother and asked if I could come home and live with my own family. She responded back right away. OF COURSE YOU ARE WELCOME TO COME HOME. I HAVE BEEN PRAYING THAT GOD WOULD SEND YOU BACK TO US. Her letter was all I needed, and I announced to the Trueblood family that I was going back home to live with my real parents.

Even though I had caused a lot of disruption and drama for the Trueblood family, they were hurt when I left them They had shown me more love and kindness during my year and half stay with them than my real family had shown me in my lifetime. But my inability to accept love always sabotaged my life. Even worse, I never bothered to talk to Bud or Betty about my decision to leave and go back home, and that seemed to hurt them deeply.

God had opened the windows of Heaven and blessed me with good foster parents. Living in the farm atmosphere with three other children was an amazing experience; yet, I did not comprehend the goodness which had come my way. Instead, I always wanted a change, because in my mind it was the environment that brought on my problems. It never occurred to me that I was my own worst enemy—even though people tried to tell me so.

Even worse, I could not trust in anyone enough to take advice. I struggled to find my way as I entered adulthood, not realizing my perception of the world around me was flawed. I was flawed because I viewed the world around me based on my childhood experiences of distrust and fear.

*   *   *

THINGS CHANGED FAST ONCE I ARRIVED HOME. My idealistic image of home life with my mother and stepfather did not match up with reality. I was home only a few hours when I began to suspect things were not as they seemed. Soon my suspicions were verified.

The devil has many names, and I suddenly confronted a devil I had assumed was deceased. My stepfather's blatant cursing and hateful comments about the church congregation where they attended let me know he was not the Christian I had imagined.

On the other hand, my mother prayed and read her Bible every day and never spoke a negative comment about anyone.

The only way I knew to manage my new predicament was to revert to my old method of hiding and keeping to myself. This was a drastic change from my life with the Trueblood family where there were always cheerful noises, and lots of jolly action around the house. I should have ran out the door, called the Trueblood family and begged for forgiveness, but at that time it never occurred to me the Trueblood family would consider taking me back.

The first few hours back home, I slowly felt the hysteria worming its way up my spine. It was like fingers of pressure formed around my throat, and a steel belt began tightening around my chest. But I had no choice but to endure my new environment.

I attended church services with the rest of the family at the Apostolic Pentecostal church. No one forced their beliefs on me, and no one tried to indoctrinate me, but from the start I believed these people were sincere. I listened to old-fashioned sermons about God's oneness, the steps of salvation, and the potential of prayer. It was clear to me that God's power was on this little church they called Christ Temple.

Attending church was in itself a big change in my stepfather's life. Through the years, Mom had tried to get him to take the family to church, but he always blatantly refused. Mom had been in the church and filled with the Holy Spirit when she was fourteen-years old, and she had often tried to get back to God. But Junior would have none of it.

Twice she succeeded in getting the family inside the church doors, but we never made it more than half way through the service. Both times were the same; as soon as the minister took up an offering, Junior used it as an excuse to leave. "All they want is your money," he'd say and march the family out the door.

That visit to the Christ Temple Pentecostal church took me by surprise. My main source of church experiences came from attending the Methodist church Earl and Louise pastored. Although good people, the Methodist congregation was not demonstrative in their worship, and the only musical instrument in the church was the acoustic piano.

This Pentecostal church was on the opposite end of the spectrum. They had a piano, an organ, numerous guitars, several accordions, and a full set of drums. And if the huge orchestra was not enough for a congregation of seventy people, someone from the audience often played a tambourine.

My first impression of the Pentecostal worship service struck me funny. I began laughing uncontrollably and could not stop. It was even more embarrassing because I had sat on the second row from the front. I covered my mouth and closed my eyes, but the laughter would not stop. To me, their demonstrative worship seemed so humorous and out of place in a church.

Later in the service, my laughter dried up quickly when the congregation grew extremely quiet and suddenly the short lady behind me let out a high-shrill scream. From where I sat in the pew, she stood even with my head, and her scream brought cold shivers along my spine. My mood went from humor to fear in one-half second. At the time, I did not know what was going on, but later I learned screamers were a rare type of Pentecostal worship.

In my heart, I truly wanted to get saved and live right, especially at that moment. As far as I could tell I had no other option. According to the minister's sermons, the Bible was plain on the matter of salvation. Once I knew what God expected of me, I wanted to obey.

During that first service, I whispered to God, *if I ever became a Christian, I wanted to be an Apostolic Pentecostal Christian.* These people enjoyed church. It was not quiet and boring; instead, it was lively and spontaneous.

In addition, the friendly congregation always treated me as if I was part of the church family. I felt at ease around them and at the same time I admired Pastor Dewey Allman because of his straightforward preaching manner.

Pastor Allman was kind and personable, but when he preached about sin, he preached plain and straightforward. I liked that. No one walked away from a church service wondering what was right or wrong. That straightforward approach was appealing to a young teenager searching for answers. Until then, my life had been full of uncertainties, and I began to understand that the Bible was the foundation to judge right and wrong in all things of life.

Every church service found me in the pew, even when the rest of the family was not there. I also attended every special function, which often meant I was in church five nights a week. My hunger for biblical knowledge became insatiable. I read the Bible and began memorizing Scriptures, and I always took notes during the sermons. More importantly, I began to pray again.

My attitude in prayer changed. In the past, my prayers consisted of begging God to help me out of a problem, but now the content of my prayers turned toward seeking what I could do for God.

My mother had a great influence on me as I witnessed her quiet commitment to live right—especially while she lived in the same household with Junior. She spent her spare time in the evenings reading her Bible and her early mornings in prayer.

On the other hand, I never heard Junior pray a single prayer, and I never knew him to own a Bible. His common past-time was cursing, smoking cigarettes, and ridiculing the church members.

His hypocrisy bothered me a great deal, but I understood that I had no choice but to ignore it. Even so, I was shocked when I watched him stand in the church and testify about how God had given him the strength to quit smoking cigarettes.

That he could stand and lie to the congregation was appalling to me. In a strange way, his hypocrisy inspired me to live as a real Christian. I knew from the start I did not want to be like him, and I was willing to go to great lengths to make certain I did not.

After attending a few church services, I clearly understood my need to repent. When I knelt at the altar, I abandoned all pride and prayed with everything in me. Usually, some encouraging parishioners knelt beside me and prayed with me. They would say things like, *Raise your hands and worship him*, and *Just talk to him.*

Occasionally, a person would grab my hands, hold them up above my head and lean close to my ear and whisper, *Say Jesus, Jesus, Jesus.* I always obeyed anything they asked. By the time I finished praying each night, my clothes were saturated with perspiration.

Finally, I asked Pastor Allman to baptize me. I had never witnessed a baptism in my life, but my mother instructed me to, "Close your eyes, concentrate on God, and when you come up out of the water, just raise your hands, and worship God with all of your heart."

Her plan made sense, but things worked out differently. During the baptism everyone sat in the pew to observe the baptism while Pastor

Allman stood outside the baptistery and helped me into the water. All I could think about was the cold water. He put his hands on me and prayed, and then said something along the lines of, "According to the confession of your faith, I now baptize you in Jesus' name."

I stood waist deep in water, and he pulled me backward and laid me down into the water. I tried my best to focus on God even though the water was icy cold. The jeans and cotton T-shirt weighed me down, and I slipped out of the minister's hands and went straight to the bottom of the baptistery where I stayed—a long time.

In my mind, I envisioned Pastor Allman reading some liturgy or Scripture over me as I remained on the bottom of the baptistery. Later, I learned the seventy-year old minister stumbled, fell backwards, hit his head on the wall, and slumped to the ground. It took him a good while to compose himself and stand back up again.

Meanwhile, under two feet of water, I was wondering how long they kept a person under water during baptism. My mother did not mention that part, and since I had never witnessed a baptism, I had no reference point to know things should be any differently. Fortunately, I had taken a deep breath before going under, but my lungs were beginning to scream for more air. *Maybe I'm supposed to stand on my own*, I thought.

Determined to hold out as long as possible, I remained very still. I did not want to void the baptism and have to do it over again. Finally, I was about to give up and climb out of water on my own, when suddenly, someone reached into the water, clasped onto my T-shirt and pulled me upward. It was all the signal I needed to stand up and breath.

I later learned, the youth leader of the church, had been sitting in the pew watching my predicament when he realized I might drown. He ran from his pew to the platform, reached over into the baptismal rail, and pulled me up. I felt badly that he soaked the sleeves of his suit jacket, but at the same time I was grateful to breathe again.

I raised my hands in worship as Mother had instructed me and did my best to focus on my new life. "Thank you Jesus, thank you Jesus," was all I could say. As I stepped from the baptistery I glanced at the audience. Everyone was smiling over my dilemma.

Baptism was a demarcation point for my spiritual growth. I knew I had a long way to go to be a good Christian, but I was determined to keep growing in the right direction. My spiritual growth was slow, often I made mistakes, and occasionally I gave up. But like a basketball under water, I could not be held under long before I would rise again and give it one more try.

Sin was an alien concept to me. As a newborn child in Christ, I struggled to accept that certain things were actually sin. In my mind, sins could be counted on one hand; stealing, lying, cheating, murder, and maybe fighting. Later, I learned the list was much longer—almost endless.

*　　*　　*

JUNIOR LOVED TO DRESS FLASHY and hobnob with the wealthiest church members. It wasn't long until he purchased a big red Cadillac. Nearly every church service required the congregation to testify, and I would sit in my pew and want to hide when he stood to testify.

That bothered me because at home he gossiped and ridiculed these same people with whom he worshiped. I knew better than to speak my mind or to say anything. The only way I knew to deal with the problem was to shut myself out from the family so I would not witness as much of the negativism.

Of course, I had serious problems too, some were much worse than Junior's problems. I had not completely gotten over the *bad-boy* persona, and the desire for acceptance among my school peers still held a strong pulled on me. I notice many of the tough guys around town wore tattoos, and I decided I needed one too.

At the time, it did not occur to me that many I had seen with tattoos had gotten them while in prison. In 1969 there were no tattoo parlors in our community, but somewhere I learned how to create a crude prison-style tattoo with India ink.

At home in the bathroom, I drew a cross on my shoulder with a new razor blade and then saturated the wound with India ink. I also carved out my initials on the arch of my foot. For the next few weeks, I kept my shoulder covered with a gauze and wore long-sleeved shirts to keep Mom from knowing what I had done. It was a stupid idea, but I was too immature to know any better.

My stepfather hated me as much as he ever did, and he never tried to pretend otherwise. Apparently, he did not want me to come back home when I left the Trueblood household, but Mom had insisted on it. Fortunately, after I returned home there was no physical abuse.

My mother had finally gotten her driver's license, and it was my job to start her car and back it out of the garage each morning. My stepfather's car-pool ride often picked him up while I was outside getting her car ready. One of the men in the carpool was the father of Jerry, a student in my class.

During school lunch break, Jerry grinned as he approached me outside the school. "You won't believe what my dad said last night."

"Now what?"

"You were outside starting your mom's car yesterday morning when my dad asked your dad about the teenager starting the car."

"Probably didn't say anything good," I said.

"Your dad told my dad that he had only one child and you were just a visitor."

I laughed. "So the old man is ashamed of me."

"He must not like you so much," Jerry said.

I nodded. "That's more true than you know."

Friction at home increased until I decided I did not want to take it anymore. One evening I did not go home after school. I had no plan, I only knew I didn't want to take the hypocrisy from my stepfather any longer. I went to my girlfriend's house but did not stay long, because I knew it was the first place the police would look for me.

It was a cold fall night and to keep warm I went to a farm sales parking lot and climbed inside one of the tractors that had a weather shelter installed on it. I slept miserably, because I could not get comfortable sitting upright in the tractor all night.

The following night was church night, and I wanted to go to church, but I knew my parents would be there. If they saw me they would call the police and I would get arrested. Instead, I went to my girlfriend's house while her mother was at church. That turned out to be a mistake, because her mother left church early and caught me while I was at her house.

She promptly took me to the church and turned me over to the pastor. He counseled me to go back home and do what was right. That was not what I wanted to do, but I respected the pastor and succumbed to his advice.

Pastor Allman went inside my parent's house with me and tried to sooth their anger. Junior and Mom were both all smiles and pretended they were grateful for the pastor's help. As soon as he walked out the door the atmosphere quickly changed.

Their first complaint was that I had embarrassed them among their church friends by running away from home. Their second complaint was my arriving late at night with the pastor had upset their evening, because they had to get up early for work the next morning.

Never in my life had I seen Junior so angry. First, he threatened me physically as he cursed me with every sentence. Then he berated me and acted as if he intended to hit me with his fist. At one point he went as far as to pull out his wallet and offer me a fifty dollar bill. "You can keep this fifty-dollar bill. All you have to do is stand up, so I can knock you down."

Naturally, I did not want him to hit me. I feared that one punch from him might knock me into a coma. But even if I stood and let him hit me, he would never have given me the money. I sat and listened without moving a muscle. I could not whip him in a physical fight, and even if by some miracle I did get the best of him, I would certainly go to jail.

My mother disappeared into the bedroom and left me at Junior's mercy. Still at the boiling point, he continued to curse and threaten me as he made it clear he wanted to kill me.

In the few months I had been back home, they had allowed me more freedom than I had ever experienced while living with them when I was younger. I could walk to church early, go outside when I wanted, and of course visit my girlfriend's house once a week as long as I respected the curfew they established.

All of that immediately changed. "When you come into this house, you go straight to your room and stay there," Junior said. "I don't want to see your face any more than I have to. You don't come out to eat supper until after the rest of us have eaten and gone to bed. Do you understand me?"

I nodded. "Yes sir." From that point forward, my life at home became one of oppression, but I obeyed. Mom would not speak a kind word to me, and Junior would only call me out of my room to berate me from time to time. I was fifteen-years old and once again living under Junior's oppression just as I had done as a child.

A few days later, I was in bed one night when I overheard Junior and Mom talking quietly before they went to sleep. "She's no good," he said. "She's just like her mother—white trash. You'll see. Look at her mother and grandmother. Both fat slobs who don't amount to a hill of beans. She'll grow up to be just like them."

I soon realized they were talking about my girlfriend and her mother. I was no physical match for Junior, but he had always told me; "Be a man, and if you got something to say, you say it to my face."

In addition, my mother had always said, "Don't run away from home. If you have a problem, come and talk to us about it."

This was the first and only time I acted on their advice. I decided to call Junior out on his hypocrisy. Maybe he would respect me for standing up for myself. "Dad?" I called out from my room. I avoided calling him *dad* as much as possible.

"What do you want?" he answered.

"I want to talk to you."

"Now?"

"Yes, now." I dressed and waited in the kitchen.

Junior came into the kitchen wearing only his briefs. He sat at the far side of the table where he could face me. Mom took a seat between us. Both parents wore expressions of concern. This was new territory for them and me.

I got straight to the point. "I heard what you said about my girl-friend."

His expression indicated he could not believe I had the nerve to confront him. Mom's head swiveled back and forth from me to him as I talked.

"You don't have a right to judge them," I said.

His eyes narrowed as he locked onto my gaze.

My heart beat like a jackhammer in my chest. "You're supposed to be a Christian, not a gossiper."

He arched his brow and set his jaw. "What are you saying?" His voice level and deep.

"You've always said for me to speak up and tell you what I think, so that's what I'm doing right now." My stomach twisted as the words left my mouth. I envisioned him nodding and telling me how proud he was of my backbone and confidence.

Instead, he shot me a scalpel-sharp glance just before he sucked in a deep breath and clamped his jaw shut as if he was having difficulty controlling himself. "Don't you ever—ever!" He paused for effect. "get me out of bed again. I pay the bills in this house and—" He stabbed his index finger on the table as he emphasized each word.

I interrupted him. "But you profess to be a Christian." My voice rose an octave. "And you smoke cigarettes and then lie in front of the whole church and tell them how God delivered you. That's wrong!"

He straightened in the chair, pointed his finger at me, and raised his voice. "Don't you—"

Anger surged through my veins. "Shut up old man, and listen to me for a change," I shouted. I was not much of a communicator when angry.

His eyes bulged as if he'd been electrocuted.

I felt as if I had just taken a step off a dangerously high cliff.

The words were more than Junior could take. In one fluid movement he slid the chair back, stood, and lunged toward me. My mother was ready for it and reacted instantly. She slid her chair back and blocked his path.

My muscles tensed like loaded springs as I stood to face him. This was indeed unfamiliar territory, and I was ready to fight in order to save my life. I accepted I was going to get beat up, but I intended to defend myself as much as possible.

Mom kept herself wedged between us like a determined guard on the basketball court. Junior went left and she went left too. He went right and she countered.

Whatever happened, I was ready for it. All of my life he had pounded into my young mind how tough and dangerous he was, and if I so much as made a squeak in rebellion he crushed me like a puffball under foot. For the first time, I crossed the line and I would not go back.

He tried to push my mother aside, but she pressed herself against him, and tried to hug him, all the while talking softly in a desperate tone. "Don't do it. Sit back down. It's not worth it. Don't do it. Honey, please."

Finally, she turned her head toward me. "Get out of the house." She raised her voice. "Now! Get out."

I obeyed, and rushed outside. It was early November and I wore only my T-shirt and jeans—no shoes or socks. The ice cold concrete on my bare feet forced me to raise one foot and then the other in a slow dance. I tested the grass, but it was just as cold as the concrete.

Finally, I took off running up the sidewalk toward the police station ten blocks away. Inside the station, I paused a moment to let my lungs catch up. When I could breath normal again, I approached the desk where a uniformed officer sat writing on a notepad. I waited for him to acknowledge me.

"I just left my home."

He didn't say anything.

"My stepfather was going to hit me." My words came between short gasps for air. "We were arguing and he came at me, but my mother told me to get out of the house."

He nodded. "So you came here?"

"I've ran away five times during my childhood, and you guys always told me to come to you instead of running way, so that's what I'm doing this time."

The officer puckered his lips a moment as if processing my words. The phone rang and he answered it. "Okay. I understand. Thanks for calling." He hung up. It was my mother reporting I had ran away again.

The officer slowly shook his head. "I don't have a place to put you for the night, except in jail."

I lifted a shoulder. "I guess that's okay."

He glanced up at the clock. It was three minutes after eleven o'clock. Three minutes past curfew. "I'll have to arrest you for something, so I'll arrest you for curfew." It was more of a question than a statement.

I nodded. "Whatever." At least I was doing the right thing for once. Running had never worked in the past, so this time I intended to depend on the authorities to help me. It was a bold step, and one I would never have been able to take except for my fledgling relationship with Christ.

*   *   *

THE OFFICER DROVE ME TO THE COUNTY JAIL in Brownstown where they locked me in the same cell I had stayed in three years earlier. I had no cell mates, which was fine with me. Living alone was something I was accustomed to doing.

A few days later, my new probation officer came to counsel me. "I've had a talk with your parents, and they're willing to take you back. You willing to give it one more try?"

I nodded. "I guess." What choice did I have? I would have been perfectly satisfied staying in the jail cell, especially if they allowed me to go to school.

When the probation officer took me back to my parents, things were rocky from the start. I did not really expect it to be any different. Nothing was said of the incident, but Junior was constantly on edge with me. I managed to stay out of his sight as much as possible. It was clear, he only allowed me to come back home to appease my mother, and possibly because he wanted to look good among his church friends.

Occasionally, Mom called me out of my room to sit in the living room with them and watch television. It was awkward. I did not understand her reasoning unless she wanted to experience some facsimile of family time, or perhaps she was trying to slowly unite the family.

One night not long after I was back home from jail, I sat on the sofa watching television with the rest of the family when the phone rang. It was my probation officer. Junior stayed on the line with him a long time. Naturally, I could not tell much by the one-sided conversation, but Junior seemed to be very congenial and agreeable while on the phone. He mostly responded with, "Yes, I understand. I'll do that." Finally, he hung up.

"What did he say," Mom asked.

Junior grinned and carefully positioned himself in the recliner before he finally responded. He acted like a man who had just won an old argument and wanted to tell the story as slowly as possible. "He told me I should do whatever it takes to keep this boy in line." His gaze locked on mine as he spoke.

He paused as if he wanted to have more effect. "He also said if I needed to use physical force then to go ahead and knock the boy's head off his shoulders, and if I put him in the hospital, then not to worry about legal repercussions, because he would take care of things for me."

Mom looked at me and then back at Junior. "Then he had better walk the line."

Junior chuckled as if enjoying himself. "So I am to do whatever I want and not worry about it." He stared hard at me while he talked. "You understand what I'm saying, boy?"

I nodded. My eyes probing his face like you might test an ice field before you walked out on it.

Mom had a flicker of pain in her eyes. "Well, we won't have to go that far. Kenny is going to church and he's going to be a good boy from now on, aren't you, honey?"

I nodded in agreement. Why did she think I had not been a good boy? Running away from home did not make me a bad boy. They obviously didn't see the world as I saw it. All the while I sat on the sofa and pretended to listen to Junior talk, but inside my head I asked myself why I had left the warmth and loving Trueblood family.

They had been so good to me, and for the most part we all got along well. All of the problems I had experienced at the Trueblood household were my own fault. I had no misconceptions about that. I lacked responsibility. I had the false concept that I was a mature adult, but I was wrong.

Now, I was under extreme oppression from Junior, and things had escalated to a dangerous level. At times, I sincerely feared for my life.

A couple days later while at school, my friend Jerry searched me out during lunch break again. He gave me some valuable information that changed everything. "I hear you got a phone call from your probation officer," he said.

I frowned. "How'd you know that?"

"Your house is on the same party line as my house. My dad picked up the phone and listened to the conversation between your probation officer and your step dad."

I was embarrassed. "So I guess you know, I might be dead any day soon."

Jerry's brow furrowed. "What do you mean? Your life should get better."

"What do you mean?" I asked.

"The probation officer raked your step dad over the coals," Jerry said. "He told your dad to let you get out of the house and have friends. He said let the boy live a little and have fun."

I laughed. "Are you lying to me? Did he really say that?" I told Jerry my stepfather's version of the conversation.

Jerry shook his head. "My dad heard the whole thing. Your probation officer was bragging about how you have been going to church, and how he thinks you have been doing a lot better lately."

Relief pulsed through me as Jerry's news gave me hope. I laughed. Not because it was funny, but because I was surprised. "That man is so evil and such a liar," I said. I had known my stepfather to be deceitful and even to bluff and bully others, but I had not imagined him lying to this extent.

When I went home, I kept my secret to myself. I feared to do otherwise. But even though I never said anything to my stepfather, just knowing the truth made me feel better. Not only did life take on an entirely different perspective, but it also made me wonder just how many other times Junior had lied so blatantly.

By the time April arrived, I was ready for a change. Life with Junior was more than I wanted to take. The few years I had spent with foster parents had given me a taste of real life, and I could not stand to live under Junior's oppression any longer. He hated me so much that he threatened me even when he was not angry.

"I met a man who can put a contract on your head, and I'm going to do it, too," he said. "You'll never know when nor where you'll be when you take your last breath. It'll be worth every penny of the money, too."

I never answered back, but it concerned me. I wanted to believe this was another one of his lies, but as I walked to school every morning, I kept a constant look out for any stranger in the neighborhood who might be a sniper or a hit man.

Some nights I feared to close my eyes. I would lie awake listening to the quietness and wondering if it I was hearing Junior sneaking out of bed and coming to smother me in my sleep. I didn't think Junior would actually follow through with his threats, but I did not want to take that chance and be wrong.

Hundreds of times, Junior had promised, "The day you turn sixteen-years old you are out of my care. I don't care if you have to live on the streets. My obligation is done when you turn sixteen."

That was fine with me, but I did not want to wait until my sixteenth birthday. It was time for a major change in my life. I had been mowing yards for the neighbors, and I also had a paper route which provided money to buy my own clothes. I had seventy dollars saved, which was equivalent to two day's pay at that time.

One morning, instead of going to school I packed a bag and left a simple note; I WILL NOT BE BACK. It was 1969 and I believed I looked old enough to travel alone, so I took what I had saved and purchased a Greyhound bus ticket to Louisville.

As I sat on the Greyhound bus in front of the Maid-Rite diner waiting to leave, a heavy sadness saturated me. Everything I knew would soon be left behind, and I did not expect to come back. My parents would have the police looking for me, and according to my stepfather, I was already on the police's list of bad people.

One good thing had come as a result of my returning home for a few months; I had been introduced to Jesus. The introduction to the Gospel message proved to be the most valuable incident of my life. I was saddened to leave my hometown, but I knew I was not leaving alone. God was with me.

I had a long way to grow as a Christian, and if you had asked me, I would have been reluctant to say I was a Christian. Not that I was ashamed, but because I felt so unworthy to be compared with so many good people. Fortunately, I was growing, and at least I was growing in the right direction.

CHAPTER SIX

Forget the past. You are not going back there.

When my father and my mother forsake me,
then the LORD will take me up. Psalm 27:10

THE GREYHOUND BUS BECAME MY HOME for the next two to three weeks. From Louisville, I purchased a ticket to a town in another state and then purposely boarded a wrong bus that would take me in a different direction than my ticket destination. This worked quite well, because most of the time, the drivers merely glance at my ticket and did not pay attention whether I was on the right bus or not.

Sometimes, I'd stay overnight inside the bus station just to have a shelter out of the rain. Once my ticket required me to change buses at a stop over, but I stayed on the bus and didn't switch. That resulted in me going many hours completely away from my ticket destination.

I expected God to make a way for me. As I rode the bus, I imagined meeting someone who wanted to mentor a young Christian and who would give me a permanent home. I was willing to work too. I imagined living with a big family with plenty to eat and lots of joy. It was only a dream, but the dream sustained me.

When a driver finally did check my ticket, he wrote on my ticket and put me on the correct bus to take me to my ticket destination. This gave me even more time on the buses.

I had no plan in mind, but I prayed a lot and promised to give God my life and soul if he would only help me through this. From that first night I had knelt at the altar in church a few months earlier and repented, I had sincerely tried to do what I thought God expected of me.

Of course, I never really done what God wanted, because I would have been a better witness if I had stayed, endured the struggles, and let my light shine. But in my young mind I was making an effort.

In many ways I had grown up on prayer even though I knew so little about God. Since prayer had helped me in the past, I knew it was my only friend now.

During my Greyhound-travel days, I tried to manage my money as well as possible. But I was soon broke, hungry, and walking the streets of Mobile, Alabama. In desperation, I took my suitcase of clothes, to the pawn shop and sold some of them to get a little money for food. I slept in the bus station that night, and a day later, I was broke and hungry again.

While in Mobile, I walked the downtown area a few hours until I noticed a middle-aged man following me. At first, I assumed his showing up everywhere I went was a coincidence. I was already paranoid about the police looking for me, and I feared this man might be an undercover officer. At fifteen-years old, I did not understand that a runaway was the least of the police force's worries.

I quickly turned and walked the opposite direction in an attempt to get away from the stranger who followed me, but there was no evading him. Panic rose up in me as I walked faster along the sidewalk. When I stopped and looked back, he was a block away staring at me.

I ran another block before I stopped and looked back again. He was still behind me. I ran up the sidewalk, turned at the next block, turned again, and zigzagged my way across town. All the while praying for God's help. I never saw the man again.

Mobile, Alabama did not appear like a friendly town to me, and I began walking away from the downtown area. After walking all day and much of the night, I found an unlocked car parked outside a bar where I slept on the backseat for several hours. Sleep was fitful knowing I might get caught any second, and possibly beat up or abducted. Finally, I left the car in the early morning hours and began walking farther away from town.

I had no plan, and I did not know where I was going, but I kept a constant dialogue of prayer as I asked God to help me. I was so tired, hungry, and lonesome, that I began to wish I had never left Seymour. At least at home I had food to eat and a warm bed. In my exhaustion, the Cinderella life didn't seem so bad compared to the homeless street life of hunger and loneliness.

I walked through the rest of the night, and by mid-morning I found a dime on the pavement in a parking lot. This was nothing less than a miracle as far as I was concerned. Ten cents would purchase a candy bar, a soda, or I could use it to make a phone call in a pay phone booth. I chose to make the phone call.

I took my bag of clothes, stepped inside the phone booth and shut the door. After a few minutes of intense prayer for the right words to say, I framed in my mind the conversation I would have with my mother. *I'm sorry. *I should not have left. If you will send me the money to come home, I promise to never run away again.* I was sincere, but things did not work out the way I wanted.

I dropped the dime in the slot on the pay phone. "Operator, I want to make a collect call to this number."

"One moment, please," she said.

My mother answered on the other end. Hearing her voice nearly reduced me to tears.

"I have a collect call from Kenny Noble?" the operator said. "Will you accept the charges?"

There was a short pause. "No, I will not," Mom answered.

My heart sank.

"Where is this call from?" Mom asked.

"Mobile Alabama."

The click of my mother hanging up crushed my spirit. I had believed that the one person in the world I could depend on for help and mercy was my own mother, but I was wrong. Tears flowed freely as I stepped out of the phone booth and headed toward the interstate. I should have bought a soda.

Discouragement overwhelmed me so much that I left my bag of clothes inside the phone booth and began walking. At that moment, I did not care about anything. With my head down, and my energy drained, I walked up the exit ramp toward the interstate. I had done wrong by leaving home, but I didn't know what to do to fix it. All I knew to do was to pray.

In the last twenty-four hours I had walked several miles and my body was low on energy, which also affected my mind. Eventually, a car load of teenage boys pulled over on the side of the road and offered me a ride. "You going to the beach?" one of them asked.

"Anywhere out of this town," I replied. "I didn't know there was a beach here."

"Dauphin Island isn't much of a beach, but we like it," the driver said.

It had to be a better place than the downtown area. I hoped and prayed God was leading me to the right place by sending this ride. The boys chattered like a bunch of hyper women while I sat quietly in the back seat.

When we arrived at the beach, I walked the opposite direction from the boys who had given me the ride. From their conversation, I gathered they intended to party and have a lot of fun. My problems needed solved, and a party did not interest me.

After walking a good while on the beach, I spotted an abandoned picnic table with a lone brown paper bag on it. Acting as if I was the bag's owner, I walked confidently to the table, opened the brown bag, and looked inside. Several hot dogs and buns were inside. They looked better than gold to me.

I closed the bag, and took off as quickly as I could without attracting attention. It was wrong to steal someone's picnic, but I was so hungry, my stomach pangs overrode my guilt.

The sun began to drop over the horizon, and I needed a place to sleep. I prayed as earnestly as I knew how, knowing I was a praying thief. Finally, I found a secluded spot on the sandy beach where I expected to spend the night.

I stretched out on the sand and quietly prayed for two hours or more. Suddenly, I heard someone speak. "Go to the bus station and get on the bus."

The man's voice was very clear and distinct. I opened my eyes and sat up. There was no one around me. At first I thought the voice was my imagination; yet, it sounded so real.

"God, if this is you, then I am going to obey," I said, as I stood and looked around. "If this is not you, then I have nothing to lose. My life cannot get much worse than it is right now." Immediately, I walked to the nearest Greyhound bus station. When I rounded the corner of the building, the first bus I spotted had the door open and several passengers were already inside. I boarded the bus and took a seat halfway toward the back on the driver's side.

A few minutes later, the bus driver stepped on the bus and looked over the passengers. There were about ten of us sitting quietly and waiting. He frowned as he used his index finger to point at each passenger and count. "Let me see your ticket," he said to the lady in front of me.

I decided if he called for my ticket, I would just stand up and leave without a word. He examined her ticket and returned it to her,and then walked back to the front of the bus and dropped behind the steering wheel. Soon I was on the road again, but I did not have the slightest clue where I was going. I stayed on the bus and road all night.

Numerous times, the driver pulled into a Greyhound station where he picked up additional passengers. Finally, he pulled into a station and announced, "This is the end of the line. Everyone must get off and board another bus."

After I got off the bus, and learned I was in Jacksonville Beach, Florida. With no clothes, no money, and nearly a thousand miles from home, I desperately needed to find a job. But that was difficult since homeless people don't have an address or a phone, which causes employers to shun away from hiring you.

Jacksonville beach had an unusual boardwalk which was built fifteen feet above sea level in order to protect the shops from the incoming tide at night. April was spring break for most colleges, and Jacksonville Beach was flooded with young people. Of course not all were in college. To my surprise many young people were just like myself. It was nineteen-sixty nine, and thousands of America's youth had run away from home only to live on the streets.

After walking along the beach for a couple miles, I discovered an old house with CONDEMNED posted on the front and back entries. Windows were broken out and doors were missing on the old house, but it was a shelter. Inside was a dirty sofa someone had left behind. I figured it was better than sleeping in cars, and I made it my new home.

On the main street of town, the window of a Chinese restaurant held a HELP WANTED sign in the window. The owner said he needed a dependable dishwasher, and they hired me on the spot. The pay was only thirty-four dollars for six days work, but I could also eat a meal while I was there each day. I was grateful for the job.

Since I had to wear the same clothes every day, my first paycheck went for a pair of generic pants and T-shirt. The left-over money from my paycheck went toward renting a room, which was twenty-five dollars a week.

The restaurant owner and his family were kind to me, but I had difficulty accepting their habit of recycling food from customer's tables. For example, if the customer left the bowl of white rice untouched, it went back into the pot. Often, someone did not eat their egg foo young, and it went back on the warmer.

After working at the restaurant a month, I was ready to find a job that paid better. I also wanted to find a church, but there were no Pentecostal churches in the area.

I quit my job and for some reason chose to purchase a bus ticket to Fort Lauderdale, which was a much larger town. Upon arriving, I had just enough money to rent a small room in another boarding house. The move from Jacksonville Beach to Fort Lauderdale proved to be a life-changing event, which was undoubtedly a divine intervention from God.

* * *

I HAD MADE NO FRIENDS, even though I had been gone from home for over a month. Thousands of tourists jammed the sidewalks of Fort Lauderdale, but I was as lonesome as if I lived on the desert.

I prayed almost constantly—not because I was a good person. I prayed out of desperation. I prayed in order to survive. Although my maturation and spiritual growth was extremely slow, that bus ride taught me one vital lesson about prayer; the possibilities were limitless. I had prayed—God had spoke to me—and now I was in a new town unsure if God had something planned for me or if I was on my own.

Right away, I searched out phone booths until I found one that still had a phone book inside (most were torn out or missing). The yellow pages of the phone book had several advertisements for Pentecostal churches. Of all the advertisements in the phone book only one announced in its belief in the Holy Spirit infilling. My heart lifted, because I knew that was the church for me.

The church was eight miles away from where I was staying in downtown Fort Lauderdale. It was Sunday, and they had Sunday night services. Immediately, I began to walk south toward the church.

When I arrived, the church service had already begun, and I took a seat near the back. It was a big church with possibly a thousand or more in the auditorium.

Two ladies in the pew in front of me talked about how anointed the singers were that night. "They're Spirit-filled. That makes a difference," one lady said.

That comment assured me I was in the right place. I waited patiently until the sermon ended, and then I hurried down the long aisle to the altar. As soon as my knees touched the floor, I burst into tears and prayed my heart out.

I did not know these people, and I really did not care what they thought about me. I needed a touch from God and I believed the altar was a sacred place where I could connect with him.

Of all of the dozens of people around the alter, no one prayed with me, and after about twenty minutes, I stood and wiped my swollen eyes. People stood huddled in groups around the altar and stared. No one said anything.

I turned and walked back down the long aisle and out of the church to begin my eight mile walk back to my room. I could have prayed in my room and saved the sixteen mile round-trip, but even I understood that the strength I received at the altar that night was worth more than the sixteen mile walk.

The next day, I continued to pray as I walked the sidewalks of Fort Lauderdale. I was nearly in tears, because I needed direction from God, I needed a job, and I needed a friend—mostly I needed a friend. The sidewalk was swollen thick with thousands of people—mostly tourists.

Suddenly, out of the crowd emerged three teenage girls who blocked my path. "Do you know Jesus?" one of them asked.

"Excuse me?" I could not believe my ears.

"Do you know Jesus as your savior?" she repeated.

Of all of the thousands of people on the sidewalk, they had singled me out. I was shy, but I was hungry for a friend and it was obvious this was another act of God. I wagged my head and lifted my shoulders. "I don't know. How are you supposed to know the answer to that?"

I had lived in a Methodist pastor's home for nearly a year, and had regularly attended a Pentecostal church in my hometown for six months, but I did not feel my heart was right with God. Worst of all, I did not know what to do about it.

The tallest of the three girls, Julie, pulled out a gospel tract and handed it to me. "We're having a Bible study at our house tonight, and it'd be great if you'd come and worship with us," she said. "The address is on the back."

I looked at the address stamped on the back. "World Ministry Outreach? What religion are you?" I asked as I folded the tract and shoved it inside my pocket.

"We're not a religion, but we believe in God's infilling of the Holy Spirit and speaking in tongues as evidence," Julie said.

My heart brightened. "I'll be there."

The girls turned and left, and I walked back to my room, thanking God for what he had just done for me. It was another miracle.

When I arrived that evening, the house was full of teenagers with Bibles. It was a big two-story Spanish-style building. A middle-aged man stood at the head of the dining table teaching Scripture.

The congregation of about twenty-five sang, worshiped, prayed, and read more Scripture. There was nothing in the world I wanted more than to be in the exact place where I was that night. God had given me common ground with others my age.

After the service ended, every person in the room shook my hand and made me feel welcome. One of the guys handed me a Bible. "Here. This is yours to keep. I see you don't have one."

"Thanks," I said. "You're right I don't own a Bible."

"I hope you wear it out." He patted me on the shoulder and left.

The pastor introduced himself and shook my hand. "Most of the people here tonight were strung out on drugs and God delivered them. Like yourself, no one is a local. They came here from all parts of the U.S., and God cleaned them up. Now, each one is doing God's work."

"I've been baptized," I said.

"That's a start. But you need the infilling of the Spirit."

I nodded. "I want that more than anything in the world."

"Have you spoke in tongues?" he asked.

I shook my head. "I pray every day."

"We have more formal church services in Hollywood, which is down the road a few miles. I'd like for you to go with us on Sunday. If you'll meet us here, we'll get you a ride."

I agreed and headed back to my room. Later, I learned that nearly everyone at the Bible study lived inside the house. The girls lived upstairs with the pastor and his wife, and the guys had numerous bunk beds downstairs.

Some of the teenagers had jobs and brought in their money and turned it all over to the pastor. Those who did not have jobs went out on the streets with their Bibles each day and witnessed to anyone who would listen.

On Sunday, I was back at the little mission. We all ate breakfast before we car-pooled and headed to the church building in Hollywood. Once service began, the congregation swelled to nearly fifty people.

I felt comfortable hanging out with the group and soon they had me going with them out on the streets and witnessing. Mostly, I just carried my Bible and listened to the others share the Gospel message.

Julie was full of the Holy Ghost, and she would often lead a person in prayer right on the sidewalk. Sometimes, she would even lead them in a confession prayer before they departed. I knew salvation required more than a confession prayer, but I also knew Julie was walking in the only light she had been taught.

From my first contact with the Pentecostal church in Seymour, I had been taught that Spirit infilling was mandatory and evidenced only by speaking in tongues. Everyone in this mission group was filled with the Holy Spirit and spoke in other tongues, but even though they had the Holy Spirit infilling, they believed it was optional. You could take it or leave it.

I had spoken in tongues, but I was not convinced I had received everything that was available to me. The Spirit would have to slay me or the lightning of God strike me before I could be satisfied. There was a dark spot in my soul that always made me feel as if I had done something wrong. All of my life, I had lived in fear, and I could never get adjusted to giving up that foreboding inside my chest.

What little money I had soon ran out, and I had yet to find a job. I needed a place to sleep and the pastor agreed to let me to sleep on the floor in the guy's dorm for a few days. The friendship of these other teens provided a strength for me. These teenagers were sincere about living for God. No one talked about sports, fun times, or personal passions, every conversation centered around Scripture or around a convert they were trying to win to God.

Hanging out with the guys and talking about the Bible late at night encouraged me greatly. We always ended each night with group prayer and worship in the main living room. This was followed by handshaking and men hugging men and encouraging each other while the women did the same with the other women.

One night after prayer, everyone moved around the large dining table as they hugged and prayed with each other. Julie crossed my path and before I knew it, she hugged me. I felt awkward, but I also felt awkward when I hugged the men, so I did not think much of it. After all, I was Julie's new convert.

The pastor's wife said something to her husband, and he immediately pulled me aside and reprimanded me.

"I didn't do anything wrong," I said. "She's the one who initiated the hug."

"We don't allow that here, so I'm going to ask you to pack your things and leave the house," he said bluntly.

"Now?"

He nodded. "It's a bad example for the others."

"But I don't have anywhere to go."

"People could start talking," he said. "I have no choice but to nip this in the bud."

I could hardly believe what was happening. I picked up my Bible, gathered up my few belongings from the floor and left. I had no place to stay and no money. Sleeping in someone's unlocked car was too frightening in this big town. Fort Lauderdale, Florida was much different than rural Jackson County, and I didn't want to take a chance of getting caught in someone's car and going to jail.

* * *

I WONDERED THE STREETS until I came to the beach area. Near the beach were large sales lots with dozens of new cabin boats. None of them were locked. Inside each of these houseboats was a nice bed, and the boat lot became my home for the next few weeks.

After my humiliating experience with the mission, I was too embarrassed to return for the Bible studies anymore. As a result, I spent most of my time walking the beach.

Hunger soon overtook me, and I had to improvise. Early one morning I walked by a hotel pool and discovered the remains of a chicken dinner on the patio table which someone had left the night before. The chicken was cold and dry but it tasted good to a starving man.

In order to survive, I visited the bakery's dumpster each day. Usually, I would find partial boxes of two-day-old pastries which they had tossed out. Many times, the pastries were still in plastic wrappers. I was often so hungry, I did not care much whether they were wrapped in plastic or not. At other times, I would boldly walk into a home owner's yard and pull a ripe mango from their tree.

Finally, an ice factory hired me. The pay was thirty-dollars a day—a big improvement over the thirty-four dollar a week I had been making. Working inside the ice factory all day and coming out to the extreme Florida heat in the afternoon was quite a shock to my body. The factory had a lot of employee turnover, and I quickly understood the reason.

My first check was over a hundred dollars, which went toward renting a room. I also purchased another cheap outfit from a thrift store. The rest of my money went for groceries. I always searched diligently for the best food bargains possible. Usually, my meals mostly consisted of oatmeal, hot dogs, and peanut-butter sandwiches.

My shift at the ice factory started early in the morning, which meant I got off work at two o'clock in the afternoon. On the way to work, I would stop at a large grocery store and hide a soda somewhere in the freezer department. That evening when I passed the store, I'd go in and purchase the single can of soda.

The ice-factory job was easy, but the shock of going from below freezing temperatures to a sudden one-hundred degrees bothered me. After work I kept job hunting until I was hired at a restaurant as a dishwasher.

Manny's Restaurant paid seventy-six dollars a week with the bonus of two free meals each day. It was a great relief to get out of the ice factory. Two other teens also worked at Manny's Restaurant during my evening shift. While on a break one day, one of the teenagers pulled out a match box and offered to share his marijuana stash with me. I declined and told him I didn't do drugs.

It didn't take long before I noticed Manny, the restaurant owner, had a lot of visitors who entered through the back door of the restaurant and slipped inside his private office. Visitors stayed only a couple minutes and then left. My dish-washing station was near Manny's office, but he always kept the office blinds closed which prevented me from seeing what was going on inside the office. But I was confident Manny was selling drugs.

Money was so tight, I could not afford a clock of any kind and Manny's wife expected me to be punctual. It took all of my weekly paycheck to pay rent and buy food necessities. The restaurant was a long walk from my room, which meant I had to get up long before daylight to make it to work on time. The only method I had of telling time was to get up and go outside where I could see the giant clock on the courthouse tower several blocks away. It was a nuisance, but it was my only means of a clock.

One day, I accidentally overslept. I jumped out of bed and rushed to get ready, but midway through the process I decided I was already in trouble and would likely lose my job anyway. Manny's wife was my supervisor and she was a no-nonsense type of woman.

I went back to bed and slept through most of the day. That evening I worried how I would find another job, and finally decided to go in to Manny's Restaurant and tell them the truth; that I had overslept and figured I was fired, but after thinking about it I wanted to ask them for a second chance.

When I entered the restaurant, Manny's wife met me at the door where she began upbraiding me before I had a chance to speak a word. "No, you are not welcome back," she said.

"I'm sorry. I had a problem."

"You left us in a bind, and I can't trust you anymore."

"But—"

She handed me the little pay I had coming and I left, and then made a twirling gesture with her hand. "Just turn around and go back out that door."

The money would not last long, and I needed to find another job as quickly as possible. But finding a new job turned out to be more difficult than I expected. I searched for employment, but without success. Soon I was sleeping on the street again.

I had to do something, because I did not want to live on the streets. I never once asked anyone for money, and I never stood on the street corner with a change cup or a *Please Help Me* sign.

As a last resort, I determined to join the Army. At home, I had often visited the post office where I picked up military brochures and read every detail over and over. President Kennedy had just begun a new branch in the Army called the Green Beret. Years earlier, I had determined I would someday be a Green Beret.

In my research, I discovered that the members of the Green Beret were chosen from the Army's pool of paratroopers. My dream was to join the 82nd Airborne and become the best paratrooper possible in order to move up the ranks and become a Green Beret. I was only fifteen-years old. But since I was big for my age, I believed I could convince the recruiter I was eighteen. At that time, the U.S. was in the middle of the Vietnam War, and I hoped their need for new troops would make it easier to get through any closed doors.

It was the middle of July when I walked into the recruiter's office. Boot camp during the hot months of summer would be challenging and possibly deadly. But I was tired of living on the streets, and what they did to me in boot camp was the least of my worries.

"I wanted to join the paratroopers," I said when I showed up at the recruiter's office with my Bible in hand.

The officer behind the desk wagged his head as if he felt sorry for me as he bent over and pulled the paperwork from his desk drawer.

He gave me an application to complete along with a series of entrance exams. Once I finished, he asked me to wait while he graded the exams. It was a relief when he announced I had passed.

"How soon can I ship out," I asked.

"It only takes a day or two to for me to get the paperwork done and arrange for your transportation to boot camp. But you'll have to bring a birth certificate to prove your age. Bring that with you and you can be at boot camp in a couple days."

I immediately went to the store and began looking through magazines until I found a source that sold blank birth certificates for a dollar. I ordered one right away. As a backup plan, I ordered my real birth certificate from my hometown hospital. If I could not forge a blank birth certificate, then I would try to alter my original birth certificate.

*   *   *

THE BLANK BIRTH CERTIFICATES never arrived. When my real birth certificate came in the mail, I took it to the mall where I found a typewriter sitting on the counter in the cosmetic section.

Using all the stealth I could muster, I tried to type over my birth date and change it to an earlier date. It didn't work. It only marred the certificate and made it look worse. After several attempts, I finally gave up.

Living on the streets, I slept anywhere I could. Once, the lawn furniture at a motel became my bed, another time I slept on the pool table inside a motel's recreation room. One night, a sudden rain storm caught me on the streets, and I had to sleep under a table outside a diner with my head between my knees and my hands over my head while the rain poured down around me.

I was not alone on the street. So many teenagers were homeless that the local Holiday Inn allowed teens to sleep on the building's sun roof after hours. A tourism canal boat also allowed teens to sleep on the boat deck at night.

Hunger and fatigue eventually wore me down. One day, as I walked down the street, loneliness overtook me. My face crinkled up and the tears would not stop. The words of my stepfather were never far from my mind; *You'll never amount to anything. You're just like your real father. He ran off and left his family, and you're just like him.*

I tried to consider the source and cast the thoughts away, but the words were deeply implanted inside my mind like a little demon who always sat on my shoulder and whispered negative thoughts in my ear. I had never been good at anything in life. I certainly wasn't good in relationships. No one really liked me, and here I was a thousand miles from home with not a single person to call my friend. But what could I do?

God's timing has always been perfect. A car tooted it's horn and pulled over to the side of the road. It was Dave, a man I had met at the park a few weeks earlier. He had been friendly and had wanted to talk. I mostly listened, and he had encouraged me to go back to school and continue my education. I had suspicions he was gay, but he never bothered me in any way.

He got out of his Volkswagen and gestured that we sit on a park bench. "You look disheartened," he said.

"I feel kind of down."

"What's the matter?"

I lost control of my emotions again. "I am such a loser," I said between sobs. "I don't know anyone here, and I get so lonesome at times."

"You're homesick. You should go back home."

"I don't have any money, and I'm afraid to go back home."

"Afraid? Why?"

"They'll put me in jail."

"You're emotionally distraught. You need to talk to someone qualified to help you. If I can get you an appointment with my priest, would you be willing to talk to him? He might be able to help you."

"I'm at the point, I'll do anything. I don't even know what to think about myself anymore."

Like a man on a mission, he promptly drove me to a large Catholic church and took me inside the rectory. I waited in the lobby as he talked to the secretary. A few minutes later, he returned. "The secretary made an appointment for you to speak with the priest. He's in mass right now, but you can wait for him here."

I nodded. "Thanks."

"I've talked to him a few times, and I think he might do you some good," Dave said.

I sat up straight and ran my hand through my long hair. I had not cut my hair in several months, and I had not showered in weeks. I also felt self-conscious about my dirty clothes.

"I told the secretary your story, and if you want to go home, she volunteered to pay half of your bus ticket to Indiana. She thinks the priest will pay the other half."

"Are you serious?" I thanked him for his help.

He smiled, shook my hand, and said goodbye. I never saw him again.

As I waited for the priest, my mind was a swirl of emotions. I had been gone from home for over three months, and it was frightening to think of going back home. But things were not working out for me.

Sleeping on the streets and eating only when I could had drained every bit of enthusiasm and life out of me. Life was so lonesome and miserable that I was willing to put myself at the mercy of my probation officer—even if it meant going to jail again.

After waiting nearly an hour, a priest came into the rectory and spoke with the secretary for couple minutes. I saw him nod and look in my direction. Finally, he crossed the room and offered his hand. "Hi Kenny, I'm Father LaPenny. I understand you've been down on your luck today."

I shook his hand and nodded.

"You want to go back home? he asked.

I nodded again. "I'd like to."

"I think we can help you. "Sister Morene and myself are considering buying your ticket home, but I would like to chat with you first. Is that okay?"

I looked down. "Yeah, I guess." I assumed he would try to convert me to the Catholic faith or council me about my sin of running away from home. Either way, I was willing to take the risk.

He gestured for me to follow him. "My office is in the other building. Have you contacted anyone from home since you've been here in Florida?" he asked as we walked along the sidewalk.

"No." In truth I had written to one of the neighborhood girls who lived near Acme, and she had written back a couple times.

The Catholic church property reminded me of a college campus with several buildings all connected by perfectly trimmed sidewalks and dark-green grass. Father LaPenny led me to a building where we went up stairs to his office.

Once inside, he gestured to a couple oversized pillows on the floor. "Have a seat on the floor if you want. I'll fix us something to drink. I have orange juice, soda, or milk."

"No thank. I'm not thirsty." I was too nervous to drink or eat. With my legs crossed under me, I sat on the floor beside the pillows and waited.

He fixed himself a soda and positioned himself on one of the giant pillows in front of me—too close for my comfort. "Do you have many friends here in town?" he asked.

"Not one," I said. "When I ran away, I didn't know where I was going. I traveled with Greyhound all over the southern states." I glanced around the room. The apartment walls were covered with giant photos of movie stars—most with large flashy signatures on them.

He saw me examining them. "Those are my clients. I'm a professional hypnotist. That's what I do for a living."

I frowned. "I thought you were a priest?"

"Of course, but I also counsel people." He looked up at the photographs. "I've worked with all of these stars you see on the wall. They have to memorize a lot of dialogue for movie scripts, and I hypnotize them to help them with their lines."

I nodded as I thought ahead. Suddenly, I did not want to be here. My decision to follow the priest up to his apartment may not have been such a good idea. Even worse, I had unwittingly informed him that no one knew my whereabouts.

He took a sip of his drink and set it on the end table near him. "Do you know Dave is gay?"

"I didn't know, but I suspected it. I've only talked to him a couple times."

"He doesn't want to be gay, and I've been helping him." He sipped his drink again and stared at me. "I have a theory that post-hypnotic suggestions can help gay men."

"I'm not gay," I said quickly. Where was he going with this?

He nodded. "I believe you. But I understand you're a religious man. Is that true?"

I glanced at the Bible beside me. "I'm trying. But I still have a lot to learn."

He tilted his head to one side slightly. "Would you like to help gay men overcome their problem?"

I lifted a shoulder, not sure what the best answer was. "I guess."

He produced a gold pocket watch with a long chain. "It's quite obvious, you have a serious inferiority complex."

I arched my brow and looked away. "It's that obvious?" I pointed to my missing front teeth. "How could I be any other way? I try not to talk, because I don't want people to see my two fangs in front, and I never allow myself to smile. When I do talk, I have a bad lisp."

"So that's why you bite your upper lip all the time," he said.

"I trained myself to do that. I also trained myself to talk fast and cut my sentences as short as possible. That way I get my words out before anyone looks at me."

"I can help you." He pointed to the photos that lined his office walls. "I helped them."

"I didn't think that hypnotism stuff really worked."

He smiled and nodded. "Oh, it works, and it can help you, too." He reached back and grabbed a couple pillows. "Lay back on the floor and put those under your head."

I hesitated. Should I even trust this man? After all, he was a priest, but before anyone hypnotized me, I wanted a trusted friend in the room. "I'm not sure about that," I said.

He smiled. "I normally charge people for this, but I'm willing to help you."

I shifted on the floor and glanced at the door. From where I sat, I could not tell if the door was locked or not. "Maybe I should go."

Father LaPenny had positioned himself higher than me. He was a big man and could likely over power me if I tried to run, and I could not be sure what he would do if I tried to escape. My only alternative was to pretend I was hypnotized and go along with him, but I had no idea how to do that.

* * *

I SUCKED IN A DEEP BREATH and glanced around the room. There was no other way out except through the front door. "Dave is probably tired of waiting on me. I should probably should go." I lied. Dave was long gone.

"You'll do fine," he said softly. "Lay back and focus. This will help you have much more confidence in yourself." He arranged the pillows behind me.

Reluctantly, I slowly leaned back on the pillows and watched the pocket watch swing back and forth in front of me like a pendulum. My heart beat like a rabbit trying to get out of its cage. There was no way I intended to go through with this.

I knew nothing about hypnosis, but I did not trust this man, even if he was a priest. We were alone in his apartment, and I had no one who cared about me if I happened to turn up missing.

He talked softly and after a moment he told me to close my eyes and concentrate on his words. His voice grew increasingly quiet until he spoke in a whisper.

Inside my mind, thoughts were raging in panic, and I prayed like a man on fire. In the last few months I had developed a serious street-smart sense and right now my danger meter was buried in the red.

My eyes finally closed, but panic continued to rise up inside me like a wild animal. For all I knew this man could be a serial killer.

Inside my mind, I prayed for God's help as I agreed to anything Father LaPenny said. I decided to fake it as long as I could and then make a run for the door at my first chance.

"Kenny, you are under my authority. You must do anything I say. Do you understand?"

"Yes," I whispered. What else did he expect me to say?

He continued talking softly. "I want you to have sex with me."

My muscles tensed. "No!

He repeated his words, louder this time.

"I will not do that." I kept my eyes closed. Did he think I was already hypnotized?

"You are under my power. You have to do what I say."

"No. I won't do that."

"I have a knife in my hand. I am going to stab you in the stomach unless you agree to have sex with me."

I hesitated.

"Do you understand me?" he asked.

"Jesus, help me," I whispered.

"Kenny, stop praying."

"I need your help right now, Jesus," I prayed louder.

"Kenny, stop praying. You must listen to me."

I raised my voice even louder. "Jesus, help me. I need your help. Deliver me, Jesus. You are my protector."

He poked his finger into my navel. "I am stabbing you, Kenny. This knife will kill you unless you consent to acts of sex with me." As he spoke he jabbed his finger deeper into my stomach.

The pain was excruciating. I rolled over on my side and tried to curl up in the fetal position in an attempt to escape the pain. Now, I wished I had tried to run, but it was too late. I feared he might have a gun or other weapon in the drawer of the table near his shoulder.

He spoke quietly for another minute as if he was trying to deepen my trance. Suddenly, he jabbed his finger deeper into my stomach as if he had grown angry. "Kenny, I command you to obey me."

The pain was nearly unbearable. It was as if he had gone through training to find the most vulnerable spot on the human body in which to inflict the greatest pain.

I continued to pray loudly. "Lord Jesus, You are my master. You are my strength. Help me, Jesus."

"Stop praying. You are not allowed to pray. You must do what I say," his voice grew louder and harsh. "You are under my power."

"No. I am under Jesus' power. I worship you, Jesus. You are my helper." The ordeal continued for more than an hour as he continued to hurt me, and I continued to pray as intensely as possible.

Finally, I burst through speaking in fluent tongues. I had received the Holy Spirit several weeks earlier, and I had read the Scripture where speaking in tongues was a prayer for the things we did not know we needed. Right then I needed a way out of this man's power, and only God knew how to give it to me.

He immediately grew quiet.

With my eyes closed, I did not know what to expect. I feared he might hit me or produce a gun.

Once I stopped praying, there was a long moment of silence before he spoke. "Okay, Kenny. It's over. I am going to awaken you now, and when I do, you will not remember anything I have said to you. At the count of three you will wake up. One, two, three."

I was not sure what to do, so I did not do anything.

"Open your eyes, Kenny."

I opened my eyes and sat up. "I can kind of remember—"

He interrupted me. "Don't try to remember. You were praying in what you called speaking in tongues. He spit out the last three words as if they burned his tongue.

As he wiped his brow, he looked away a moment. "I've been doing experiments with gay men trying to help them. I believe hypnosis has the possibility to change a person's sexual desires."

He rambled on about his experiments and theories. Apparently, he had experimented on a few men, but so far he had no certain success.

I was not listening to him. Inside my head, I was still praying and thinking about how to get out of the apartment—alive. If I pretended I had to go to the bathroom, then maybe I could run out the door as I passed by the entry.

His demeanor instantly changed. "Come on, I'm going to take you to the bus station. He picked up his keys from the table.

I stood and hurried to the door. It was not locked.

At the Greyhound bus station, he purchased a one-way ticket to Seymour, Indiana in my name and wrote NOT REFUNDABLE across the front of it. "Here's ten dollars for food. I hope things go well for you." He shook my hand and quickly left as if he wanted to be rid of me.

I boarded the bus, not knowing what awaited me in Indiana. The police might arrest me as soon as I arrived, or even worse my probation officer could insist I go back home and live with my parents. All I wanted was for the authorities to leave me alone and let me live my life free from Junior and his oppression. I dreamed of getting a job and living on my own, but I knew that was nearly an impossibility.

CHAPTER SEVEN

Don't let mistakes become memorials.

For in the time of trouble he shall hide me in his pavilion: in the secret of his tabernacle shall he hide me; he shall set me up upon a rock. Psalm 27:5

FEAR GRIPPED MY HEART, when the Greyhound bus pulled into Seymour on Thursday evening. Daniel Luckey and his family had always been kind to me, and I went straight to his house, which was only a few blocks from the bus station. Marie, his mother, was active in the church, and I considered her a true Christian. Although, the family was friendly to me, I'm certain they called my probation officer right away in order to protect themselves.

Marie insisted I go to church with them that night. I wanted to go to church more than I wanted anything else in the world, but I knew my parents would be there, and I did not want to face them.

My hunger for a connection with God won out, and after service started, I slipped in the door of the Pentecostal church and sat near the back. My mother and Junior were in their regular pew near the front on the left side. When everyone stood to pray, Mom turned and spotted me.

I made eye contact across the church and smiled, but she didn't respond. When church was over, I left before anyone had a chance to question me. The Luckey family let me spend the night with them, for which I was grateful.

The next morning I called the Trueblood family. It had been nearly a year since I had left them, and I was worried they would reject me, but I did not have many options. Betty answered the phone and like usual, I was direct and to the point. "Hi Betty. This is Kenny Noble. I just got into town from Florida and I need a place to stay. I was wondering if I could come and live with you and your family again?"

She hesitated. "I don't know, Kenny. You need to ask Bud that question." She handed the phone to her husband.

"Hi Bud. I need a place to live now that I'm back in Seymour. I was hoping I could come back home to live with you guys."

He was silent a long moment before he released a long sigh. "I reckon, Kenny. Is your parents okay with this?"

"I'll have to talk to my probation officer, but there's no way I am going back to live with my parents."

"Well, run it through your probation officer and have him give me a call me first," Bud said. "As soon as you get that taken care of, we'll be glad to have you back with us."

I was elated. The Trueblood family had been so good to me, and I felt as close to them as I did my own family. They did not try to put on a front or impress people as my parents did, and everyone in the family always got along well.

Once again, had they known the trouble I would bring to their household, I'm sure they would not have taken me in again.

Things turned sour my first week living with the Trueblood family, and it was all my fault. I was expected to help with the chores, which was reasonable, because everyone worked on the farm. I didn't mind doing chores, but I had changed a lot during the trip to Florida. Now, I was attempting to be the best Christian possible, but I had a lot to learn about how to accomplish that deed.

I had developed the habit of reading at least ten pages from the Bible each morning and praying before I did anything else. Of course, living on the street gives a person a lot of extra time to accomplish that goal when they are not inhibited by regular job hours. Now, it bothered me that I was out working when I had not completed my religious devotions first.

In reality, I should have gotten up earlier and done my devotions or waited until that night to do them. But I had this self-imposed discipline, and in my mind, I believed God expected this out of me. My guilt would not leave me alone.

Bud sensed my negative attitude toward working, and he became frustrated with me. It never crossed my immature mind that I would have been a much better witness for God if I had worked hard and prayed while I worked. In this situation, I was an example of being so heavenly minded I was no earthly good.

We were taking bales of hay off the wagon, busting them open, and spreading the hay just inside the fence for the cows to eat when Bud questioned my quietness and we began arguing. "What are you mad about today?" he asked.

"I haven't even read the Bible today," I burst out in frustration, as I tossed a bale of hay to the ground.

Bud stopped what he was doing. "Then get yourself back to the house and read your Bible." He pointed his finger at me. "You're messed up, kid. You got a lot to learn."

I plodded back to the house, certain Bud was the one who was messed up for not understanding me. I took my Bible to the bedroom and tried to read, but I could not focus on the words. The argument had upset me, and I was not certain if I was in the right or wrong.

Soon Bud came back to the house and told Betty about my attitude. "Kenny come out here," she said.

I went to the kitchen where they both stood, their hands fisted on their hips. "Kenny, working is part of life," Betty said. "We all have to work. The Bible talks about that."

"I know, and I want to work. I just feel so guilty not reading my Bible first. If I die, I want to go to Heaven, and how will I make it if I'm not doing the things I'm supposed to do?"

Bud shook his head. "Betty is a Catholic. She has been to school to study the Bible. You should take her advice."

I looked up at the ceiling and sucked in a deep breath. "You don't understand." I turned and went back to my bedroom.

The World Ministry Outreach group in Florida had embedded in me the idea that a person needed serious Bible reading and prayer every day. Sadly, they had not taught me the importance of a work ethic, and that was something I needed to learn.

In my spiritual immaturity, my dedication to God was portraying a bad example of the Christian life. In some ways I had grown up too fast. Even the Trueblood children didn't seem to relate to me anymore, and it was my fault. In my own way I was very legalistic, because I thought living for God had no margin for error and grace.

Sadly, people often perceive their heavenly father in the same manner as they perceive their earthly father, and I was one of them. The harsh environment of being raised under Junior's tutelage without any grace or affection had transferred into my attitude toward my Savior. But it would take a long time before I understood I had that flaw.

Bud assumed since I was having conflict with him that I would automatically revert to running away again. That idea had not entered my mind, and I told him so, but he did not believe me. As a safety precaution he moved my little duffel bag that held all of my personal belongings to his room at night. "I know you won't leave without your things," he said.

He was wrong. I had ran away without even my shoes at least twice in the past. But he was trying to manage me in the only way he knew. Once again God had given me such an amazing opportunity, and I was too immature to see it.

Betty attempted to convince me that I was confused and needed help. She did her best to teach me that God was not one who condemns us when we don't measure up, but rather God is merciful, and he always tries to show love and help us with immeasurable grace.

My mind could not comprehend that concept. In addition, Bud and Betty were now the authorities in my life, and automatically I considered any authority the enemy. Even though I tried, I could not buy into their advice. I had never once been able to measure up to Junior's approval, and in my mind, I had to measure up to the highest standards possible before even God would save me.

As usual, I was wrong and did not know it. God was not only trying to teach me, but through Bud and Betty he was also demonstrating his grace and mercy. Sadly, I was not able to see it.

The Luckey family volunteered to drive the ten miles from Seymour to the Trueblood's house in Acme to pick me up for church each Sunday night. I was grateful for their sacrifice, and it was probably the only element that helped me through those hard times.

As the weeks passed by, my relationship with the Trueblood family deteriorated, I realized my stay with them would not be long term. They were so good to me, but they were at their wits end and did not know how to help me.

I got along well with the Luckey family, and they agreed to let me move in with them. Marie had several long talks with Betty, and soon I was living with yet another foster family.

After moving into the Luckey household, I continued to attend church and grow, but I was far from the person I should have been. Fortunately, the Lord moved on numerous people and gave me favor in their sight—undeserving as I was.

At that time, I owned very few clothes, but one man in the church gave me several of his good suits. Another elderly lady saved her change all week long and gave it to me after each Sunday night church service. It was humbling to take money from an elderly lady, but she insisted and I needed the money. Another man in the church gave me a job working on his construction site where he began to mentor me.

When one of the men in the church discovered I had an interest in guitar, he purchased a nice electric guitar and handed it over to me. His only rule; I had to leave it at the church. As a result, I spent much of my spare time at the church practicing.

I am not certain if he realized what he was doing, but this resulted in my having a lot of interaction with the parishioners who would come and go from the church for various reasons.

The pastor lived next to the church, and I often found him sitting under the shade tree in his back yard. I would stop and talk with him, which proved to have a tremendous effect on my spiritual growth.

Technology and media was limited in those days. Eight-track tape players had just been invented, but I did not have access to any kind of albums, videos, or recordings.

Occasionally, the pastor left a big reel-to-reel tape player in the church kitchen. On it were several recordings of formal religious debates, usually on the godhead. I listened to the debates over and over and took notes. More important than what I learned from listening to the debates, was the tremendous desire it gave me to study the Bible.

Without God's mercy and tolerance, others could not put up with me for any length of time. The Luckey family understood my commitment to spiritual growth which seemed to help, and they allowed me to be myself and grow at my own pace.

Of course, that was not necessarily a good thing. I was extremely immature—even for a fifteen-year old. I was not sure who I wanted to be and my attitude was not that great. In addition, I was constantly pulling pranks and teasing others. Pulling pranks was the only way I knew to interact and make people like me.

Dennis, a teenager from school, lived on the same block as the Luckey family, and he also lived with foster parents. We became friends, and one evening we began talking about how we'd like to run away and live out west. The talk quickly turned into making serious plans.

The next day, we each told our foster parents we were going to stay all night at the other person's house. We packed our bags and carried them out the front door, our guardians non the wiser.

Freedom and adventure was our chief goal. We had no money, but our plan was to jump a train and ride it out west. I was seriously committed to the plan, but it turned out Dennis only wanted to have a little fun.

That night we went to the rail road tracks behind the State Police station, and hid in a petroleum-tank train car. At the end of the train, the petroleum tank was supported by several giant louvers welded on the ends. These giant fins provided the perfect cubbyhole for us to hide.

We each crawled inside the cubbyhole and waited a long time until finally the train engine took off and pulled our car forward. Then it slowed down and backed up to connect our car another car. The jolt from slamming into another freight car shook us so much that at first I thought it might kill us.

The train repeated the process several times, knocking us around inside our cubbyhole like we were in a steel bouncy house. Finally, we heard the engine pick up speed and called to each other in excitement. The engine puffed faster and faster and when I leaned forward to peek outside our cubbyhole, I saw we were not moving. The train unhooked our car and left without us.

We left the train tracks and walked about a mile to an auto dealership where we climbed the tall chain-linked fence to get inside the car lot. An unlocked semi in the repair lot had a sleeper built inside the cab, which Dennis took, and I slept in the driver's seat.

Later in the night, another train came by and we quickly gathered our things, climbed the large fence, and headed for the tracks. Our plan was to jump the train and ride it out of town.

Once I ran up close to the train, I discovered it was traveling much too fast to board safely. I ran alongside it and reached for the ladder on an empty car, but it was more difficult than I had imagined. In addition, the tracks were built on a rise which made it even more difficult to reach up and catch onto the train ladder while running. I feared the sudden transfer from land to train might dislocate my shoulder, but I was willing to try.

As I ran alongside the train and tried to muster enough courage to grab onto the train-car ladder, I kept calling to Dennis to hurry and come along, but he pretended he had dropped his glove and could not find it. He stalled until the train passed us by and was gone.

*   *   *

SINCE JUMPING THE TRAIN DID NOT WORK out, we walked back into town to the Pentecostal church. The door was locked, but we eased the lock back with a pocketknife and got inside. The upstairs Sunday School room over the church office was the least visited area of the church, and I felt confident we would be safe up there.

We slept on the floor of the Sunday School room, and the next morning, we left early and walked along the railroad tracks to the Persimmon Lake camping park, which was about ten miles west of Seymour. Inside the privately owned park, we chose a camper set back away from the main road and nearly hidden from view. We broke into it and spent two nights inside where we ate the owners stockpile of food and in general made a mess of his littler camper.

The third evening a car pulled up outside the camper. Our first fear was the we were caught by the camper's owner, but the car doors opened and someone called out our names. It was our foster parents. Someone had seen us walking westward and reported it to our foster parents. They wisely guessed at our hiding place.

I remained quiet, because I did not want to get caught, but Dennis began to whisper and they heard him. He opened the door and we were busted. We went back home with them, and to my surprise they quickly forgave us. After they called the police and told them we were back at home safe and sound, it was the end of it.

Since we had missed several days of school, we had to meet with the high school principal in his office. Dennis blamed everything on me. "I just went along because Kenny told me to go with him."

"You are responsible for your own actions," the principal said. "If Kenny tells you to jump in a lake, are you going to do it?"

Dennis laughed. "Maybe."

In the end, our only punishment was after school detention, which turned out to be more like a party for the high-school's bad boys.

It was only a few weeks later my brother, Steve, rode his bicycle over to the Luckey's house to visit me. It had been several months since I had seen him and I was glad he came to visit me. But when he returned home, and Junior discovered what he had done, he whipped Steve for visiting me.

I was in the kitchen when I heard what had happened, and I grew extremely angry. "It is so wrong for my own brother to get whipped for visiting me." At the time, I had a coffee cup in my hand, and in anger I slammed it on the floor and shattered it.

"What is wrong with that man that he has to whip kids?" I yelled. "What's wrong with a mother that allows her own son to get whipped for visiting another son?"

Only Daniel and Beth were in the house, and my fit of anger frightened them. They hurried to a neighbor's house where they called their mother at her workplace and explained what was happening. Marie promptly called the police.

Everything happened so fast. One minute I was venting my anger, and the next minute the house was suddenly empty. It seemed only a couple minutes later, and a police car pulled up in front of the house. I knew I was in trouble.

My first impulse was to turn and run out the back door. But with my hand on the knob, I paused and thought a moment. If I ran, I had no where to go.

Later, I learned the story had escalated from the time the children told it to their mother and she repeated it to the police. As a result, the police were considering me dangerous. I also found out later that an officer had stationed himself behind a large tree in the back yard with his gun drawn waiting for me to come out the back door. Running out the back door may have resulted in my being shot. At that time, I certainly would not have stopped if he had confronted me.

Instead of running, I went to the bedroom and stretched out on the bed where I pretended to be calm. When the officer came in and told me he was taking me to jail, I asked if I might take my Bible with me. He agreed and I went peaceably.

They locked me in a cell in the Jackson County jail for forty-nine days. The Luckey family no longer wanted me. They had held up longer than any other foster family, but I finally exhausted their patience, too. My parents did not want me either, which meant I had no place to live.

I had no visitors while in jail, but one day without notice, an officer unlocked my cell, handcuffed me, and walked me to the judges chambers at the county courthouse. The judge asked my name as he shuffled through a stack of papers. Without further conversation he announced. "We cannot find a place for you to live. Therefore, I have no alternative than to sentence you to Indiana Boy's School until you are twenty-one years old."

His words broke my heart. I had not seen it coming, and I walked out of the judge's chambers on the second floor of the courthouse with my head spinning. In my mind, it was the worst possible thing that could happen to me.

Junior's words rang out in my ears, "You'll be in prison before your sixteen years old."

As his words replayed in my mind, I crossed the balcony of the courthouse and looked down to the main floor. A strong urge came over me to jump off headfirst and commit suicide. Adrenalin rushed through my veins like firewater. My muscles tensed and I looked over my shoulder at the officer following me. He had lagged several steps behind me and would not be able to stop me. My hands were handcuffed, but I sucked in a deep breath and edged closer to the balcony rail.

Something stopped me. I told myself I was not afraid to do it, I just was not certain it was the right thing to do. Finally, I decided I could always hang myself later while inside my cell.

I hurt more than I had ever hurt in my life. Never had I felt so alone and helpless. Junior's prophecy had come true, which made me believe Junior might be right about his other predictions he had made over me too. I began to question if God had rejected me also.

I sat alone in the jail cell and beat myself down each day. After sitting in the Jackson County jail for forty-nine days, they transferred me to Indiana Boys' School. I walked through the doors with my hands and feet chained together like a hardened criminal on death row. My heart was broken, because it was less than a month until my sixteenth birthday. Junior had been right all along.

In the depth of my depression, I began to grab onto the possibility that God was still my friend. My fledgling relationship with him was the only thing that sustained me the next few months.

Those first days at boy's school were frightening. The only way I knew to deal with harsh situations was to take the humble path and assume the attitude of submission. Junior had forced me into submission all of my life, and I was good at it.

During the first seven weeks at boy's school, they locked me inside a small concrete cell with only a toilet, a bed, and a lavatory. They called this building the Orientation Building. Here they kept new inmates until they were tested and the counselors decided which campus cottage best suited an inmate.

On occasion, they let me out to socialize with thirty other inmates who were in the same predicament as myself. The guard unlocked our cell and we would all march down the hall to a recreation room which had a television, a ping-pong table, and a pool table. I chose to sit quietly and watch whatever was on the television.

Only one man supervised the thirty rowdy teenagers in the big room, and he spent most of his time at his desk reading and studying. He always acted oblivious to the events going on around him, even though gay sexual acts were taking place less than twenty feet from his desk.

I kept to myself and did not socialize at all. But my presence did not go unnoticed, because one mid-morning, I was watching television and about to fall asleep when suddenly a terrible burning pain in my rear made me jump from my seat and cry out. Someone had placed a burning cigarette in my seat. When I looked behind me, I spotted several burly inmates grinning and waiting for my reaction.

They acted as if they thought the prank was funny, but I knew they were just testing the new white boy. I laughed, shook my head, and sat back in the chair. When they realized I was not going to challenge anyone to fight or quarrel they all went about their business and left me alone.

The next day, two of the inmates escaped through the kitchen window while we were all in the recreation room. Apparently, they got away from the boy's school grounds (there were no walls around the campus) and wound up at a quarry where they found a parked pickup truck with a camper on the bed. One of the boys quickly hot-wired the truck and they were soon driving down the road to freedom.

But their luck went sour right away. The truck began to sway all over the road so badly the driver had to pull off the road and stop. As soon as the vehicle came to a stop, several men popped out of the camper and attacked the two boys with pots and pans. The men were on an overnight fishing trip, and had been sound asleep in the camper when the boys hijacked the truck.

The men subdued the boys until the police arrived and took the escaped prisoners back to their cells. One evening all of the inmates were in the big room when two security guards came to administer the escapees punishment. The two punishers were dressed in black and wore black gloves.

They instructed us all to line up in a large circle around the big recreation room, which we did. Next, the two guards walked around the room and gave us a lecture about good behavior and the results of bad behavior.

After the lecture was finished, the guards had the first escapee bend over and place his hands on a card table in the middle of the room. The guard drew back his paddle and hit the boy in the same manner in which a person would swing a baseball bat. Every inmate watched in fear as the boys back side went up in the air and he along with the table slid across the floor several feet.

The poor boy tried to put on a show of bravery and not cry out, but he could not help from falling to his knees and writhing and squirming in response to the pain. The room grew quiet as we all watched.

When the boy gained control of himself and his pain subsided, the big guard told him to place his hands onto the table again. The man swung the paddle once again and sent the boy and table sliding back across the room in the other direction. After the guard repeated this process three times, he put his paddle under his arm. "I'll wait about three days until you're good and sore and then I'll come back and give you the other three licks."

He repeated the process with the second escapee before he left the building. As far as I knew, he never returned to administer the other three licks. I determined then and there I would never try to escape even if I had to spend my entire life in prison.

*   *   *

IN MY CONCRETE CELL, my window was covered with bars, but I was grateful to see outside. Day-in and day-out, it was always the same routine for meal time; the guard opened the door, and I had to be on my knees waiting at the door to slide my food tray inside the room. Once finished, I slid the empty food tray under the door.

After I went through the testing and evaluation process, I requested the counselor to send me to the Henryville Honor Camp. My former foster parent, Mr. Nossett, had an older son who was the camp's psychiatrist. Apparently, the counselor contacted the Henryville Honor Camp and discovered I was telling the truth, and he arranged to send me there. While I waited for an open bed at the honor camp, they placed me in one of the boys' school cottages with forty other inmates.

Each inmate had the option of going to school, or working each day. Like most of the other inmates, I chose work over school. My job was working on the yard gang. We mowed the lawns, picked up trash, and did anything else that needed done.

After dinner each evening, the inmates were confined to the cottage where they watched television and played board games. I continued to keep to myself, and study Scripture.

Reading the Bible attracted attention from the other inmates, and one inmate was quick to inform me, "Why are you reading the Bible, man? Don't you know you can't be saved in here?"

Fortunately, I was convinced he was wrong and tried to use my time to learn the Bible and to grow spiritually.

The food truck came to our cottage twice a day, and it always left the exact amount of servings to match the number of inmates in our building. Thirty-nine inmates meant they delivered thirty-nine pieces of cornbread and thirty-nine desserts and so on. Unfortunately, the bully who worked in the serving line always helped himself to the other inmates share of food before it was served. That meant the last few inmates in the food line did not get a complete meal.

If the bully did not get to work in the food line that day, he would demand those who sat at his dinner table to give up some of their food. Once he had a share of their food, he would threaten his victims into silence.

At bed time, we all made our way to the dorm room where the bunk beds were lined up in several straight rows much like the Army barracks. A night watchman lived in an apartment adjoining our dorm, and he periodically came in to check on everyone. Occasionally, he would be gone for nearly an hour.

As soon as the lights went out each night, several inmates got up from their own bunk bed and scurried to other inmates beds—more gay sex acts. When the guard returned to check on us, he acted as if he was oblivious to what was happening. I stayed in my bed with my eyes open and prayed while I kept my fist doubled and ready to fight.

If anyone came near me, I determined to fight as long as I was alive even though I knew the consequences would be grim. Fortunately, no one bothered me.

A few days later, they transferred me to the honor camp, which was located inside the Henryville Forestry in Southern Indiana. The conditions at the honor camp were much better than at boy's school. It was more of a family-army atmosphere where all inmates worked in the forest, chopping weeds and cleaning the up dead limbs.

One day each week, I was privileged to attend a small trade school where they taught me to repair washing machines. Eventually, the instructor made me the student teacher, which I appreciated because it gave me more class time.

The honor camp allowed inmates special privileges, but our freedom was limited. We could walk outside anytime we wanted as long as we stayed within sight. The doors to the building were never locked, and as you might imagine, this made a big difference in our attitudes.

I considered myself a Christian and tried to spend my time growing spiritually by praying and reading the Bible in my spare time. Some might think it was easy to live as a Christian inside a reformatory, because there were no temptations nor opportunities to do wrong.

But even inside the walls of the boy's school there were many of the same struggles a person faced on the outside. One of the struggles was getting along with more than thirty other high-strung teenagers who lived with you twenty-four-seven.

Most of us were known by our last name, but within a few days of my arrival, the other inmates tagged me as *Preacher*. Even the guards called me *Preacher*.

My first few nights at bed call were trying times. No one was allowed in the dorms before bed call and everyone had to get up at the same time each morning. Each night, I knelt at my bed for prayer, and with very little knowledge and a lot of determination I purposed in my heart I would not be ashamed of my Christianity.

More specifically, I determined to pray in boy's school in the same way I had prayed when I was in church. As I prayed, I realized if I was at the apostolic church, I would pray with my hands raised to heaven. So, as I prayed, I raised my hands.

But while I prayed, I felt body heat radiating around me.

When I opened my eyes, a crowd of spectators had quietly gathered to watch me pray. They weren't content with watching from a distance. They wanted to hear my whispers of prayer, so they hovered around me until they were two feet from my face.

I wasn't allowed to pray very long, because the guard walked the aisles and made certain each person was in bed. Dedication to prayer and Bible reading earned me tremendous respect from the other inmates, something I had not expected. I did not curse or smoke, and I only fought twice during the five months I was incarcerated at the honor camp.

Mail call was the highlight of each day for all of us, and I wrote letters to anyone back home whom I thought might respond. My mother wrote back to me twice. In the letters she expressed her love for me and how she hoped I would get my life straightened out. I wrote back and told her that I had a confession to make. "I smoke cigarettes, but I am trying to overcome them and quit."

In reality, I did not smoke at all. In fact, I thought smoking was gross and disgusting, but I said this to test her, and see if she really did care for me, or if she was only saying those nice things. My answer was just as I suspected. She never wrote back. I decided if she really cared about me, smoking cigarettes would not matter—especially since her husband smoked and hid it from the church people.

After working in the forestry all day, we showered and ate dinner each night before we went to the recreation room. I had a tremendous desire to pray, but inmates were not allowed any privacy. We were not only monitored constantly, but every half hour the guard checked off each inmate's name on his clipboard to verify the inmate was accounted for and had not escaped.

My prayer solution became the mop closet near the recreation room. I thought it was humorous to pray inside the closet since Jesus had said to enter into the closet and pray. Yet, it was the perfect answer for me. I waited until no one was watching and then slipped inside the mop closet where I knelt among the mops and brooms.

This worked well for several days until one night I prayed too long.

"Have you seen Preacher? the guard asked. "I can't find him, and I think he's ran away."

I knew I was in trouble if I did not get out of the closet and show myself right away. But I was embarrassed for anyone to know I had been hiding in the closet.

The guard lingered in front of the mop closet door and continued to ask each passing inmate if they had seen Preacher. None had.

Finally, he stopped an inmate named Buzza. "I can't find Preacher. Have you seen him?"

"Yeah, I saw him," Buzza said. "He went inside that mop closet a few minutes ago."

I suddenly began to pray as intensely as possibly. "Please God, don't let them find me here. They'll think I'm crazy."

As I prayed I heard the guard's voice in the distance asking others about my whereabouts. That was the break I needed, and took advantage and quickly opened the door and exited the mop closet.

As soon as the guard saw me walking his direction, he seemed relieved as he put a check mark by my name. From that moment on I discontinued my practice of praying in the closet.

Although I prayed and read the Bible daily, my spiritual growth was extremely slow. So much of the Christian life and the biblical concepts were alien to me. Often I would fail and get discouraged, and occasionally I would give up. But after a few hours of self pity, I would pick myself up and try again.

In my zeal and determination to live right I took everything in the Bible literally, which at times caused hardship and confusion. I memorized the Scripture, *if a man ask for your coat, give him your cloak also."* I interpreted it to mean I should not only be a giver, but that I should never refuse anyone who asked me for something.

Unfortunately, the inmates I lived with soon caught onto my thinking and began to take advantage. I did not have much in the way of material possessions to give away, but when dinner time arrived, the other inmates learned to ask for my food. I aways handed it over even though I was reluctant. Living by this *ask-and-ye-shall-receive* policy became increasingly difficult to maintain.

The climax came during Sunday dinner. Unlike boy's school, this honor camp fed us extremely well, and like most homes, Sunday dinner was the best meal of the week. While sitting at the dinner table, one of the inmates looked my direction. "Hey Preacher. Why don't you turn me on with some of that fried chicken on your plate?"

It was more than I could take. I was hungry and I had been looking forward to the chicken dinner all day. In my mind, I believed I had a scriptural obligation to give it to him my chicken since he had asked for it.

I picked up the fried chicken leg and threw it at him, in the same manner a person might throw a knife at a target. The chicken leg landed in his food tray and splattered gravy and mashed potatoes on the table. He smiled, picked it up, and ate it like it was the most normal thing in the world to do. Another inmate quickly reprimanded him for taking my chicken. But after that experience I re-examined my interpretation of Scripture and realized all Scripture was not to be taken literally.

My most frightening experience while incarcerated came early one morning as I stood in the breakfast food line. No one talked that early in the morning while all thirty of us lined up along the wall and worked our way through the food line. In the corner of the dining room sat an old piano that was used only when visiting church groups came to minister to us.

The inmate behind me accidentally leaned on the piano keys and played a long bang of notes. Everyone, including the guard looked our way.

"Preacher!" The embarrassed inmate stared at me.

At six o'clock in the morning, I was as groggy and quiet as everyone else, and it made me angry when the inmate tried to blame me for something I had not done.

"I did not do that." I spoke loudly.

The inmate glanced at the table where the guard sat staring at us.

"You did do it," he said.

I stepped closer to him. "Say I did it one more time,—say it."

"You did." He raised his voice an octave.

With the guard and all the other inmates watching, I punched him hard in the stomach, and then stood with my fist doubled ready to hit him again if he fought back. This was my first act of violence while in boy's school.

The young man stared at me a couple seconds, wavered a little, and then the light went out in his eyes as he slumped to the ground and stayed there. Stretched out on the tile floor, he did not appear to be breathing at all.

The room remained silent, but all I could do was stare in shock. My first thought was I had killed him with one punch. My mind went straight to Billy Bud, the novel I had read in high school. Billy punched the ship's captain and killed him instantly with one blow. As a result, the crew hung Billy for murder.

I quickly thought ahead and realized this freak accident might result in me getting locked in prison for the rest of my life. As my head spun in confusion, I imagined Junior grinning as he looked at me through the prison bars. "I told you boy. You'll be locked up for the rest of your life.

The guard who had witnessed the conflict, picked up his coffee cup and took a long sip as if nothing out of the ordinary had happened. Finally, one of the adult cooks from the kitchen came out and knelt beside the boy. A moment later, the boy's eyes fluttered, he took a deep breath, and then quickly stood and looked around. He was noticeably embarrassed by the incident.

Everyone in the room let out a long sigh when they realized he was okay, but no one was more relieved than myself.

The cook smiled and walked away. Normally, the guard would write us up for fighting, and usually fighters were sent to the tank for a day or two. The tank was actually a shower stall with doors and locks on it. However, the guard said nothing about the incident, and I was never called to the office to give an account.

To save face, the boy began telling his friends how I had better never do that to him again, because he would beat me up in the worst manner. Naturally, I never worried about him.

*   *   *

TWO INMATES HAD A PERSONALITY CLASH, and always bickered and fought. McDonald was short and stocky, while Pruitt was tall and slender. Eventually, the Captain decided he'd had enough of their bickering and called them both into his office.

The captain was in charge of the little boy's school, and he was strictly a no-nonsense type person. No one had ever talked back to the captain. More realistically, no one had ever been brave enough to talk back to the captain. He was near retirement age, but he was short and stout and gave the impression he could hold his own in a scuffle with any two or three inmates.

When the captain called McDonald and Pruitt to his office, a group of us hurried and stood outside his closed office door to listen as he reprimanded the two boys. "I am tired of you two boys bickering and quarreling all the time," he said. "So I want you two to fight it out right now and get this aggression for each other out of your system."

The room was silent a moment.

"I am serious. If you two don't start punching each other, I'm going to start punching you." We heard him slap one of the boys.

I was frightened, even though I was not the one the captain was angry with. We hurried to the end of the dorm where we could watch the fight through the captain's office window. Our dorm room ran in an *L* shape from the captain's office, which meant we could go to the end of dorms and look out the window and see inside the captain's office window.

The two inmates raised their fist and danced around a little, but neither teenager became serious about fighting. Apparently, the captain was not satisfied, and he stood from his desk and slammed one of inmates against the lockers in his office.

I could not imagine what the two boys were thinking. The captain's actions were so bazaar and out of the ordinary that it was frightening just watching. After he slammed the second inmate against the lockers, the two inmates began to take the Captain's words to heart and they started punching each other in the face.

But after a few minutes they grew tired. "This is not nearly over," the Captain said. "You better get to punching each other or I'm going to start punching you both." Immediately, the two boys increased the intensity of their fighting, and they continued to fight for several more minutes.

After the ordeal was over and the Captain allowed them to leave his office. The two teenager boys came out of his office with their arms around each other's neck as if they were best of friends. They were bruised and bleeding and they both looked as if they had been in a gang fight—and lost. They could hardly walk, their lips were swelled and their eyes were bruised, but they were suddenly the best of friends. From that day forward, they never fought or bickered again. In fact, all thirty inmates seemed to get along well after that.

A few days later, the Captain called me into his office. As soon as I walked in, he got straight to the point. "Preacher, this is Mr. Welch, he wants to talk to you a while." The Captain nodded to the stranger and left the office.

Mr. Welch smiled. "Let's go for a drive." He spoke in a whisper as if he had a sore throat.

I followed him outside to his pickup truck, where he drove us out of the forestry and down the interstate for several miles. As he drove, he explained he had just gotten over a stroke and had yet to get his voice back. We made small talk a few minutes and then he turned to face me. "How would you like to go home with me and stay at my house?"

This was not something I had expected. I knew there was a reason the

Captain left me to talk with this man, but I did not expect it to happen so quickly.

I lifted a shoulder. "Sure. That'd be great."

He exited the interstate, turned the truck around, and took me back to get what few personal belongings I owned. From the time I first met Mr. Welch until I was gathered my things to leave was less than an hour.

"I live in Bloomington near the airport,"he said. "I'm a retired Navy recruiter, and my wife is an officer with the Salvation Army."

I nodded and waited for him to tell me more.

"I've taken boys into my home for several years," he said. "I've also got another foster teenager living with me. The two of you will be sharing a room upstairs."

The most humorous thing about Mr. Welch was his smoking habit, which he tried to hide from his wife. Often, he would light up a cigarette while he was in the garage, and if she came out to the garage, he would act as if the cigarette belonged to one of us teenagers.

Mr. Welch was active in the boy scout division called the Sea Scouts, which was a scout program for older teens. I loved it because we wore real Navy uniforms. Mr. Welch liked the outdoors and he often took us camping, hiking, and even rock repelling. The Welch family was good to me, but my stay lasted only four months.

I had no friends at the Bloomington High School and soon decided to run away and go back to Seymour and visit the Luckey family. I left school and walked downtown where I purchased a Greyhound bus ticket to Indianapolis.

My first night I stayed inside the Greyhound bus station in downtown Indianapolis. The second day, I purchased a bus ticket to Bedford, Indiana. The police would be looking for me at Seymour, so Bedford seemed an unlikely place for them to look for me. From there I walked around town the first few hours before I began the forty-five mile walk to the Luckey's new residence near Jonesville, Indiana.

*　　*　　*

THE TRIP TOOK ME TWO LONG DAYS, but I finally arrived at the Luckey's residence late in the evening, where I spent the first night in an old car parked behind the house. The next morning, I watched from the back seat of the car as Daniel and the other children boarded the school bus. I rested and slept most of the day.

Late in the afternoon, I walked to the woodlot across from the house and hid until the bus dropped them off that afternoon. When I saw Daniel and Charlie in the yard, I could not contain myself. They were my friends, and I finally called out to them. Daniel and I talked while Charlie rushed straight inside the house and told his mother I was outside.

Marie called me to come into the house where she welcomed me and gave me a good meal. They all treated me so well I wanted to stay with them, but before I knew what was happening, a police car pulled up in front of the house.

I turned to run out the back door, but Marie stopped me. "Don't run, Kenny," she pleaded. "It's not the right thing to do."

I struggled with indecision for several seconds. Finally, I nodded. "I know. It's not the right thing to do. Running is useless."

When my probation officer came inside Mr. Welch was with them. He was ready to forgive me and take me back home with him. At one point, he even offered to let me to participate in school sports if I wanted. I refused to go back with him, and he looked hurt. Mr. Welch had been good to me, but in truth I felt very disconnected living in a strange town.

When they questioned me as to why I had ran away, I did not know what to tell them. In truth, I was lonesome for the people I knew. At Bloomington I had zero friends, and zero social life. The police took me back to the Jackson County jail and locked me in the same cell I had been in several times before.

Living with the Welch family was a good experience, but I was sixteen, and I wanted friends. In my mind, I considered myself an adult and thought I should be allowed to live on my own and not be accountable to the law. Of course I had a lot to learn.

Eventually, they transferred me back to the Henryville Camp facility, and when I walked in the guard on duty stood grinning at me. "I knew you'd be back here, Preacher," he said.

The comment was like a stab to my heart. I had been a good inmate and had not caused any trouble; yet, the guard did not have any confidence in me.

After I was incarcerated at the honor camp for several months, the Luckey family came to visit me on several occasions. One weekend the captain granted me a Saturday-evening pass to go to church with the Luckey family. They drove the forty-mile trip to Henryville to pick me up, and took me to the apostolic church service in Seymour. After the service, they drove me back to Henryville that same night.

It was quite an exciting evening for someone who had been incarcerated for several months. In addition, I was humbled that different inmates loaned me their personal clothes to wear so I could look good when I went out.

The Henryville Camp staff recommended my release after I had been incarcerated for four months. Along with my time in the county jail, I had been locked up for five months this second time. The Luckey family had made arrangements for me to live with them, but instead of allowing me to leave straight from the Henryville Camp and go back to live with the Luckey family, the state returned me back to Indiana Boys' School where I had to spend my last ten days going through their exit process.

At Plainfield Boy's School they once again, they put me on the yard crew where I mowed lawns each day with an old-fashioned rotary push mower. About twenty inmates made up the yard crew who were all supervised by two older guards. The guards lined us up with our mowers in single file in such a manner that each inmate offset his mowing path from the person in front of him. Each inmate cut a two-foot swatch and the inmate following cut another two-foot swatch to the left.

Mowing in this manner was a difficult job during those hot summer days, and conditions were worsened because the guard forced us to push our mowers at a fast walk. This meant that if a person slowed down he would get his heels clipped by the mower behind him. No one wanted that kind of pain, so we all pushed our mowers as quickly as we possibly could.

The ground was rough and uneven, and the mowers were old and worn out, which was not a good mix. Sometimes, we would go so fast that our bouncing mowers would break the handle. Eventually, we broke so many mower handles that there were not enough mowers for each inmate. This made the guard angry and he accused us of breaking the mower handles on purpose. "The next man who breaks a mower is going to push it anyway," he said.

Less than five minutes after he made this threat, my mower handle snapped off at the base. I did not do it on purpose. I had three days left before my release, and I did not want to do anything to hinder that release date.

I looked down at my broken mower. All that remained was a little stub of a handle. "It was an accident. I didn't do it on purpose," I said.

The guard crossed his arms. "I am a man of my word, and I said the next one who broke a mower handle would push it anyway, and I am going to keep my word."

"But it was an accident," I protested.

"Don't you argue with me," his voice escalated to nearly a shouting level. "I can keep you in here for the rest of your life, if I want to. Do you want me to do that?"

"No sir," I said humbly, as I bent over and grabbed onto my mower's stubby handle. I was hot, tired, and mad, but I had plenty of experiences like this with my stepfather, and I knew submission was once again my best strategy.

After five minutes of pushing the mower, my legs and back began to hurt so badly I could hardly keep up with the person in front of me. But I stayed in line and kept crawling along. After ten minutes the pain was excruciating, and I knew I could not bear it much longer. I began praying desperately for God's help.

One of the inmates spoke up. "Sir? Let me push his broken mower and he can push mine."

"Nothing doing," the guard said. "He broke it. He can push it."

I kept pushing and praying. Seconds before I was about to collapse, another inmate spoke up. "Let me push it."

"I'll do it. He can have mine," two others said in unison. It was like the Spartacus crowd all over again.

The guard sucked in a deep breath. "Okay, you can trade off with him. I just want to get this yard mowed."

I could barely stand up. I thanked the boy and traded mowers with him. Several of the other workers continued to trade off and use the broken mower until the end of the day. I have never forgotten the kindness of those inmates who took my place and suffered my pain for me. If they had not interceded on my behalf, I may not have survived that day without incident, and it is possible I would still be incarcerated today.

*   *   *

I WAS ELATED when the Luckey family made arrangements with my probation officer to take me in as their foster child. They were not only down-to-earth people in whose company I felt comfortable, but they were also dedicated to the church. This was possibly the best thing that could have happened to me at that time.

It also goes without saying that this was a time of a crucial crossroad in my life, and without the Luckey families kindness my life may have easily went the other direction.

This was my second stay with them, so they knew what to expect. I had matured a little, but I still had a long way to go. Daniel shared his room with me again, and Beth put up with a lot of immature teasing from me. Marie was very patient, and in reality the entire family deserved a medal for their sacrifices they made for me.

Marie's husband, Merle, was possibly the most congenial and patient man I had ever met. Regardless of what I did, he never complained or reprimanded me.

During the next few months, I continued to grow at a slow pace. I attended the apostolic church regularly and although I had the infilling of the Holy Ghost evidenced by speaking in tongues, I kept questioning my experience. I worried that I had deceived myself and had not received the Spirit infilling. I wanted more. I wanted God to slay me in the Spirit and make me unconscious in the Holy Ghost.

I prayed at the alter for nearly an hour after every service and begged God to fill me with his Spirit. Even though I had spoken in tongues, I wanted to be sure. Ironically, as I prayed, I refused to turn loose and allow God to speak through me. I wanted him to forcibly take control of me and make me unconscious in the Spirit.

One night after a revival service, the visiting evangelist, Elder McGruder called my parents aside. "Why isn't this boy receiving the Holy Ghost and getting satisfied?" he asked.

My mother shook her head. "I don't know unless it is because he won't live at home with his own family." She explained how I was living with the Luckey family, and how she believed God wanted me back living in my rightful home.

Brother McGruder called me aside in private and asked me about this. "Do you think your mother might be right, son?"

I lifted a shoulder. "I don't know."

"Are you willing to go back home and live with your parents?"

I nodded. "I'll do anything to get right with God."

"Anything?"

"Yes. I'll even go back home if I have to."

I certainly did not want to go back home, but since the man of God implied I needed to go back home, I began to seriously consider it. I had been living with the Luckey family for nearly a year, and they certainly treated me well. I could not have asked for better conditions.

Of course, Brother McGruder did not know the conditions I would face if I went back home.

A few days later, I contacted my mother and asked about coming back home. She must have been expecting my call, because she agreed right away.

This time I was fully aware that I was putting my head in the lion's mouth. I was seventeen- years old, and it had been over two years since I had lived with my parents. Even though I felt confident things had not changed for them, I was desperate to do anything in order to please God, and since the ministry implied I needed to return to my real parent's home, I determined it must be God's will.

After I moved back with Junior and my mother, my passion to grow spiritually intensified. I never missed a church service. I fasted several days a week, and since the church was kept unlocked during the day, I often walked to church where I had long prayer meetings. It was all I knew to do in order to grow spiritually.

Finally, I realized I was fighting against God's Spirit, because I refused to speak in tongues. I surrendered myself to him and accepted the Holy Spirit infilling. I did not go unconscious as I wanted, but I realized I had the Spirit of God in me all along. I also realized that I was not in charge of what God wanted to do in my life. It was not up to me to decide how God manifested his Spirit in my life.

In truth, this two years of soul searching while I sought the Holy Ghost helped me to mature more than any other period in my life. The next morning after I spoke in tongues and claimed the infilling of the Holy Ghost, I opened my eyes and thought to myself; *that was not real. You deceived yourself last night.* The devil was talking in my ear, and I wrestled against him with my faith.

At the same time, I happened to be reading a book by Elder G.T. Haywood. In the book, he explained his own experience about fighting the same battle I was fighting. The morning after he received the Holy Ghost, the devil spoke in his ear and said, *You did not get the Holy Ghost, that was just your imagination.* Reverend Haywood recognized it was the voice of the devil and rebuked it and went on with his day.

I did the same.

The last two years I lived with my mother and stepfather were difficult years emotionally. The worst minutes of each day were at the dinner table where Junior usually sat making degrading remarks about my pastor. I loved my pastor and Junior knew it. Even so, he seemed to take joy in hurting my feelings.

I always hurried to eat my dinner and get away from him, but often tears slipped down my cheeks and onto my dinner plate. At times, I sobbed uncontrollably and could hardly swallow my food. Occasionally, Mom would tell him to be quiet, but he would chuckle and pay her no mind.

When I finally turned eighteen-years old, Junior still hated me as much as he ever had, and he let it show. If I took out seconds on my plate during dinner Junior would give me dirty looks as if he resented me eating his food. I walked a fine line around him and did not say much because I wanted to be a good Christian.

I had matured enough that the pastor put me in charge of the Saturday evening youth service. Several other youth were more capable, but I was grateful for the opportunity and tried to do my best. Sadly, my best was rather crude.

Youth service was well attended, and as the youth leader I spent a lot of time behind the lectern. Occasionally, Mom point-blankly asked that I say some nice things about Junior during the service. I was appalled to hear her ask such a thing. Of course, I did not have anything good to say about my stepfather. Living at home and trying to live as a Christian was like jumping through hoops of fire everyday.

Like most teenagers, I was eager to get a driver's license, but Junior would not sign his consent for me, because he did not want to be responsible. I had to wait until the day I was eighteen to get my license. But once I had my license, Junior occasionally allowed me to drive his old work car to church. That privilege was a big deal to me.

However, Steve was two years younger than me, and Junior signed for him to get his driver's license as soon as he was eligible. We both obtained our license at the same time. In order to have the privilege of driving Junior's work vehicle, he made Steve and me pay his auto insurance.

My part-time job at a local warehouse brought in a weekly paycheck of one-hundred and twenty-five dollars. According to Junior the insurance rate to add me as a driver in the family was eight-hundred dollars every ninety days. In nineteen-seventy two, nearly a hundred dollars a week for insurance was extremely high.

Like most teenage boys, I did not care. I wanted to drive regardless of the cost. Later, I learned Junior had been scamming me. My hundred dollars a week was going into his pocket.

While I was in my senior year of high school, Junior habitually haggled me to quit school and get into a full time job at a factory. I wanted to quit anyway, but I realized I needed to finish and get my diploma. Eventually, I faced struggles at school and I gave in to the pressure and quit school during my senior year.

As soon as I got my first paycheck, Junior demanded I begin paying room and board. I did not resent it, but the twenty dollars a week I paid was nearly a day's pay for me.

I was nearly nineteen years old when one night during youth service

I sat on the platform playing the guitar and spotted a teenage girl on the back row. At first glance I thought she was beautiful. After service one of the ladies from the church introduced us to each other and then abruptly walked away and left us alone.

The girl gave me a smile that made me feel like a fish dropped on a rock. I was so shy, I could hardly speak a coherent sentence to her. A few days later, I asked around and obtained her phone number.

I picked up the phone to call her, prayed, and then hung up. It was a big step for me, and it took several attempts before I actually made the call. As I talked, my tongue seem glued to the roof of my mouth, and I could hardly speak coherently. I invited her to a church function at our church, she agreed, and that began our relationship.

While dating her, I worried she would reject me once I told her about my past. My stepfather had repeatedly pounded into my mind that I had ruined my life because I had been to boy's school. It was actually a reform school; yet, Junior made certain to imprint upon my teenage mind that I had been in prison and ruined my life. He called it the *penitentiary.*

Finally, the second week after I met her I explained my rocky past. I was prepared for her to politely tell me she did not want to see me anymore. After all, her father was an apostolic minister, and from what I had learned so far, her parents were old fashioned and very strict. But when I explained that I had been in boy's school twice and that I had lived in numerous foster homes, she did not seem to mind. From our first time together I always believed she was the one for me.

Nearly all of our dates consisted of attending church together. Her church had services on Wednesday, Friday, and Sunday, and my church had services on Tuesday, Thursday, Saturday and Sunday. After three months of dating, I asked her to marry me. She was hesitant, and the only answer I could get out of her was, *I'll think about it.*

I did not give up. Two weeks later, I repeated my proposal. Once again, she would not commit. I did not blame her for not wanting to rush into a commitment, but I was confident from the start that she was the one with whom I wanted to spend the rest of my life. I have never had any doubts.

Finally, the third time I proposed to her, she had a weak moment and agreed to marry me. We met late in December and were married the following June.

CHAPTER EIGHT

We might be finished with the past,
but the past is not finished with us.

Wait on the LORD: be of good courage,
and he shall strengthen thine heart:
wait, I say, on the LORD. Psalm 27:14

MY FIANCÉE DID NOT UNDERSTAND what my home life was like during our courtship. Her parents were friendly people and always made me feel welcome in their house, but my home life was different than hers. My stepfather often ridiculed and slandered her, even when he knew I was listening.

I desperately wanted to speak up and confront him, but I knew it would only escalate into bigger problems, so I kept my peace and tried to be a good Christian. At this point of my life, I was finally past the running away solution for my problems, but I struggled with the idea that I was not being a real man if I did not fight against his verbal abuse.

At the same time, my fiancé insisted we spend time at my house so she could get to know my parents better. I did not want her to spend more time with my parents, and they certainly did not want her company. Yet, I felt that as a Christian I should not speak negative about anyone, so I could not tell her the truth; I was in the rock and hard place situation.

Even after we were married, my new wife did not understand the emotional baggage I brought into our home. I was insecure, backward, and lacked confidence. Getting away from my parents was the best thing to happen to me at that time in my life, but I still had a long way to grow before I could consider myself a normal person. My emotional bruising affected every area of my life.

Sue and I were very poor when we first married, and I was determined to stay out of debt. We were fortunate that a business man from the church helped us finance a mobile home for five-thousand dollars. We had a generic bed that came with the mobile home, and my mother-in-law purchased a dinette set for us. In the living room, all we had were two used end tables and a lawn chair. Being poor did not affect our marriage. My emotional baggage did.

Soon after we were married, I began to experience depression for the first time. This was a new battle for me, because I had never experienced anything like it in the past. This battle worsened, because as I grew spiritually, I developed a tremendous passion to be involved in the work of the Gospel; yet, I believed I was a failure.

Even so, my potential was like an oxymoron compared to my desire. I was so anti-social that I did not have the basic skills I needed to interact with others; yet, at the same time, I possessed a tremendous desire to minister. I wanted to be used of God; yet, I had little ability. This brought on tremendous guilt which turned into depression and fear.

As months of guilt manifested into fear and depression, I became afraid something terrible was going to happen to me. I never told anyone about my feelings, but I lived under a constant dark cloud of fear. Distrust was an issue for me, which meant I could not bring myself to talk to anyone about it. This battle went on in my mind for several years.

At times, my suppressed guilt came out in anger, and the frustration that haunted me seemed unbearable at times. I tried to grow spiritually, but I made little progress. It seemed God demanded productivity from me; yet, I was not able to perform.

Matters grew worse as well-meaning ministers visited the church and preached how every Christian should win others to Christ. I wanted to obey that Great Commission, but I did not know how, and no one showed me how to do so.

I knocked on doors and invited people to church, but I was not good at it and as a result had no success. Several times, I took handfuls of gospel tracts and stood on the street corner downtown where I passed out tracts. A few times, I had fliers printed at my own expense, and I put them on car windshields at parking lots. In all of my efforts, I saw no fruit from my labors.

Working within the church was actually doing a work for God, but I never understood that concept and no one explained it to me. Everything I heard from the pulpit was about the need for a dynamic ministry and how everyone needed to be used of God in a great way. Condemnation continued to follow me every day of my life.

On our first wedding anniversary Sue and I went to Williamsburg Virginia, along with her mother and Sue's two younger siblings. Before we left I fought with a terrible foreboding that something horrible was going to happen on the trip. I prayed and prayed, but it would not go away. I finally accepted that fear would be a part of my life, and I would have to live with it.

Fortunately, nothing bad happened on our vacation trip, and we returned home safely. I should have realized then that my fears were a trick of the enemy, but I continued to live in fear.

At the time I was ridiculously shy. One weekend, I drove Sue and her mother to Kentucky to visit her relatives, but I stayed in the car and read until bedtime. My shyness made people think I was abnormal, but I learned it was easier to let them think I was abnormal than to try to communicate and fail. Too often socializing became awkward, and I was embarrassed even further for my efforts.

A year after our marriage, I began to feel a call to the ministry, but like so many other areas of my life, I was confused. Contrary to the report of many others who have been called to the ministry, I never had a defining moment where I could point to a specific day and say that was the day I was called.

First, an idea came to me that it might be possible God was calling me; later, I began to think in terms of what if I am called to a pulpit ministry. Finally, I began having a type of haunting in the back of my mind that I could not get away from the calling.

The ministerial call added more confusion to my life. I wanted a lightning bolt sign or experience for my calling or a blinding light to strike me, but all I received was a still small voice whispering in my heart. Finally, I got to the place where I felt I was a hypocrite if I did not accept the call to the ministry; yet, at the same time I felt inadequate.

I was sincere, but confused. Scripture helped me, because I learned from them that ability had little to do with a calling from God. We only plant the seed—God makes the seed grow.

As a way to prepare myself for the ministry, I spent as much time as possible studying and memorizing Scriptures. For years, I would not allow myself any type of recreation, because I evaluated everything according to the question; *how important will it be in eternity?* Naturally, my life was dull. Even so, I kept trying and I slowly grew as a person.

Sue and I thought it would be best for me to attend Bible college in order to help me grow. She volunteered to work a full-time job while I attended school full time. I was elated at her suggestion, but when I approached my pastor, he was adamantly against it.

"I don't understand why you are against me going to Bible college," I said during our private meeting.

"Bible college is not what it appears to be. People backslide at Bible college," he said.

I frowned. "But you went to Bible college."

"I know, but your place is right here on the pew in this church."

I did not understand, but I succumbed to his advice. Bible college seemed the perfect solution for me. I was serious about working for God and I felt the Bible college training would help me. Nevertheless, I accepted his advice, remained at the church, and tried to grow and work in the local church.

About that time, I learned first-hand about intercessory prayer. My brother had disappeared when he was twenty-years old. This was not his first disappearance, but it was his longest. Twice before he had left town without telling any of his family where he was going or when he would be back.

In the past, he had been gone for a few weeks, but this time he had been gone for more than two years. I assumed something had happened to him in another state and without identification on him, the authorities did not know who to notify.

One Sunday after church service, Sue and I went out to eat and did not get to bed until nearly midnight. I had barely drifted off to sleep when I began dreaming about someone weeping. In my dream, it was dark and all I could see was a distant silhouette.

Immediately, something awakened me and I lay wondering, *who cries like that person in my dream? The person weeping in my dream reminds me of someone I know.* A moment later, I realized it was my brother, Steve.

I had heard Christians tell stories about God waking them in the middle of the night to pray for someone else, and how God used them to intercede for a person in need. Since I had to get up at four a.m. the next morning, I began to argue with myself. *I have to have some sleep tonight. I can pray for him tomorrow. But what if this is God wanting me to pray for him?*

Finally, I reasoned that I did not want to take the chance of missing God's will. I threw the covers back and climbed from bed. We lived in a mobile home, and I walked to the end of the hallway and closed the accordion curtain to keep from waking my wife.

The instant my knees touched the living-room carpet, the Spirit of God came over me and I began to weep and sob for my brother. Conviction was so strong, I could barely speak. All I could say was, "I plead the blood. I plead the blood on my brother's life." This continued for nearly an hour.

Finally, the conviction lifted and I went back to bed. The next day, I told Sue about my experience. "I don't know what happened our how it will work out, but my brother is alive, and I believe God used my prayer last night to intercede for him. It may be months or years, but one day we are going to hear that he was in danger and God spared his life."

We did not have to wait long. I had not heard from my brother for two years, but a week later we received a letter from him. I read it and wept.

DEAR KENNY,

YOU WILL NOT BELIEVE WHAT HAPPENED TO ME. I HAVE BEEN MANAGING APARTMENTS FOR A MAN, BUT A FEW DAYS AGO A PROSPECTIVE TENANT CONFRONTED ME ABOUT A DEPOSIT, AND OUR ARGUING ESCALATED INTO A FIGHT. THE MAN HAD SEVERAL FRIENDS WAITING, AND AS SOON AS THE FIGHT BEGAN, THEY ALL ATTACKED ME AND BEGAN TO KICK AND BEAT ME WITH THEIR COWBOY BOOTS. THE APARTMENT OWNER CAME TO MY RESCUE, BUT THEY OVERPOWERED HIM ALSO. THE APARTMENT OWNER'S WIFE BROUGHT A 357 MAGNUM OUT TO HER HUSBAND AND THE ATTACKERS ALL RAN AWAY.

MY COLLAR BONE WAS BROKEN AND AS THEY LOADED ME INTO THE AMBULANCE, THE POLICE TOLD ME I WAS FORTUNATE, BECAUSE THEY HAD EXPERIENCES WITH THIS GROUP BEFORE AND I WAS LUCKY TO BE ALIVE.

THE DOCTOR X-RAYED ME AND VERIFIED MY COLLAR BONE WAS BROKEN AND PUT MY ARM IN A SLING. I BEGAN TO THINK HOW MERCIFUL GOD HAD BEEN TO ME AND DECIDED TO HUNT A CHURCH TO ATTEND THAT NIGHT. I SAT IN THE BACK ROW UNTIL THE EVANGELIST TOOK THE PODIUM. BUT HE ANNOUNCED HE WAS NOT GOING TO PREACH BECAUSE GOD WANTED TO DO SOMETHING SPECIAL FOR SOMEONE. "IF YOU'LL COME DOWN TO THE ALTAR AND WORSHIP GOD," THE EVANGELIST SAID. "GOD WILL FILL YOU WITH HIS SPIRIT AND MEET YOUR NEED.

I HAD NOT BEEN ABLE TO RAISE MY ARM, BUT AS I STEPPED INTO THE AISLE AND BEGAN TO RAISE MY ARMS IN WORSHIP, GOD INSTANTLY HEALED ME AND FILLED ME

WITH THE HOLY GHOST BEFORE I EVEN MADE IT TO THE ALTAR.

I could not stop sobbing as I realized God had used me to intercede in prayer for my brother. If I had not obeyed God that night, I believe that event in his life would have turned out much differently.

* * *

MY REAL FATHER CALLED me when I was twenty-three years old. When I answered the phone, a deep voice spoke on the other end. "This is Ed Brock. Do you know who I am?"

"Yes." My voices sounded weak, even to my own ears. I had dreamed of that moment many times, but I was speechless once the opportunity arrived. I stood with the phone to my ear and let him do most of the talking.

"I work on the pipeline here in Alaska," he said, and went on to talk about and his job. He then invited me to come to Alaska. "I can get you a job on the pipeline, if you want. We need to hire an oiler for the crane I operate. It's good pay, and it's long hours, but it is not hard work."

I wanted to ask why he forsook me when I was a child, but I was too awestruck to think clearly.

"I didn't want to leave you," he volunteered. "But when you were three years old your mother and grandmother refused to let me see you. You loved sucking the charcoal off burned matches, and I would burn a match and then give it to you to suck on. They claimed I was doing a terrible thing, and used it as an excuse to prevent me from visiting you. So I left."

Instantly, I forgave him and was ready to pack up and move to Alaska, but my young wife did not want to leave her family—and rightly so. She had been raised with structure while surrounded by her parents and twelve siblings, and she did not want to leave that.

In contrast, I had moved nearly every year of my life, and many times I lived with a new family each year. Relocating would not have been a sacrifice for me at all, but it would have been devastating for her.

About a year later, while working for a seamless-gutter company, I finished installing gutter on a house in the rural area of Kurtz, when I received another shock. As I was about to leave the job site, the homeowner saw my signature on the invoice and asked my father's name.

"I should know you," he said. "Who is your father?"

"Oh, you wouldn't know my father. He doesn't even live around here anymore."

"I know a lot of people," the homeowner said.

As I put the paperwork on the dash of my work vehicle, the man continued to pry about my family. "My real father is Ed Brock," I finally answered.

"Sure, I know Ed," he said.

I shook my head. "No. My father's name is actually Pearl Edward Brock and he lives in Alaska."

The man nodded. "Yeah, I know him. He just died."

I frowned. "What? How do you know?" It was as if darkness suddenly began closing in around my peripheral vision. Surely, this was not true.

"His obituary was in the local paper. Ed knew he was dying, and he came down from Alaska to be with his family during his last days. He died just a few weeks ago."

At first, I assumed he was mistaken. But I had to force myself to accept the possibility. Processing the information was difficult, because I still dreamed of meeting my real father. I went home and called my mother on the phone.

She seemed nonchalant. "Yes, I knew it. Your grandfather called me and told me your father was in town. He had sclerosis of the liver and he knew he was dying."

"Then why didn't you tell me?"

She paused. "I didn't want to stir up a lot of questions and old memories."

That was not a good answer to me, and I struggled to forgive her. The number one dream I had harbored all of my life was to meet my real father. Now that dream was an impossibility. Apparently, she did not understand how important it was to me—or she did not care. Even worse, I had to hear of my father's death from a stranger.

In the end, I chose to believe that God managed the situation for what was best for me. My real father had married while in Alaska and produced six additional children. He did not bother to divorce his first wife in Indiana.

My half sister from his first marriage who attended the funeral informed me that neither family had known about the other until the funeral viewing. Altogether, my real father had at least fourteen children—(that we know of) by three different women.

As an adult, my negative attitude seemed to control my life. Everything I did reflected my poor self image. Even my body did not respond well to my negativism, because I became lethargic in everything I did.

Faith was an alien concept for me, and when things went wrong, I was not surprised. I expected bad things to happen in my life. My friends were few, but I did not mind living as a loner. Life was more simple that way.

Any disappointments that came along usually sent me into depression. During those times, all I wanted to do was sit and stare at the wall or go to sleep in order to escape my depression. Fortunately, I continued to practice the ritual my probation officer had taught me years earlier; that is, to think about things just before going to sleep.

But during my times of depression, instead of thinking about thing- before going to sleep, I yielded to gloom and succumbed to sitting and staring at the wall as I thought about my problems.

My wife was a very positive person, and she would always try to talk to me and cheer me up. I knew I was making her life miserable too, but I could not bring myself to change. Every difficulty became a catastrophe in my mind. Negativity colored every areas of my life including my job.

Getting out of bed each morning was a struggle, and sleep became an escape. Eating was my only pleasure, which resulted in my gaining an extra fifty pounds and making me even more sluggish and lethargic.

I did my best to avoid every social situation possible except church services, which I knew I needed. Most of the time, I did not look forward to attending church simply because it was a social situation, and I experienced a great fear when I was in the company of people. Often I would have anxiety spells where I would have to force myself to breath when among people.

Eventually depression became so great, I began to pray for God to take my life. I truly did not want to live, because it appeared as if God was not going to use me in his work. In my mind I had no other real reason to live. Oddly, it was not important that I be used of God in a glamorous way; I just wanted to be involved in his work. In some strange way, I hinged my self worth onto God using me.

During this time, we were very poor. Of course, we had everything we needed, but we struggled to pay our monthly bills. We were so poor we went on only one vacation the first ten years of our marriage. When the guys at work took an afternoon break and purchased twenty-five cent sodas, I usually declined and drank water instead. Even if I did have twenty-five-cents in my pocket, I wanted to keep it.

During my twenties and early thirties I went to a new job every five or six years. Sometimes I outgrew my job and it became boring, and other times a new job was a better opportunity. Sadly, I did not like any of my jobs, because I did not like myself.

My first job after high school was in a warehouse as a stock boy. Soon I gravitated toward different construction jobs for several years. Leadership opportunities came from time to time, but I feared leadership and the conflicts that often came with it, so I avoided leadership. It never occurred to me that these leadership opportunities were chances to be used of God. To put it mildly, I was a slow learner when it came to spiritual areas.

During childhood, I had missed a lot of school as a result of running away from home and spending time in jail. Growing up, I attended a different school each school year, and that alone put me behind in my school work. Missing so much school left a lot of blind spots in my education.

As I continued to grow spiritually, I read and studied a lot. I often visited the library and checked out books to study in order to improve my intellect. I kept notes of my studies and reviewed them occasionally in an effort to retain what I had learned.

For years, the weakest link in my Christian growth was the lack of a consistent prayer life. I did pray, but my prayer was sporadic. I prayed ever day, but I was not consistent. When I had a big need, I found it easy to pray, and often I prayed out of fear—fear that God would be angry with me for not praying.

As soon as I arrived home from work each evening, I tried to pray, but I was always tired and had difficulty focusing on prayer. The time-window after work was not a good choice, because often things came up and my prayer was interrupted. I would go back to prayer later in the evening, but many times I did not get my prayer finished until late at night. As a result, prayer became more of a burden than a joy.

Finally, I learned a valuable lesson; *prayer is best when done in the morning.* I read biographies of ministers and discovered that most rose up early for prayer every day. I took a clue from them and began to put God first in my day.

It made sense to give my most uninterrupted time to prayer. Only then did I begin to develop a serious prayer life. That in turn, changed my life. Not only could I focus better on prayer in the morning, but I also felt good all day knowing I had reached my praying goal.

Another milestones in my adult life came from a single book someone gave me. Until then I had never heard of self-help or motivational books, and I was surprised to learn that most bookstores had an entire genre of self-help books on display. After reading *See You at the Top*, I realized that type of instruction was exactly what I needed. I began devouring every positive thinking and self-help book I could buy, borrow, or read. My determination became so strong, I would highlight thoughts from the books, record them in a notebook and memorize the notes.

As I read books by Zig Ziglar, Dale Carnegie, and Norman Vincent Peale, my attitude began to change dramatically, because I began to gain knowledge about the need for an attitude change. In only a few weeks after I made this amazing discovery, I had an epiphany. Suddenly, I understood that I alone controlled my future—no one else. I came to understand that the purpose of my scars were to remind me of where I had been, not where I was going. I could change, but it was up to me.

As I flooded my mind with huge amounts of positive input, my mind began to change me. I also had an epiphany; words matter. I learned that I was engaging in self-defeating habits by my negative talk—even the inner speach in my head.

It took years of training, but I finally reached the place where I avoided all negative talk and replaced it with positive affirmations. I learned to purposely say positive things like, *I am going to have a good day today. I am a man of God. I have a good self image. Good things are happening in my life.*

Even today in my prayer, I speak positive affirmations like; *The Lord Jesus is my God. I have strength from the Lord. Jesus is my savior, I walk in the strength of the Lord. God is for me. I trust in the Lord.* As I began to fill my mind with positive words and thoughts, my inner being began to change. I have never looked back, adn it has been one of the most valuable lessons I have learned in my life.

In my new positive attitude, the possibilities of life suddenly seemed endless. I began the habit of writing down both small and large goals and then reviewed them habitually. It took a lot of mental struggle and it did not happen over night, but as I reached a few small goals, my enthusiasm for life escalated. The large goals I dreamed about became possible in my mind, and it was like a snowball effect of positiveness. The more I dreamed, the more my dreams came true, and the more they came true, the more I dreamed.

Not only did I dream, but I began to dream wildly. My dreams were so large and outstanding that I was embarrassed to share them with anyone. I had two list of goals; on one list was the goals I could likely reach with effort and discipline. But the goals on my second list were goals that could only be described as hilarious. Not that I wanted to do anything like become the president, but the simple concept of leading a productive life and becoming an asset to society was suddenly a realistic possibility for me. Considering the childhood I survived, the likelihood of my becoming a productive asset to society had always seemed an improbability.

During most of my adult life, I had worked various construction jobs, but I did not really like construction. I liked the creativity of woodworking in a wood shop, but I did not enjoy building houses. I came to the conclusion that it was possible to have any job I wanted. Why not? I asked myself. I was approaching thirty-years old, and of all the professions available, I really wanted to be a photographer.

Later, I would dream about becoming a teacher and an author, but at that time, even though I considered it, I could not conceive those lofty dreams as possibilities for me. It was too far away from my mindset to even imagine, and if I had told someone that I dreamed of someday authoring a book, they would have thought it hilariously impossible considering who I was. My grammar was horrendous, I had not even finished high school, and I could hardly engage in a coherent conversation, let alone write a book.

Even during those short flashes when I first dreamed about authoring a book, I often reprimanded myself because it was such a higher noble dream that seemed certainly out of my reach.

Photography had been my hobby, but I had no serious skills that could land me a job. But I set out to reach that goal, and believed it was possible. As I searched, the largest photography business I found was Olan Mills Inc. This company employed more than ten-thousand people, and I decided that was the company for me.

First, I enrolled in a distance learning photography course from New York Institute. When I finished it, I obtained the phone number to Olan Mills, Inc., and called the main office.

The secretary was obviously trained to brush off wanna-bees like me. "We're not really hiring right now. If you want to send in a resume, I'll make certain it gets in the right hands," she said.

I had prayed intensely before I made the phone call, and I prayed while she was talking. Fortunately, during the short conversation, I said something that changed her attitude toward me. "I had my own photography studio for a while, but I would really like to work for your company," I said.

In reality, while I had been between jobs, I had boldly (and hilariously) rented a building for eighty-dollars a month and put out a small sign in hope that God would miraculously send business my way. It had been a total waste of time and money, because I had no serious photography skills and certainly no business skills.

Even so, that one sentence I said to the secretary changed her attitude toward me, and God gave me favor with her. She arranged for me to have an interview with a couple executives who were driving from Springfield, Ohio to Indianapolis, Indiana to set up a day of interviews.

On the day of the interview, the two executives from Olan Mills interviewed me very thoroughly. Before the day was over, they told me they had planned to rehire a former employee for the one job opening they had available. "We used this opportunity to interview several applicants for potential hires in the future," one of them said. "We know we can hire the former employee any time we want, and we'll keep him on the back burner. But today we have decided to give the job to you instead of him."

I was elated. For a thirty-year old who did not finish high school, God gave me an good-paying blue-collar job with excellent benefits. The company sent me through several weeks of training, furnished me with an elaborate studio, which was worth more than ten-thousand dollars and provided plenty of customers. Even better, I was not involved in portrait sales in any way.

The job also had a couple unusual perks. I worked away from home three or four days a week, and I took family portraits in churches for yearbooks. My first appointment was usually around three-thirty in the afternoon, which meant I had several leisure hours in the mornings to study. This allowed me a significant time for spiritual growth.

Another important perk from this job was that each day I was required to meet and communicate with approximately one-hundred strangers. Although difficult, this purged me of shyness more than any other period in my life. Alone, and a hundred miles from home, I was thrust into interacting with a group of strangers each and every work day.

On occasion, customers would cancel their appointments and during my leisure time I always visited the church library to read and study. I would also wander around the building, peek into the classrooms and try to get a sense of the teacher's burden for his or her class. Working in two or three different churches each week was a tremendous learning experience.

When I discussed my opinions with other photographers, we all agreed that a person could quickly learn a lot about the church members just by walking through the building. It turned out that pastors were a representation of the congregation. Almost without exception, he or she reflected the same friendliness and burden (or lack of it) of the congregation.

I dedicated myself to the job and set out to be the best photographer the company employed. My commitment paid off. After my first ten months into the job, the company had their annual regional meeting where all the photographers in the five-state area met for several days of lectures and training.

At the meeting each regional manager was allowed to award one employee with a large gold trophy they called *The Olan*. My regional manager covered a three-state area, and not only was I awarded The Olan that first year, but I also received it for three consecutive years.

The job was actually physically demanding, but I thrived on it. Part of my success was due to the great management of the company. Everyone was positive and helpful. My supervisor was the best manager I had ever met. His positive-affirmation management style was new to me, but I responded well to it.

Each morning, I used my three to five extra hours of leisure time to study the Bible. In addition, I read every theological book I thought would help my spiritual growth. I wanted to grow in sermon preparation, but all I knew to study in that area was English and writing. I assumed if I wanted to prepare a better sermon then I needed to learn how to construct speeches and essays.

My huge (and hilarious) goal of attending college seemed out of the question for me at that time, but Sue and I visited the Indiana University campus bookstore where I purchase textbooks for several of their on-campus courses. I took the books home and studied them, but I was never satisfied I was getting the right knowledge I needed. I had a calling to minister, and I wanted to learn how to communicate as effectively as possible. But God already had a plan even though I could not imagine it.

*　*　*

I BECAME INVOLVED IN WOOD CRAFTING as a means of creating gifts for others, and soon it became a hobby. Together, Sue and I made shelves, bookcases, and other home decorations for gifts. She learned to use a band-saw and sander better than myself, and eventually people began to give us orders for our wood crafts. My job with Olan Mills paid well, and we did not need the extra money, but woodworking was fun and supplementing our income was nice.

We invested all the profits from our woodworking endeavors back into tools, and eventually we had a full-fledged woodworking shop in our basement. Sales increased to the point where we even had to refuse orders for several months.

I always enjoyed my job at Olan Mills, but after a few years I began worry about not being home enough for my twelve-year old son. In addition, the company began to habitually work me six days a week, and I became very lonesome when I was gone from home for six days at a time. This was long before cell phone and email, and often I left on Monday morning and would not get back home until late Saturday evening.

After five years with the company, I politely asked them to give me a few days off work in order to catch up on our woodcraft orders, but they adamantly refused. "We don't do that," my supervisor said and laughed.

Next, I called and asked if they would give me a temporary leave-of-absence. "I'll come back to work anytime you need me, or if you never need me to come back, then that is okay too," I said. "I just need a few weeks or months to catch up on my woodworking orders."

They refused again.

God had blessed our little business, and I felt an intuition that it was time to take advantage of the opportunity to work at home. After I discussed it with my wife and learned that she felt comfortable with my decision, I went to the pastor and explained how I felt. "If you feel like it's what God wants you to do, then you better do it," he said.

That was all I needed. I called my regional manager back. "Since you will not give me time off, I am turning in my two-week notice." Two days later, he called me back. "We've changed our minds and have decided to work with you. We are willing to give you as much time off work as you want. We will work with you in any way you need, whether it's a few days or a few months."

"Too late," I said. "I wish you had told me this before I had to wrestle with the decision to quit. But now that I've made the decision, I'm not backing out."

I really liked the job, but it made so much more sense to take advantage of the opportunity God had given us with our little business. More importantly, working at home allowed me to spend more time with my son, and that alone was reason enough to make any financial sacrifice my job change might entail. In hindsight, it is easy to see this was one more step in a multifaceted plan of God.

Events in my life were like a row of dominoes that God had set up, and he was tipping them over one at a time. Yet, I was not aware of what he was doing. Had I known what he was doing, all of the internal struggles I was going through would have vanished, knowing that God had a plan. But the struggles were part of the growing process, and I still had a lot of growing I needed to do.

About that time, one small event took place has been forever burned into my mind. We lived in an old house which had wooden floors that creaked with every other step. One afternoon, my son and I were in the basement working on a woodworking project when we heard someone open the upstairs entry door and boldly walk into the house. Their footsteps were easy to hear as they walked across the floor and stopped in the kitchen.

I was not concerned, because most people knew we had our little wood shop in the basement, so Jonathan and I kept working and assumed whoever had come in upstairs would come down to the basement and find us.

After three or four minutes went by and we did not hear them go back out of the house, I assumed they were sitting at the kitchen table waiting on us. "Let's go upstairs and see who is here,"I told Jonathan.

We went upstairs, but there was no one in the house. I checked in every room, inside the closets, and even under the beds, but whoever came inside the house could not be found. Both of us were quite certain we had heard someone open the door, walk across the floor, and stop in the kitchen. Yet, what happened to the person was a mystery—until a few nights later.

After the family went to bed, I often stayed up late and walked the floors in prayer. As I said earlier, I learned to pray in the morning, but many nights I would pray extra after everyone else was asleep. That night, during prayer, I did like I had done so many times before and went into my son's room where I placed my hands on his head and prayed for him as he slept.

"Lord Jesus, I plead the blood on my son's life. Would you keep him safe and in your care. Help him through the struggles he faces in his teenage years. Send an angel to this household to minister to us and keep us in harmony with one another."

When I said that prayer that night, cold chills ran along my arms and my breath seemed to leave me a moment. I suddenly understood that God had indeed answered my prayer and sent an angel to our house. I realized the reason we had heard someone come inside the house but did not hear anyone leave was because that person had not left. God had answered my prayer and sent one of his ministering angels to our house.

I believed that with all my heart, and years later, when we moved to another house, I could not bring myself to put our house up for sale because I knew it was such a sacred place. We left our old house set empty for nearly eight years until I felt a release from God that it was okay to sell it.

I can also promise you that as soon as I moved into our new house, once again I walked the floors throughout the house and prayed that God would once again send his holy angel to our house to minister to us and to keep us safe and in harmony.

At the same time, my ministry seemed dead in the water. I had been so excited to become self employed, thinking I would have more time to minister and work in the church. However, after nearly six years of working at home, I grew frustrated because I did not seem to be making progress in that area. The frustration affected my marriage and every other area of my life. I knew I was called to a ministry, but my ministry seemed sterile and unproductive.

My passion to be used of God had never left me, and with all of my reading and studying about great men of God, I dreamed of nothing less than being used of God in a great way too. Years later, I would learn that most of God's work is always done by faithful men and women who work in the shadows and never receive recognition. In fact, God's greatest work is done by the humblest people who never consider themselves great men or women of God.

But I was still growing and learning, and part of my growth was facing that *rock and hard place* where I became so frustrated with myself until I was finally able to look deep inside my soul and examine my motives.

One afternoon during an intense prayer time inside the house, I prayed about my failing ministry and cried out to God with everything within me as I had done many times before. Finally, after more than two hours of prayer, I broke through the barrier and knew I had touched God for my ministry. For several intense minutes, I could hardly get my words out as God saturated me with his Spirit and washed me of my personal interest.

I stood up from prayer and spoke out loud. "God, I don't understand it, but I believe this prayer on this day is a demarcation point for something you are doing in my life. I don't know how, but I firmly believe that from this point forward everything is going to be all right." I believed it too. It was not a matter of my having to grasp for faith, something inside me made me feel like everything was going to be all right.

When my wife came home that afternoon, I cried as I told her exactly how I felt. "I don't know how it's possible, but I believe God wants me to go to college and learn to write," I said. "I'm feeling that maybe my ministry is more in writing than in a pulpit ministry." She was congenial and agreed to support anything I wanted to do. At that time, not only was I a high-school drop out, but college was financially out of our reach also.

In addition, we were both getting discouraged about our wood-working business. Our five years in business had been a good experience, and we were still making a good wage, but we were tired. Not just physically tired, but long-term tired.

The disadvantage of self-employment was working extra hours every week. I worried that hard times might come upon us, and I felt responsible to work twelve hours a day. Sometimes, I even worked six days a week. But after five years, we were both worn down and tired of the stress of maintaining the business.

Sue got a full-time job and a couple months later, I did the same. We faded out our orders, and we both agreed it was much better to work forty-hours a week and not have the self-employment stress.

My new warehouse job was rather difficult work, but later I learned it was another falling domino in God's plan. After working there a year, I discovered the company offered employees the benefit of tuition reimbursement for college. I took advantage of it and first finished my GED, and then enrolled in two college classes that met at night. As long as I made a grade of A, the company reimbursed me one-hundred percent. It seemed almost too good to be true.

However, during my second semester in college, the warehouse began working late every night and most Saturdays. This conflicted with my college classes. "You have to be here Saturday to work," my supervisor said.

"But I have classes that I have already paid for," I said.

"You will just have to work something out with your professor, because you have to be here in order to keep your job."

"Can't you at least let me finish this semester, and then I'll be available to work weekends and evenings next semester?"

He shook his head. "Working at this job is top priority, not your classes."

Graduating from college had been a life-long dream, and I did not want to quit. I was on a roll and I knew if I quit attending classes, I might never start back up again. The determination to finish college was greater than my desire for prosperity.

The warehouse paid extremely well, and also provided good health insurance, which made it a tough decision, but I turned in my notice and began looking for a new job.

To say the next few months were tough times is an understatement. I applied to twenty-four places and the only one who would hire me was McDonald's Restaurant. I was discouraged to have to work for near minimum wage, but I had to have a job and I intended to work there until I found something better.

When I came home with my McDonald's T-shirt and work schedule, my wife shook her head. "You are better than that. Take that shirt back and tell them you don't want the job."

I was somewhat relieved and thankful for her belief in me. We both believed it would take only a few days until someone called me for a better job, or at least for an interview. We were both wrong. I continued taking college classes and praying a lot for God's help, but no one called me to come to work. Stress built up to an all-time high.

At the time, I was enrolled in a psychology class where we studied nervous breakdowns and suicide. The professor gave us a list of warning signs that we should look for in people who were about to go over the edge. On the one-to-ten checklist she gave us, I was at a ten on nearly every item.

It was a difficult time, both financially and emotionally. One day I shared a feeling I had with Sue. "I have this odd intuition that God wants me to work at a motel. I don't have any experience in that area, and I don't see how I can possibly get a job in the motel industry, but that's how I feel."

She agreed to go with me, and we got in the car and drove to town where I stopped at a motel and went inside. She stayed in the car and prayed. When I finished filling out the application, the on-duty clerk called the general manager and asked about interviewing me.

When the general manager stepped out of the office, I was surprised to see it was a woman who had been my mother's best friend. She hired me on the spot and even though the pay was much less than what I needed, I went home elated.

God had indeed guided me to apply at the motel for a job. If I had doubts about God's directing me, then it faded away that day. Another domino had fallen.

That weekend, all of my built up stress left my body like fast moving water. Sadly, when I reported to work the next week, my bubble of enthusiasm burst. I learned I had been hired for a part time job. My wage was only seven-dollars and fifty cents an hour, and suddenly I learned I would get only two day's work a week. I was devastated. When I confronted the general manager, she did not appear concerned.

"Don't worry. Someone is always quitting around here, so you'll be full-time before you know it," she said.

I believed God had given me the job, and I had no choice but to continue and wait for better opportunities. Waiting was tough. It took six months before I was able to go full time as a motel desk clerk. But God gave me favor, and in a few weeks after becoming a full-time employee, the manager promoted me to assistant manager. My pay increased to nine dollars an hour.

In addition, the promotion was an answer to prayer, because as the assistant manager I was allowed to schedule my own shift in order to have the most convenient hours for college classes.

I had worked at the motel nearly a year when the general manager announced she was retiring. That was not good news for me, and I tried to convince her to stay another year or two, but she would not reconsider. The next general manager might not treat me so well, and I would have conflict with my college classes again. At that point I was about two years into a four-year degree.

It turned out God had a plan from the beginning, because the corporation who owned the motel could not find a new manager. It was almost as if they had no choice but to promote me to *temporary acting manager* while they continued to look for a qualified general manager.

The corporation owned forty different hotels; but even so, six months later they still had not found anyone to install as the general manager. When they promoted me to general manager, I considered it a divine act of God, because the pay increase was substantial, and I was still able to work out my own hours for my college classes.

I worked at the motel until I completed all my college classes to earn my bachelor degree in education. However, a giant obstacle loomed over me. I still needed to finish my student teaching in order to earn my teacher's license. That was a problem, because I would be gone from work during the day. Teaching in public school meant I would only be available to work at the motel in the evenings and night shift.

I called my regional manager and explained my problem. "I know this is an unusual situation, but I am committed to finishing my degree. If you will allow me to finish my student teaching, I can work here during evenings and nights. If this is not acceptable for you, then I respect that, and I appreciate your kindness to me, but consider this my official two-week notice."

I was blunt and straight to the point, but that was the only way I knew how to communicate. If they allowed me to do this, then it had to be an act of God. But if not, then I knew God had already provided so much for me in this endeavor, and I intended to trust his management.

As I held the phone to my ear, I waited and prayed. My regional manager was quiet a long moment. "Okay, let's give it a try and see if it works," he said.

That was it. As far as I was concerned, it was a miracle. I went on to complete my bachelor degree in education and graduated with honors. The dominoes were falling, and I was almost in a daze at what God was doing in my life.

On the morning of my last day of my last college class to earn my degree, I walked out the door of our house and was nearly to the car when my wife called out for me to come back inside the house. "I just received a phone call," she said. "Junior died last night."

I was not emotionally moved. Nor did I shed a single tear. Yet it did seem significant to me that he died on the day of my last class to earn my bachelor degree. It was significant, because hundreds of times he had made me stand at attention in front of him while he plainly told me, "You'll never amount to a hill of beans. You're no good, just like your father, and you'll never be worth anything."

I did not go to his funeral. I had no desire to go, and I knew he would not want me there. My wife printed the obituary, and although he listed my brother as his son, my name was never mentioned. It never bothered me in the least.

At night, when I close my eyes, I am often back home under his oppression. In my dreams, I try to stand up to him and fight back, but I can never do it because I fear I am doing wrong. He does not punish me any more, but he is still in my head—still telling me how I will fail. Only by the grace of the Lord Jesus have I been able to ignore that inner speech of his voice and goon to function in life like a normal adult.

My graduation commencement seemed like an unnecessary event—given my age, so I stayed home and waited for them to mail my degree to me. It was a memorable day when I took that bachelor degree out of my mailbox, I went into the house and carefully opened it and placed it on the table. Next, I read it very thoroughly as tears filled my eyes and ran down my cheeks.

Finally, I picked up that degree, walked outside, and looked up into the cloudless sky. "Where are you now, Junior?" I cried out, sobbing almost uncontrollably. "You said I would never amount to much. You said I would never accomplish anything." I held the degree up to the sky "Where are you now? You were wrong. You were wrong."

I TRIED TO BELIEVE God had a plan for my life during the last years of college. Every day, I tried to review my list of goals, but there was one goal on my list that seemed so high and so big to me that I felt humbled to even write it on paper. If I could do anything in the world I wanted to do, it would be to teach. Not only teach, but to teach in a Christian atmosphere—preferably in Bible college.

I felt confident this was the best way to minister and affect others for Christ. Teaching the upcoming generation who would in turn affect the world offered the greatest returns on my efforts.

I applied for a teaching job at public schools in the area, but my heart was not in it. I talked to my pastor about working in my home church's Christian school and turned in my resume, but they weren't interested in hiring me. The public school system was not for me. At one point, a public school called me to come in for an interview, but I turned them down.

The summer after my graduation with a bachelor degree in education, I continued to work as the general manager at the motel and take graduate classes toward my Master's degree. One day my son, who attended Bible college, called and advised me to apply at the Bible college he attended.

"I want to apply, but I am waiting until I obtained my Master's degree," I said. "I doubt if they will hire me with just a Bachelor degree. In truth, they probably want a celebrity-type minister, and I'm just a regular guy."

However, it turned out that an employee at the Bible college had just resigned who taught English and computer. My degree was in English education with a minor in computer education. Another domino had fallen.

I applied for the job, and after a couple interviews, the school hired me. I finished my Master's degree at the University of Indianapolis, and continued to work at Indiana Bible College. One of the professors at the University where I was taking classes approached me about working for the University in the publishing department. The invitation was flattering, but I flatly turned him down too. After he asked me the third time, and I told him I was committed to the Bible College, he quit asking me.

It was a testimony of God's delivering power, because I doubt at any time during my youth and teenage years that anyone expected or even imagined it was possible for such a troubled child to actually receive an invitation to teach at the academic level. God blessed me to work at Indiana Bible College for sixteen years. Not only have I been fortunate to work alongside a great group of ministers and teachers, but I have also been privileged to have a small part in the lives of thousands of young students. There is no greater privilege than to affect the upcoming generation.

Through the years God has blessed me beyond measure. Everyday, I remind myself that my story is not over, because I continue to grow and learn as much as possible, even in my senior years. I am convinced my best years are still ahead of me, because I firmly believe that the greatest accomplishment in life is daily walking in the Holy Ghost and anointing. (I know some will not understand my *churchese* and what that statement really means.)

As I look back on life, I realize it was not time or chance, or even others who kept things from me—it was myself. Too many times I held back in fear instead of walking through the door God had opened for me.

The external challenges in life have certainly shaped me, but Satan's plan was never a match for God's promises. It has taken me a long time to learn that simple lesson.

Although, this is my testimony, I know you have your own story to tell. God has his hand on your life and that means the possibilities are endless. Your story is not over yet, either. I hope you are encouraged to throw off the restraints and imagine the possibilities God has for you.

The person you are now is who you have become in life—not necessarily who you are. With God's help you can change your life and blossom into the person he created you to become.

I believe that each of us are born with the potential to reach a specific ability. Some are created to become ministers and some are created to become house painters, or a thousand different abilities that God uses. But if you do not reach the potential for which you were created, then you have not only failed God, but you have also failed yourself and mankind.

Why not raise your sails, cut the anchor loose, and take a risk? It is no telling what God will do in your life. What if nothing happens? What if it does?

LESSONS I HAVE LEARNED IN LIFE

1. Making mistakes is part of the learning process. When you fall, eat your pity cake if you must, and then get up and try one more time.

2. Do not allow mistakes to become memorials.

3. Difficulties are certain to come, just remember, your future is determined by how you respond to those difficulties.

4. Dream big. Believe the impossible. You will never be more than you dream.

5. You will be disappointed if you fail in your goals, but you are doomed if you don't try.

6. God will take care of what you go through in life. Your job is to take care of how you go through it.

7. People like you, not for who you are, but for how you make them feel. Always give the other person grace. Always give them a chance to save face.

8. Pray every morning; give God your first hours, when the day is fresh.

9. Plant the idea (seed) in your mind, water and fertilize it with expectancy, and it will manifest itself in your life.

10. By God's blessings, nothing you imagine can be kept from you. There is not such thing as impossible.

11. Remember that everyone has a strong need to feel appreciated. Most conflict is a result of someone's need to feel for appreciation.

12. Always keep your mind busy with great expectations for yourself.

The following materials are sample chapters taken from other books written by the same author. All books may be ordered from www.amazon.com or directly from; Kenny Noble 6973 Meredith Drive, Seymour, IN 47274 All books are $15 including postage.

Cinderella Boy
The Mentor
Chef Boy or Me
Rite of Passage
Devotions for Spiritual Growth
(This devotional book will not be available until August 2018)

Rite of Passage

Maddy Hampton receives a cryptic voice mail that an unknown uncle is in an intensive care unit, and she's suspicious. Yet, her dream of meeting her family provides all the motivation she needs to make the trip from Los Angeles to Anchorage. Since her mother always kept the family a secret, Maddy prepares herself for the worst. What she does not expect is a high-stakes game of life and death where Alaskan poachers use her for leverage against her uncle who has stolen their contraband money.

Her only help arrives in the form of a handsome trooper who rescues her from the poachers. However, to get out of the wild bush country where the poachers have kept her prisoner, the couple must hike twenty-miles through bear-infested wilds to get to a village where they can find help. The odds are not in their favor, and the only hope she has to live another day is the trooper's unwavering commitment to protect her. Right of Passage is a story of overcoming abandonment issues and learning to trust.

RITE OF PASSAGE

CHAPTER ONE

"I am not afraid, just concerned." Maddy Hampton nearly shouted into the phone as she wheeled her suitcase through the noisy airport. She stopped and glance over her shoulder. The man who followed her stopped and stared her direction. Her stomach tightened as the crowd closed in around her.

When the man in the fedora saw Maddy looking his direction, he quickly looked the other way. His dark sunglasses were too big for him, and his clothes looked a size too large. How did such an old-timer manage to keep up with her?

Unaware of her predicament, Jasmine laughed on the other end of the line. "Calm down girlfriend. There's nothing wrong with you being afraid to take a risk. Only your friends will tell you the truth, you know?"

"Don't start talking to me like a greeting card." Maddy slipped around a steel column to avoid crashing into a lanky teenager who abruptly stopped to text on his cell phone.

"I'm talking to you like a friend," Jasmine said.

"Don't forget, you are the one who talked me into doing this," Maddy said into the phone as she wove her way through the crowd. "I blew off my schedule today only because you insisted I take that voice mail seriously. It's probably a hoax anyway." She glanced over her shoulder again. Fedora had disappeared.

"And you'll thank me when this is over," Jasmine said. "A day off work and a three-thousand mile trip is a small price to pay for meeting your first family members."

Maddy swallowed back her worry. "I should be back in L.A. right now in case Mom has a spell and needs me."

"Maybe your new uncle needs you too," Jasmine said. "Follow the crumbs and see where the trail leads. For once, trust that God always looks out for you."

Maddy released a pent up breath. "Like I said, you are the only one I trust." Jasmine believed in that religious stuff, but not her. Based on the way her own life had turned out, God acted as if he did not know she even existed. "Not so sure I want to meet my real family, whoever they are. Henry will be only the second family member I've met in my entire life."

"Which means this will open up a new world for you." Jasmine's voice escalated.

Someone bumped into Maddy's backside, nearly knocking her into the crowd. The knot in her stomach tightened, but she quenched her emotions and pasted on a smile. "Excuse me," she said.

"You're a nurturer." Jasmine's voice was barely discernible above the noisy crowd. "You have this need inside that you have to take care of others."

"It's called compassion. And what's wrong with that?"

"Nothing, except you also need to get a life of your own. When was the last time you and Jack went on a date?"

"You don't have to preach to me. I know it's been a while." Maddy's tone was sharp. Fedora stood at the exit door now. He'd gotten ahead of her. Maddy bit her lip and looked the other way. "All I care about right now is meeting this new uncle." She searched for the exit farthest from Fedora.

The old man stepped outside the building and stared into space as if waiting for someone. Maybe she was too paranoid, after all. He was probably some grandfather looking for his family to arrive and take him home.

A slow sigh escaped Maddy's lips. "You won't forget to check on Mom tonight, will you?

"No worries. I'll be your granny nanny while you're gone. I've been thinking. You should get a cat. A baby kitten would be good company for your mother."

"Animals always run off," Maddy said. The crowd near the exit thickened in front of her. "You're breaking up, Jasmine. I'll call you later."

"Praying for you, girl," Jasmine called out just before the signal dropped.

Maddy disconnected and dropped her phone inside her handbag. The raspy intercom overhead barely registered as she searched for Fedora. She considered herself relatively street smart, but an inner intuition made her wary of the old man who had followed her.

If something happened, she would depend on the crowd for her protection. As long as she stayed close to other people, she was safe. Near the exit, taxi's lined up outside along the curb like little yellow chicks waiting for their mother. Another minute or two and she would be safely inside one of those taxi's and away from this place.

A few steps from the exit door, a tall man wearing a black T-shirt and a blue-jean jacket took two steps sideways and blocked her path. The man's blond hair and smooth skin gave him a magazine-cover handsomeness, but his ice-blue stare quickened her pulse.

Pins and needles jabbed the tips of her fingers. Too late to change direction and avoid him, she yanked the suitcase behind her and leaned hard left to step around him. The fragrance of leathery cologne touched her senses, and for a flash reminded her of Jack's absence.

"Ma'am, you'll have to come with me." Black T-shirt's voice was soft, yet firm. From what she could glimpse under his jean jacket, the man had a serious workout commitment. But it was the big bulge below his left shoulder that had her attention. He was either airport security or some joker causing trouble—like the old man who had been following her. Eight years working in the airline industry had taught her to watch for such things.

Her next few hours had no room for free time. Visit her uncle in the hospital, make friends, trade contact information, and get back to the office by morning; that was her goal.

Black T-shirt's hand reached for her arm. Not in an attack sort of way, more like a gesture to stop her.

She ducked to avoid his grasp. "Not going to happen, Mister."

Like a dancer who'd been quietly waiting for the music to cue, black T-shirt went into action, pivoted on the balls of his feet, gripped Maddy's bicep, then lifted her onto her toes. "Wasn't a request, lady. Now, do us all a favor and don't make a scene."

Adrenalin spiked through her veins as she pulled against his grip. "Let go of me." Her efforts were useless. You—" She bit back a word she had not used in a long time.

His blue eyes locked on her pupils and trapped her gaze. The muscles in his jaw twitched a moment until finally, the thin line of his lips relaxed. He pushed back his jacket to reveal a badge clasped to his belt. "Alaska Wildlife Trooper, Chase Barnes," he said. "Keep quiet and take it easy. No need to alarm the crowd."

"What's this all about," she asked.

Several uniformed officers converged around them, guns drawn, walking slowly and if expecting trouble. Relief coursed through. Thank God, they'd seen her trouble.

Without speaking a word, one of the officers pulled her handbag from her shoulder, while a second took her suitcase. Their coordinated actions looked like a well-rehearsed routine.

Any optimism she'd had earlier suddenly fell in shards at her feet. The officers were not coming to her aid; they were part of Trooper Barnes' team. She had done nothing wrong, so why were they doing this to her?

The crowd stopped to stare, their hum of activity gone eerily silent. Obviously, this airport was not accustomed to random searches. Truthfully, she had not expected it either; at least not in Alaska, and definitely not like this. A lone baby's cry echoed through the cavernous room. Any hope of maintaining her tight schedule floated away like a helium balloon in the wind.

The trooper with her suitcase dropped to one knee and unzipped the cover. The onlooker's expressions were tense and expectant, like children watching a jack-in-the-box.

Once again, she tried to twist free, but Barnes' grip tightened and burned her skin. A hot flush crept up her neck as she watched the trooper open her suitcase. "Hey pervert," she called. "If you like snooping through women's clothes, go back home to your mama."

"No need to get nasty," Barnes whispered. "Trooper Henderson is only doing his job."

Henderson was thirtyish, dark hair, and looked to weigh less than a fashion model. When he raised the suitcase's lid, his eyes widened. He looked up at Barnes, his brow arched, a slow whistle escaped his lips. "Jackpot."

Maddy touched her bottom lip with the tip of her tongue. Her years working in the airline industry had drilled one thing into her above all else and that was the importance of following security policies. On duty or off duty, she packed her luggage according to the same rules every other passenger followed. She never carried more than two ounces of fluids, never brought food on her travels, and always kept her baggage size and weight limit within the required standards. Anything they found in her suitcase had to be a minor offense.

Henderson spun the suitcase around to reveal neatly packed bricks of one-hundred-dollar bills. "We got a winner, boss."

The sight of the money slapped her. For several seconds nothing made sense in her brain. Her breath caught in her throat. That was not her money. She had never even seen that much money before.

Henderson continued shaking his head as if amazed. "Looks like an easy million. Probably more."

Maddy looked at Trooper Barnes and shook her head. "This is a mistake," she finally managed to blurt out. Her voice sounded weak and raspy even to her own ears. "Would someone listen to me?"

Barnes slowly released her arm. "I am listening. Start talking."

She worried her lip with her upper teeth while she struggled to organize her thoughts. "Apparently, I picked up the wrong suitcase from the luggage belt."

Barnes laughed, but it wasn't real. "You're lucky day, I guess.

"I'm telling you the truth."

"Your mouth says you're telling the truth, but those red ears of yours tell me you're lying."

"Cute. Maybe you should have your mother crochet that on a pillow for you," she said.

Barnes locked on her gaze a moment. His eyes seemed to penetrate into her soul. "That kind of attitude won't help you. You cooperate, and it goes easier for you. Nothing complicated about this."

Maddy closed her eyes and involuntarily swallowed back the lump in her throat. She was innocent, and her employer could get her out of this easy enough. But if she called her office and asked for help, they'd know she had lied about being sick this morning. Not that it was a major crime, but at this stage of her career it was a serious enough problem to make her boss question her integrity. Especially, with the hard-nosed boss she worked for.

A lot of good Jasmine's prayers had done. The meeting with the CEO tomorrow was possibly the most important day of her career. If she did not resolve this situation immediately and get back home tonight or early in the morning, then she'd miss that meeting and forfeit everything she'd worked for during the last eight years.

God knew how much she needed that promotion to support her mother's medical expenses. Right now, nothing else in life was more important to her than that meeting tomorrow. But like always, God never got involved in her life.

*   *   *

Chase Barnes fought back the surge of adrenalin that pumped through his body. Catching this woman could turn out to be a major step in the investigation of his brother's death. He'd worked long and hard to obtain the smallest clue about Andrew's accident, and today God had rewarded his efforts.

He kept his eyes on the woman's expression. She was a good actor, he'd give her that. A person in her situation would normally be desperate as a goldfish in a leaky bag, but her demeanor exuded confidence. Not the reaction he wanted. If he could ratchet up the tension and get her to panic, then maybe she'd break. Nothing would make him happier than to get a confession right here and now. "You ever been arrested before?"

She forced a smile. "Of course not. My record's spotless."

Frustration coursed through him. "Was spotless. It looks like you'll be spending the next few days in a jail cell. You understand that?"

Another flash of perfectly white teeth. "I understand you're desperation to find a suspect in all of this, but I am not that person, and I don't have anything to tell you."

Dressed in a navy business suit and white blouse, she looked as if she belonged in a corporate office somewhere. Why would any woman wear high heels on a three-hour flight? Especially, if she'd known there'd be a lot of airport walking." Either this woman was meeting someone she wanted to impress, or she was one of those gals who are always OCD about their appearance.

The crowd had gone silent. Their silence brought an eerie surreal atmosphere. Many stood frozen like a group of manikins. He methodically searched the faces. He spun back to his suspect. "Tell me Maddy, what is it you do for a living exactly?"

"I look after my mother for one thing." Her eyes averted as she shifted her feet.

What was she hiding? With his hands fisted on his hips, he took a step closer to her. "You know we'll be checking into it? So anything you lie about is only going to come back and bite you in bad places."

A woman this attractive was probably accustomed to getting anything she wanted from men. But her pretty face wouldn't affect him. Her arrest was the break he needed to bust Andrew's case wide open, and he would not be deterred this time.

The memory of his brother sent a knife-like pain though his heart. If only Andrew could witness this victory. "I assume you knew Andrew Barnes?" he asked.

She shook her head again. Her expression unaltered. "Should I?"

Did her pupils dilate or was it only his imagination? He lifted a shoulder. "We'll go down that road later. You came in on a flight from Los Angeles. That your place of residence?"

She nodded. "I'm only here overnight to visit a family member in the hospital."

"Listen Maddy, I'm going to ask you a few more questions. How you answer them will make a big difference in how you spend your time here in Anchorage."

She arched her brow. "I'm an open book."

Her arrogance touched a nerve inside him. He'd known her type before. They always believed they were the smartest person in the room. Maybe that would be to his advantage.

"Tell me about your meeting with your contact here at Ted Steven's Airport."

She didn't hesitate. "I am visiting a relative in the hospital today. Tomorrow I catch my flight back to Los Angeles. Anything else you want to know, Mr. Barnes?"

He bit his lower lip. After a long moment, he signaled to the trooper holding her handbag and waited for her driver's license. "What were your plans for that money?"

"There were no plans, because it isn't my money," her tone low but firm.

He examined her license. "So what? You carrying a million dollars around with you for fun?"

No answer.

His heart pounded hard against his ribs, but he purposely kept his voice calm. The last suspect he'd questioned about Andrew's accident had gotten him so angry he'd nearly lost control. He would not allow that to happen again. "You have someone to share this money with? Maybe a significant other?"

Maddy's brow wrinkled. "No offence, Mr. Barnes, but—"

"Call me Chase," he interrupted.

"And you can call me Maddy. No offence Chase, but you act like you're stuck on stupid?"

He ground his teeth together, but remained silent a moment. "Explain."

"First, I told you that money is not mine. Second, I am not the kind of person who'd get so attached to a significant other that I'd risk going to jail for them. And third, if I had known there was money in that suitcase, I'd have called the police myself—or troopers, whatever you guys call yourselves."

"It's trooper. You make a good impression, Maddy, and I think you're intelligent enough to know you're not walking away from this."

She groaned and let her head fall forward. "I told you," Her tone escalated. "I—" She went suddenly silent and released a long sigh.

He scanned the crowd again. Any person in the crowd could be her accomplice. A few yards away, several men sat on benches, seemingly undisturbed by the troopers' presence. Outside, an old man wearing a fedora hat with an identical suitcase stood just outside the exit door as if waiting for someone to give him a ride.

A tall woman in the crowd stood with her mouth agape, also holding the handle of a black suitcase. From where he stood, at least a dozen people had the same exact black suitcase.

"Did you check any other luggage on your flight?" he asked.

"Only my one bag."

"Because we'll find out."

"I'm sure you will," she said.

"That's a lot of money. I'm surprised you checked it. I wouldn't trust anyone but God with that much money."

She rolled her eyes. "Then we're different, because I wouldn't even trust God. Besides, our luggage is supposed to be scanned. How is this even possible? Why wasn't that suitcase confiscated before it was put on the flight in L.A.?"

He knew the answer but he wouldn't tell her yet. If she was guilty, then she already knew the answer. If not, then he'd tell her eventually. Security at L.A.X. had made an arrest. At least one security agent had taken a cash payoff to ensure the suitcase slipped through the baggage scanner.

Once the jet was in the air, the man's fear got the best of him, and he confessed his wrongdoing. The worst of it was the security agent they had arrested claimed he didn't know the contact's name. Technically, a person can carry as much money as they want on a flight, but they have to declare it. As soon as they declare it, the authorities will want to know why a traveler is moving so much cash, and they always assume it is connected with criminal activity. Which means most criminals never declare large sums of cash.

"Anyone traveling with you?" he asked.

Maddy blinked hard and glared at the gawking crowd, her posture erect, lips pressed together in a tight line. Like so many perpetrators he'd arrested in the past, she was following a common cycle. First, she'd be indignant and maintain her innocence. Later, she'd soften and act as if the two of them were best friends. When that didn't work, she'd lawyer up and suddenly grow silent.

Chase pulled out his smart phone, took a photo of her license, and sent it to the station. They'd begin a background check right away, and by the time he arrived with her at the station, he'd have access to more information on her than her parents. She might refuse to comply now, but a long day of questioning and isolation in a cold jail cell would make her tame as a week-old kitten.

His phone buzzed, and he glanced at the screen. It was his contact from LAX. He gave Trooper Henderson the signal to stay close to Maddy, as he took several steps away to talk in private.

"Any luck up there?" the man on the other end of the line asked.

"We have a suspect," Chase could not keep from smiling.

The man would razz him when he saw a photo of his suspect.

"And you got the money?"

"Looks like a million dollars," Chase said.

"You keeping the passengers on ice?"

Chase stepped farther away from his suspect. "The Chief decided against isolating the passengers. Afraid it would scare off the perp's contact."

"Great. That's how I see it too."

"Bigger fish are a better catch," Chase said.

"Your suspect talking?"

"Not yet. But then, we didn't expect her to talk yet."

"Wait. Your suspect's a woman?"

Chase looked back at Maddy. "Definitely a woman."

The man let out a loud laugh. "Tell me about her."

"Blonde, five-foot four, in her early thirties. Every time I look at her I think I've seen her before … on the magazine rack."

"Such a waste."

"I know. But she can't be working alone."

"Her accomplice might be female too. Wouldn't that be a bust?"

"I doubt it," Chase said. "She's dressed like she's meeting a man."

"Keep me posted."

Chase said goodbye, walked back to the suitcase of money.

Maddy sidled up closer to him. "Look, can't you just take the money and let me go?" Her voice became a soft purr. "You have my contact information. And you'll discover my background is flawless."

He fought back the urge to laugh at her. How could she be any more transparent? Not going to happen."

"I have to get home tomorrow to check on my mother or she'll go spastic."

"Should have thought of that before you got involved in this," he said.

"She has Alzheimer's, and she gets disoriented easy."

"She alone?"

"She's lives with me, but she's under nursing care."

"You just said you took care of her."

"What I said is that I look after her. I manage her affairs. Some days I do spend my entire evenings to feed and bathe her, which takes a lot of time."

"Then I'll ask you again; what is your occupation?"

She looked away and remained silent.

He folded his arms and waited "You understand you're not going anywhere until you give us legitimate answers."

She turned back to face him. "You want answers? Talk to the snitches who told you to check my luggage. Obviously, they know more about this than either of us do. Maybe you're being duped, Trooper Barnes. How did you know about this money anyway?"

Chase watched as Trooper Henderson took multiple snapshots of the crowd around them.

"You don't get to ask the questions."

"My bag was checked in properly at L.A.X. and scanned. I know all of the workers there. I can even give you most of their names."

"Good to know. We'll get that from you at the station."

She groaned. "I don't have time for this."

"You'll have to take the time. You have some reason to be afraid?"

"I told you, I'm an open book. Just tell me what chapter you want to read. I don't like being treated like a common criminal."

Sharp anger rose up in his throat and Chase suddenly stabbed his finger in the air inches from her face. "Then give us something to work with, some bit of truth." Six months working Andrew's case and all he knew for certain was Andrew had been working undercover with poachers before the accident.

Tension gnawed deep inside him. He needed her to be the perp. He needed her cooperation. He needed a good lead on Andrew's death. If she knew the security agents at L.A.X. and they vouched for her, then there was a slim possibility she was telling the truth. Unless, the entire security team at L.A.X. was corrupt.

Too bad he couldn't let her go and put a tail on her and see where she went. But this much money required serious answers. A couple nights in a jail cell seemed the better option for her. If she did have a sick mother as she said, then he would use that to his advantage too. The sooner he got inside her head and found out what tripped her hammer, the better leverage he'd have to make her cooperate.

*　　　*　　　*

Maddy tried to infuse her voice with confidence, but her mouth was dry as tissue paper. During her career in the airline industry, she'd experienced a lot of difficult situations, but this was possibly the worst. Even so, she would not allow these troopers to intimidate her when she had done nothing wrong.

Barnes snapped a cold handcuff on her right wrist. "Let's save the chit chat for later. We're going to the station where we can talk privately. He twisted her around and handcuffed her other wrist behind her back.

"Ouch." Maddy squealed as the cold steel cut into her wrists. "That's a little tight, trooper. Do you have to be so rough?"

A ghost of a smile touched his lips. "Don't worry. Their new, they'll stretch."

"I'm trying to tell you the truth, but you're not hearing. So how—" Her cell phone chirped interrupting her.

Barnes nodded to Henderson who dug inside her handbag and pulled out her phone. Chase took the phone, pressed the speaker phone icon, and held the phone close to Maddy's lips.

Maddy cleared her throat. "Hello?"

"I forgot to ask you about the natives up there," Jasmine said. "You spotted any hunky lumberjacks yet?" Her voice rang with laughter.

The two of them had a running joke that Maddy might find a potential boy-friend in Anchorage and spark jealousy into Jack, Maddy's current boyfriend.

"I'm still at the airport," Maddy said. "I'll have to call you back later."

"Why you still there? Don't tell me they've lost your luggage," Jasmine said.

Maddy glanced at the suitcase of money. "My luggage is the least of my worries right now."

"You sound upset," Jasmine said.

"A little stressed is all. Listen Jasmine, I got to go. I'm kind of tied-up right now."

Chase chuckled.

Maddy rolled her eyes again. She had not intended to be cute, but it had come out that way.

"Wait a minute," Jasmine said. "I have good news. I was in Mr. Graystone's office this morning and saw a couple files on his desk. One of them had your name on it. Everyone here thinks you're a ringer for the promotion. And we all know you deserve it if anyone does."

"Got to go, Jasmine. Call you later." Goodbye." Maddy turned away. She wanted to get off the line before Jasmine said anything to incriminate her.

Barnes ended the call before he handed the phone back to Henderson. "Not many lumberjacks in the city these days," he said.

A warm flush rose to Maddy's neck. "It's a private joke," was all she said. Her relationship with Jack was as involved as she'd ever been with a man. Jasmine accused them of a static relationship, but Maddy believed Jack was a good man and he would come around in his own time.

The crowd watched Trooper Henderson zip the suitcase closed. He wheeled the suitcase toward Chase and held out a worn photograph, its edges bent and wrinkled. "Found this inside. Might be important." Henderson had put on latex gloves.

Chase looked the photograph over without touching it. "Someone's been carrying that around for a long time." He looked at Maddy. "Family?"

"I don't know them," Maddy said.

"You sure? Take another look."

She stared at the photo a moment. An attractive woman in her thirties held a toddler on her lap. Both were smiling. The child revealed a strong resemblance to the woman. "I don't have to take another look, because I never saw them before."

Henderson put the photo inside a plastic bag and handed it to another trooper. "Get this to the lab for prints."

Chase bent to examine the name tag on the suitcase. "This says Maddy Hampton from Los Angeles. Couldn't be any plainer than that."

"That's because the tag must have fallen off my own suitcase and one of the workers in baggage put it back on the wrong one. Can't you call them out here and ask if that ever happens?" Hope flashed through her mind that she might be a victim of a TV prank, and any minute a smooth-talking show host would appear and point out the hidden cameras around them. Her optimism dried up like a grape on a California sidewalk when she met Chase's stare. This was no prank.

Chase gripped the suitcase handle and wrung his hand around it. "Last chance to be cooperative. Want to tell us where you were taking the money?"

"If it isn't my money, then I couldn't be taking it anywhere, could I?" Maddy's tone was sharp. "There was an old man wearing a fedora who followed me when I got off the airbus."

Chase's brow furrowed a moment before he turned and looked at the people loitering outside the door.

"Tell me about your contact meeting." His voice level and crisp.

She swallowed back her anger. "How long is this going to go on? What is it you want me to say? You want me to start making things up?" There is no contact. This is a big mistake. Your mistake."

"That's the story you're going with, a mistake?"

It had been less than ten minutes since the troopers stopped her, and the crowd had grown larger. Their faces were a mixture of fear and relief. Camera phones clicked punctuating the silence. Some stood wide-eyed, mouths gaping. Others looked amused. They likely thought the troopers had captured one of America's most wanted.

Fear licked at her insides. She was in serious trouble, and if word got back to Mr. Graystone, he'd be furious at her playing hooky. She had not meant to lie to him this morning, but when she'd called the office and asked him to get a replacement for her today, he'd asked if she was sick. She'd replied yes without thinking about it. Only one word. An innocent lie. Now, it might cost her dearly.

This problem with the money was so much bigger than a day of hooky from work, but she intended to try and work it out if possible in order to not lose her chance at the promotion. Graystone was a hard man, and the sympathy card would not work on him.

As soon as the troopers discovered she was a commercial pilot they'd call her company for verification, and that would kill her spotless record at the evaluation tomorrow. Even worse, someone could easily leak the story to the media, and her face could be plastered on national television. UNITED TRAVEL AIRLINE PILOT CAUGHT TRANSPORTING A MILLION DOLLARS. The implication would immediately be that it was drug money.

It definitely would not be good PR for the company, and it would be quite a killjoy for her promotion too. On the average, this promotion only came along every ten years. In another ten years, they'd consider her too old for the captain's chair. "I want a lawyer, please—" The last word trailed off.

"You'll need one. Ever been to Alaska before today?" Chase asked.

She shook her head. "Not returning either."

"Sorry our welcome wagon isn't up to your expectations." He nudged her toward the exit door.

Perspiration trickled down her neck. If detective TV was anything like real life, a trip to the station was code for question and arrest. She cleared her throat as she stepped through the door. "Am I under arrest?"

"Depends."

"On what?

"Your answers to my questions when we get to the station."

The crisp morning air felt good on her flushed cheeks. "I'll tell you anything you want to know. My social security number, what I've eaten for the last five days, age, and even my weight. Just get me out of these cuffs."

"Maybe later," he said.

This morning she'd considered this day the most important day of her life. Everyone else had a family, why shouldn't she? When she got the voice mail that she had an uncle here in the hospital, she knew there was no option but to follow up on it. "I flew here to visit my uncle. Outside of my mother, I've never met another family member. This is important to me."

"Guess you'll have to put your bucket list on hold."

Thoughts of what to say raced through her brain at lightning speed. They'd discover her secret soon enough. She might as well tell him now and get this done and over with. "Would it help if I told you I'm a commercial pilot, and I work for United Travel?"

Chase glanced at her from the corner of his eyes. "You never thought to mention that earlier?"

"As a professional pilot, you understand how an arrest will affect my career?"

He arched a brow. "I'm a professional too, Maddy. As one professional to another, I'm sure you understand why I have to take you in, don't you?"

She stared at the cracks in the pavement a moment. "You're making a mistake. You'll see that when my employer vouches for me."

"A half-million dollars isn't something a person can just vouch for."

"Trust me. Once you do your forensic CSI thing, you'll discover someone put my name tag on the wrong suitcase. Not to mention, there's an unhappy person out there with a suitcase full of my pajamas and personal items."

What looked to be the beginning of a smile formed on Chase's lips. "Wish I could witness that."

"Besides, I have to get back home to take care of my puppies." It was dumb, but she'd try anything to help her chances. "I volunteer at an animal shelter. You like puppies, Agent Barnes?"

He nodded. "I do like puppies."

It was not a total lie. She did volunteer at the animal shelter, but it was filled with cats and kittens. Most of the puppies were adopted right away.

"I also like wolves, elk, walrus, and a dozen other species native to Alaska." His voice grew louder. "What I don't like are poachers who profit from innocent animals."

Her mind raced ahead to find meaning in his words. "Is that where you think this money is from, animal trafficking? I can assure you I'm not involved in trafficking of any kind."

"Here in Alaska we take abuse of our natural resources seriously. That's why we have strong penalties. Personally, I have a no-tolerance rule." He opened the back door of the SUV, put his hand on her head and gently pushed her down as she clumsily dropped inside the vehicle.

Snowsuits and oversize boots fill half of the back seat. "I'm not much on guns. And I definitely would not shoot helpless animals. Call my employer. They do extensive background checks on us."

"By us, you mean commercial pilots." He leaned inside and pulled the seatbelt across her body, the warmth of his skin radiating against her face.

Her breath come in short whispered pants. She closed her eyes, angry with herself for such a ridiculous reaction. "By us I mean female pilots. I work in a man's world, and I don't expect you to understand, but there's a woman tax every female pays in order to compete in a man's world."

He paused a moment. "I guess that door swings both ways."

"Everything I do has to be better than my male coworkers." She opened her eyes. The woman card was her only power right now, and she was not embarrassed to use it.

He clicked the seatbelt shut and paused a moment before he turned to face her. His lips inches from her mouth. "Then you must be a strong woman," he whispered.

She cleared her throat. What did that mean? A strong woman?

"If you are telling the truth, then you've nothing to worry about, and I apologize in advance for the trouble you're having."

The kindness in his voice made her eyes sting. She blinked hard and looked away. "Thank you," she whispered.

He straightened, shut the vehicle door, and loaded the suitcase in the back before he turned to the waiting troopers. "You two contact airport security and get today's surveillance video. I want a list of names of everyone on that flight." He waited until the men nodded their response before he circled the vehicle and opened the driver's door.

Maddy slid farther from the window. To think it had all started with a voice mail on her cell phone yesterday. The message had been short. Your uncle, Henry H. Tims, is in the Alaska Regional Hospital. You should visit him right away. Seventeen words. No explanation. No return number. With Jasmine's prompting, she'd quickly packed her bag and made flight arrangements.

Right now, her greatest fear was that news of a pilot's arrest would travel through the company faster than celebrity gossip. It had taken her eight long years to elbow her way into position for the captain's chair, and she could not risk losing that opportunity. Yet, without the company's intercession in this matter, the troopers would likely arrest her.

Even worse if her mother had one of those spells again, it would disorient her for days. When that happened, Maddy was the only one who could coax her mother back to reality.

The words her mother had said last night cut into her thoughts. God will help us, Dear. He's still in control. It was a nice thought, but if God was in control, then he definitely was not doing his job right now.

Somehow, she had to convince Trooper Barnes of her innocence before he called her office. Mr. Grayson was in the power position, and she would not give him the chance to bump her from the job she'd sought for all these years. Whatever the cost, she had to get back to L.A. in time for that interview tomorrow.

CHAPTER TWO

Excitement flamed inside Chase as he circled the SUV. This was the break he needed for Andrew's case. With this suspect in custody, he finally had leverage to get information he needed.

He slid behind the wheel and tossed his phone onto the passenger's seat. The spring sunshine made the SUV warm as a greenhouse. After flipping the vent fan to max, he slipped on his sunglasses and adjusted the rear-view mirror position where he could see the passenger in the back seat. At the station, she would be out of her comfort zone. Maybe then she'd want to make a deal. At least that was how he imagined the next couple of hours playing out.

She shifted in her seat and turned to stare out the side window, her eyes searching the crowd as if looking for someone. Her blond hair fell in a pale curtain around her face giving her a look of innocence. From what he gathered so far, she was one of those feminist types who lived on the verge of hating men. All she needed was a reason. Based on the tone of her voice, she'd become easily irritated when he'd asked about a significant other.

Perfume permeated the cab, causing him to close his eyes and swallow hard. He mentally shook himself and started the engine. How did an attractive woman like her get involved with poachers? The average airline pilot made seventy-five grand a year, so why she risk going to jail when she was bringing home that kind of money?

Maddy leaned forward. "How long will this take, trooper?"

"Depends." He glanced at her in the rear-view mirror. "If your story holds, you'll be visiting your family this afternoon." Possible, but not likely. He wanted to keep her in a positive frame of mind—something he needed himself.

He wouldn't try to deny how his emotions had been numb for several months. Even the simple chore of getting out of bed each morning had become a struggle. The first thought in his mind every morning was always the same; Why hadn't God taken him instead of Andrew?

"My story?," Maddy interrupted his thoughts. "It's not a story. It's the truth." She stared at him in the rear-view mirror, one brow arched. "If you call my home office, it'll put the skids on a promotion I'm up for."

He put the vehicle in gear and pulled into the traffic. "So you've said." An expensive lawyer wouldn't get her out of this. Not if he had anything to say about it. He exited onto the highway, checked his side mirrors, and merged into the traffic.

When they had received the call from L.A.X. authorities this morning, his team had gone immediately into action and were already in place before the jet landed. They did not have a name or face of the person they were looking for, but they had a description of the suitcase—even if it was a generic description.

He had driven only a couple miles on the highway when a blue sport car zoomed passed them at high speed. The small car sat low to the ground and sported wide low-profile tires, which was favored by youth. A moment later, the car weaved from one lane to the other and back again, nearly crowding other vehicles off the road.

Chase keyed his microphone. "Dispatch, I've got eyes on that blue sport car we've been looking for." He gave the dispatcher his location, and then reached for the switch to activate his emergency lights. "It's either a drunk driver or a teenager showing off," Chase said to no one in particular. "I can't risk waiting for another trooper. We've been trying to catch this guy for weeks."

He jabbed the gas pedal. "That guy is bound to cause a bad accident."

In an instant, the blue car took the next exit, sped down the ramp, and slid onto the frontage road. The car's rear wheels slid off the pavement onto the shoulder, fishtailed, as if defiantly disregarding the flashing lights behind it. Black tire marks appeared on the pavement behind it.

Once off the exit ramp, Chase stomped the gas pedal to the floor again. The SUV's engine whined in complaint, but in a high-speed chase, the big vehicle was slow and sluggish as a big boat.

The low-riding sport car grew smaller in the distance. Two miles into the chase, the car suddenly slowed its speed as if waiting for Chase to catch up with it. Dark tinted windows made it impossible to distinguish details about the driver.

As the gap between the two vehicles narrowed, Chase stared hard at the plate number and keyed the mike on his radio. "This is—"

Without warning, the blue car suddenly braked hard, sending the vehicle into a half- doughnut slide. A smoking streak of black lines appeared on the road as the car whipped around, and faced the SUV head on. Seconds later, Chase realized the car was racing toward him.

Beads of moisture formed on his forehead. He dropped the microphone and gripped the steering wheel with both hands. "What is this guy doing? He's wanting to play chicken."

Less than fifty yards away, the car slid over into Chase's lane and bore straight toward the SUV like a blue missile honing in on its target.

Chase's pulse pounded in his head like a woodpecker. Involuntarily, he stomped the brake pedal and hugged the vehicle over to the road's shoulder. Tires squealed like babies crying. The odor of burning rubber filtered into the SUV's cabin. Prayer filled Chase's mind.

From his peripheral vision, Chase noted Maddy's seatbelt was still intact. The color had drained from her face as she stared, eyes wide and blinkless. No doubt, she'd bale from the vehicle if she could get to the door handle, but that wasn't an option with her hands cuffed behind her back.

The car was less than twenty yards away, the gap closing rapidly. An angry shot of adrenalin rushed through Chase's mind and urged him to join in this game of chicken, but he instinctively steered the SUV to the edge of the road.

His safety wasn't his only concern. He had a passenger to protect. When he put those cuffs on her, it became his responsibility to protect her. "What is this guy doing?" he cried out.

The driver was visible now. He wore a baseball cap, sunglasses, and huge canoe-like grin. A head-on collision looked inevitable. At the last instant, Chase jerked the steering wheel hard right, sending the SUV into the ditch. His body jerked violently against the seatbelt as the vehicle bounced hard and lurched to a stop. "I can't believe this. The driver has to be too drunk to know what he's doing."

The blue car streaked by them, barely missing the SUV's side mirror. Harsh music with a thumping bass rattled the SUV's windows. A short breath later, the blue car was gone.

Chase released a long pent-up breath, and looked over his shoulder at Maddy. "You all right back there?"

She stared a moment as she bit her lower lip. Her hair was tussled, concealing her eyes. "Lovely." Her voice was barely a whisper.

Chase released a long sigh and unlatched his seatbelt, and then groped across the carpet for the microphone.

"Sorry you had to go through that," he said. "I'll call the station and get us a tow truck." He twisted around in his seat to look behind him. The blue car had spun in a half doughnut once again and was now traveling back toward them—slowly.

Cold chills ran along Chase's spine. He dropped the microphone and reached for his revolver. In the five years he'd been a trooper, he could count on one hand the times he'd pulled his handgun. It was not something he wanted to do now, but he had a passenger to protect. "Get down," he yelled as he cocked the revolver's hammer.

The blue car slowed to a stop beside the SUV. A moment later, the passenger window came down.

Chase kept the gun concealed inside his jacket, every muscle tense.

The driver, a skinny, pot-faced male, more kid than man, wore sunglasses and had a blue baseball cap pulled low over his eyes. The loud music was back again. The kid grinned even wider and tossed a baseball-size object out the window. "Enjoy my taillights." Tires squealed and the blue car sped away.

Instantly, pink smoke rose from both sides of the SUV engulfing them in a cloud. Chase turned to his passenger. "We got to bail."

Maddy had managed to pull her knees to her chest and looped her restrained wrists over her feet. With her hands in front of her, she unbuckled her seatbelt and wiggled toward the door.

Chase holstered the handgun, scrambled across the seat and out the passenger door. His heart thumped like a machine gun against his ribs as he jerked open Maddy's door and then half pulled, half dragged her out onto the ground.

"Get up the hill. Take cover behind those trees," he yelled.

She seemed to understand the immediate danger and clawed her way across the ground until she was on her feet again. Her shoes were on the floor of the vehicle, but there was no time to retrieve them.

On his way up the hill, Chase glanced over his shoulder. The thick cloud had mushroomed. He wiped at the beads of perspiration that ran down his temple and stung his eyes. Flashbacks from his military days crashed into his brain. He blinked hard and focused on the foggy space in front of him. His lungs screamed for air, but he kept moving until he reached the top of the hill away from the pink smoke.

Maddy stepped behind a large pine tree. Breathing in shallow gulps, her wide eyes darted from the SUV to Chase as if waiting for his instructions. Dead leaves stuck to her business suit, and a twig hung from her hair where she'd fallen climbing the hill.

The two of them stood panting, staring at the road below. The SUV was no longer visible, only the growing pink cloud. The blue car was likely long gone by now. "You going to be—"

He barely got the words out of his mouth when a popping sound from the road below interrupted him. Instinctively he pushed Maddy to the ground, covered her with his body, and waited until the explosion was over. Even in the midst of the drama, he could not ignore the fruity scent emanating from the woman beneath him.

Tires squealed again and a vehicle accelerated away. The noise had only been the sound of a vehicle door slamming.

Maddy squirmed beneath him. "Get off me. It's only a smoke bomb; otherwise, it would have exploded by now—don't you think?"

"Sorry. My military training took over." He rose to his knees and used the nearest tree to pull himself to a standing position. The dissipating smoke revealed the outline of his vehicle.

Maddy groaned and struggled to her knees, her hair disheveled, a long run in her pantyhose. "He was after the money."

"I know. Are you all right?"

"Except for the ribs you crushed. She held out her bound wrists. Can you take these off now?"

He brushed the leaves from his clothes. "Later."

"Why not?" she asked.

"I can't believe I fell for that trick. I should have grabbed the suitcase." But getting his passenger to safety had been his only thought. He extended his hand to help her to her feet. "The smoke bomb was only a diversion. I over reacted. The money's probably gone by now."

She refused his offer and stood to her feet. "Great deduction, Sherlock."

"Stay here while I go down and call this in." He sucked in a deep breath and took two steps when suddenly it seemed as if he'd stepped on a land-mine.

The SUV exploded into flames. He caught sight of the driver's door flying through the air as turned back to move uphill. The heat from the explosion propelled him along like a strong wind. "Get down," he screamed." He pushed Maddy to the ground and fell on top of her again. The deafening roar from the explosion reverberated in his ears.

Maddy clasped her cuffed hands behind her head and kept her face to the ground. They both remained quiet and waited.

He shifted his weight to his forearms and tucked his head against his chest. Long after the noise of the explosion resided, the sky continued to pepper them with debris. Fortunately, the curtain of trees around them blocked much of the flying debris.

When it was quiet again, he rolled to his knees and unlocked her handcuffs. He was breaking protocol, but this was not the typical situation. "I think it's safe to get up now."

She groaned and accepted his hand this time and let him pull her to her feet. They both stood and watched the burning vehicle.

"There goes a pair of good shoes?" her tone sharp.

213

He started to laugh until he saw the look on her face and stopped the chuckle in his throat before it came out. Women and shoes—what man could understand that?

"Not much left of your ride, Sherlock." She ran her hand over her flyaway hair and combed out the twigs and leaves.

"I doubt if there's much left of my career either. But we both survived and that's what matters." He scanned the area around them. Branches of trees nearest the road were singed and shriveled. Pieces of metal were embedded in tree trunks and bark was chewed from the tree above their heads. "Looks like someone was watching over us."

Maddy shot him a scalpel sharp glance. "Yeah, I can't help but feel the love."

He arched his brow. "You're crazy if you don't think God had his hand of protection on us just now."

"And this is the best he can do?" She waved her hands. "Look around. Your drive is burned to a crisp. We're stranded out here in the wilderness, and do I need to mention your money is gone?" She folded her arms and looked away. "And I lost my good shoes," she whispered.

He took two tentative steps down the hill and then stopped and waited a moment. Nothing happened. Pieces of metal that had once been part of his SUV lay scattered at his feet. "Well, I'm grateful," he said softly. "It could have been a lot worse."

"Look Mr. Barnes, it seems you've just lost a million dollars, so I'm guessing you got bigger problems rather than questioning me. So if you don't mind, I'll find my own way back to town and get—" Her words stopped abruptly.

Chase turned to face her and followed her gaze down to the back of his left leg. The entire backside of his pants were dark and wet. Only now did he notice the growing throb in his leg. He ran his hand along the back of his thigh to the source of the pain. A metal shaft embedded in the back of his leg, which looked like a piece of a door handle.

"You've been hurt," she said.

His vision blurred a moment, but he blinked it away. "It's minor." He twisted his frame and delicately touched the protruding shard. "These people are in the big league. Tell me the truth—off the record if you want. Are you involved with them in any way at all?"

She didn't answer—he hadn't expected an answer. Without speaking a word, she removed her blazer and began ripping out the lining.

"What are you doing?"

"We need to slow down the bleeding. This looks serious."

"You a nurse too?"

"I don't have to be a nurse to understand that wound needs attention. You're losing too much blood. Hold still while I make a tourniquet." She ripped open the leg of his jeans.

"Hey! These are my good jeans."

"I know and this is your good leg too?"

"I'm partial to it. Yes."

"You could lose it if we don't do something right away."

"I'm OK."

"Don't be such a man. I'm trying to help you." She wrapped the material around his leg and tightened. "Everyone needs help at times. You afraid you'll be indebted to me, or something?"

"And if I was?"

"I'm not the kind who expects pay back, because I learned a long time ago most men don't understand the word responsibility."

"Maybe I'm not like most men."

"Maybe I don't buy that line anymore."

"Maybe you should."

"Maybe I'm happy with my own opinion." She twisted the stick she had just inserted in the tourniquet.

He groaned. "Maybe you have issues," he said between clenched teeth.

"I'm not the one who let a teenage boy dupe me out of a million dollars."

"Touché." A glance at his bleeding leg brought back the blurred vision.

He looked away. "The Chief isn't going to be happy about my ride." He wasn't happy about it himself. Maddy had been in danger, and it was wrong of him to pursue the blue sport car. He should have let another trooper ¬handle it.

The Chief had been right. He hadn't been himself lately. Maybe he did need a break from the case. The last few days his brain had been fixated on finding Andrew's killer. It was almost as if he couldn't control himself. But he had to do something. He couldn't just sit back and wait for things to happen.

He'd been the one who'd gotten Andrew into law enforcement, and as the older brother, he was responsible for Andrew's safety. He'd failed. Today, Andrew's killer was out there walking free and clear—a calculating man who would likely kill again.

Without warning, his body suddenly felt weak. He took in several quick breaths. His brain acted as if someone used a remote to put it on pause. In the distance, he heard a voice shouting for him to sit, but nothing made sense to him anymore. The edges of his vision darkened and the world faded into blackness until there was nothing--*continued*

THE MENTOR

SURVIVING THE WINTER OF 1776

Jack Baer quietly knelt in the dirt and pulled the pine branch aside. His stomach did a flip when he spotted fresh deer tracks in the creek bed below him. All he needed now was a little help from the Lord, and his life might take a turn for the better. Okay, maybe a lot of help from the Lord.

He leaned his muzzle loading rifle against a pine limb and tucked the legs of his faded camo's inside his rubber boots. The after glow of the orange sunset lingered above the horizon. Only an hour of shooting light remained. A gust of wind clawed at his booney hat, which he pulled down tight before he stood. In his thirty-eight years, tough times had never been this aggressive. Not that he was complaining, because he knew God was in charge.

The deer was several minutes ahead of him, and if his guess was correct, then it was headed to the pine thicket over the next ridge. Once inside the thicket, any chance of him getting a shot would be slim—especially since only an hour of shooting light remained. With God's help he wouldn't leave empty handed. At least not this time.

This wouldn't be the first time he'd hunted all day only to bag a deer in the last minutes of evening light. But filling his tag was not the chief concern this time; he was hunting to fill his stomach. More importantly, the stomachs of his elderly neighbors. Their retirement check wouldn't arrive for two more weeks and they had no meet in their freezer. Of course, they'd get by somehow without his help, but they'd suffer in the process. He was determined to do all he could to keep that from happening.

Last evening, he'd stopped to check on the Johnson's as he often did, and for the first time since he'd known them, they didn't invite him to stay and join them for Sunday dinner. The flicker of worry in Mrs. Johnson's eyes told him something was wrong. After he tumbled the idea over in his mind awhile, he asked flatly, how they were on groceries.

Mrs. Johnson gave a nervous laugh before she confessed they'd been living on flour- gravy and biscuits for several days. Not bad for breakfast fare, but elderly bodies needed protein every day in order to function well. Mr. Johnson tried to brush off Jack's concern with a comment about needing to lose a little weight anyway.

Jack wasn't buying it. He boldly promised them he'd bring a deer home and restock their freezer. He'd been confident last night, but now he wasn't so certain. If he hadn't been so broke and poor himself, he'd have driven to town and bought groceries to stock their freezer. But his empty bank account didn't give him that option.

The task of circling the downwind side of the ridge took him several precious minutes of remaining light. Minutes he didn't have to spare. The temperature dropped several degrees with the sun set, He stopped to quietly zip his jacket. "God, show me favor today, and deliver this animal into my hands? Not for selfish motives, but because we need the meat." Some men would laugh at his praying for success, but he stood by the belief that nothing was beyond the reach of prayer except that which was outside the will of God. Helping a neighbor eat was surely inside God's will.

Before he entered the standing pines, he stopped and took in a long breath to relax his tense muscles. Slow walking was difficult and he chose each step carefully. Time was running out, and he was desperate. No one had to tell him how desperation made a man careless. He'd been there before.

Under the forest canopy the light continued to grow dim. His truck was parked forty-minutes away, and he really needed to reach the dirt road before dark—with a deer if God allowed it.

For the next several minutes, he quietly inched through the stand of pine trees. Branches swayed gently with the evening breeze while the long shadows cast an eerie picture around him. Hands against his side and bent forward, he moved methodically and deliberately, like a ghost. He treated each step as if walking through a leaf-covered land-mine. When he came to the edge of the pines, he paused a moment to listen.

Nothing.

Only a barking squirrel and a few chattering birds broke in on the evening stillness. At the edge of the pines was a thicket of saplings and vines, a sanctuary for the deer. He mapped out his next few steps and began threading his way through the thicket. While in mid-step, a flash of white suddenly appeared and then blended into the shadows.

Jack slowly lowered his foot and then remained motionless for several long breaths. No sign of the deer. Just one shot was all he needed. With his fifty caliber muzzle loader, he could drop a deer at seventy-five yards easily, but first he had to have opportunity.

Finally, he released a pent up sigh and turned to head back toward his truck. It looked as if that wasn't going to happen. The deer was aware of his presence now, and there'd be no way to stalk it today. "Sorry Mrs. Johnson," he whispered. "I've let you down."

The thicket was difficult to penetrate anyway. A few trees and dead falls were scattered throughout, but the area was dominated with saplings and tall horse weeds. Not only was it not favorable conditions for still hunting, but the ensuing darkness made finding his way difficult.

He snapped a broken stick underfoot and cringed. Every deer within a mile range was just alerted of his presence. After he retreated and exited the thicket, he searched the area around him. The shadowy evening light removed all the familiarity of the area when he'd came through this morning. Now it was difficult to find the right direction to his truck. He made a choice and stumbled on, looking for a trail.

Minutes later, he spotted the remains of an old building at the bottom of the ridge. The fact that he'd never seen the old building before indicated he was outside his normal range. A quick look and he'd be on his way. At the valley floor, he walked a circle around the fragments of what had once been someone's home. All that remained were the foundation stones, part of the chimney, and an old well.

A cluster of frostbitten violets, their purple petals curled and wilted, indicated a woman had likely lived here too. But how long ago? Fifty years, a hundred? Probably longer.

The house had been no larger than his own kitchen. A simple shelter with room for a bed and table, nothing more. But why had they built it so far from the road? Or had they? A hundred years ago, this may have been near a well-used path.

He rubbed his eyes and looked around him. Darkness had fallen quickly. Without a flashlight, he'd likely get turned around, and possibly lost. When he'd left his truck this morning, he hadn't intended to spend the entire day inside the woods. But here he was, unsure of his location, and with no choice but to spend the night in the woods.

A heap of dry leaves would be his bed tonight, and his pack would suffice as a pillow. Once he raked a pile of leaves together for a bed, he stretched out, folded his arms across his chest and relaxed. The ground was a little chilly, but he'd stick it out and find his way back to his truck in the morning.

Night sounds around him died away as the fog of fatigue clouded and took over his mind. He imagined the family who'd lived here a hundred years ago. Maybe they were newlyweds who had built the structure for immediate protection until they could later erected a larger house in another location.

Maybe the wife was a frail woman with a simple beauty, and the young man would have likely been outdoor savvy. At least savvy enough to … . The world around him faded into the darkness until there was nothing.

*   *   *

Gideon Bounds removed the barricade and cracked open the cabin door. "I've got to see what they're doing," he whispered to his wife. A gust of icy wind took his breath away as he searched the empty valley before him. The buttery glow of the morning sun had just broke over the treetops. A deep snow had fallen and covered the long meadow grass, giving the air a scalpel-like bite. "Thank the Lord. Our prayers are answered," he said.

Violet quietly came up behind him and peeked around his shoulder, "Are they gone?"

Gideon released a long sigh. "It's over. The British Army's left our valley and moved on somewhere else."

"It's so cold." She pushed the door shut, locked it, and then stood massaging her slender neck. The wind had chilled the room several degrees. "I'll move Josh closer to the fireplace."

Gideon teased the smoldering coals into a blaze. Tension slowly left his body leaving him feeling free again. God had blessed them—saved them was more like it. It was a miracle the army had left without harming his family.

Violet placed Josh on a blanket in front of the fireplace. He whimpered a moment before he turned over on his side and went back to sleep. The growing flames brightened the room punctuating their new-found freedom with an occasional pop or sizzle.

Violet hummed softly as she tucked the blanket around Joshua. Joy had returned to the household once again. Violet's long auburn hair hung gracefully down her back. The dark summer tan lingered on her smooth complexion even though it was late into the winter. Most woman avoided the sun as much as possible, endeavoring to keep their skin milky white. But long days in the garden had complemented Violet's beauty.

The rough army soldiers would normally have considered her a prize for the taking, but by the mercy of God, the Captain had immediately ordered the family locked inside the cabin while the army camped outside last night.

She finger-combed her hair, and then smoothed the wrinkles on her blue dress. Uncertain of what the night might bring, they had both slept in their clothes. "I'll fix something to eat." She wrapped a blanket around her shoulders and opened the door. Gideon followed her outside where they entered the cellar together.

Before his eyes could adjust to the darkness inside the cellar, a gasp escaped Violet's lips. "Oh no."

Empty shelves before him seemed like an illusion. He blinked several times as if his eyes were playing tricks on him. They weren't. He'd feared the army might take some of their supply, but he'd expected they'd have the courtesy to leave them something behind.

Violet spoke first. "They've left us nothing. Our canning and all the dried meat, the potatoes, everything—gone."

"And they took my rifle too." A trickle of fear made his palms begin to sweat.

"Oh God." She put her hand over her mouth. "What now?"

Gideon wagged his head. He'd faced hard times before, but this was different. Now he had the responsibility of a family. "I—"

Violet spun around to face him, "How will we live? Don't they care if we die?" She sliced the air with her hands as she talked. "This isn't fair."

Gideon put his hands on her waist. "We'll make it. At least they're gone." Fear crept up his spine and brushed its prickly fingers at the back of his neck.

Violet covered her face with her hands, and then suddenly cleared her voice. "What are we going to do?"

"First, we'll begin trusting God." His voice was calm, but inside he wasn't so certain. If they'd only given him back his rifle, he could shoot wild game to feed them through the winter.

"How? How can we make it? There's nothing. No potatoes, no vegetables. They stole it all." Her voice quivered. "Josh has a bad cold, none of us have eaten since last night, and now you've no gun." She wrung her hands and paced the floor.

He took her by the hand. "Let's go back inside where it's warm." Behind him he could hear her sniffling. Once inside he knelt beside her in front of the fire and prayed while Violet cried.

After a long silence of staring into the fire, Gideon spoke. "I'll set a few snares, we can live on rabbit for a while."

"Really? How many rabbits have you seen this winter, or in the last year for that matter? The coyotes have killed them all." She sniffed and brushed a tear.

He took her hand. "Look, we've never had a better time to trust in God.

219

This is our opportunity to have faith. We can eat coyote if we have to. The natives do it." He laughed at his own joke, but his emotions fought a tug-of-war inside.

She looked down as if measuring his words as they sat quietly for several minutes. The flames leapt up and then died down as the wind howled outside. He knew what he had to do. There was no choice, really.

"We should have hidden some of our supplies," said Violet.

"Wasn't time. I opened the door and stared down the muzzle's of three rifles. Then that General Burgoyne told the officers to lock us in the house."

"Will neighbors help us?"

"Neighbors? The Silliman's left after Christmas to spend the winter in Philadelphia with their parents. John Middlekauff's family has all left to follow their menfolk in the Continental Army. We're stuck." As soon as the words left his mouth, he was sorry. Hope was what she needed, not his negativism.

"What about the Claycamps? They're our friends."

He considered their distant neighbors. To get to the Claycamp's will take at least two days walking, in this weather. And sadly, the army likely left them in the same situation.

"The Indian camp? Whitehawk is your friend," she added.

"Yes. Whitehawk will help," he said, tumbling the idea over in his mind.

"How long will it take to get there and back," she asked.

"In this weather, … three days."

"Josh has to eat today."

Gideon nodded. If White Hawk was here, he wouldn't give up. He had no doubt about that. He crossed the room and reached behind the stack of wood for the bow Whitehawk had helped him make last summer. He didn't have his rifle, but he'd use what God gave him do.

Unstrung, the bow resembled a walking stick. The British had seen no value in it, or they would have taken it, too. Yet, in the right hands the Osage-wooden bow would be a powerful weapon.

He attached the string and tested its pull. The orange limbs responded in a graceful arc. From the ceiling rafters, he fished out the fox-skin quiver and arrows, which he'd hidden to protect Josh from the sharp tips.

Many summer evenings had been spent shooting arrows into the hillside behind the house. At the time it was almost an obsession. He'd wanted to learn the Indian culture, and White Hawk appeared elated to be his mentor. What he learned on those summer evenings might keep his family alive this winter.

He crossed the room and removed the large buffalo robe he'd traded from a French traveler. Violet, in her nervous tizzy, searched every corner as if by a miracle she'd find food the general had overlooked.

Not until he picked up the bow and quiver did she turn a sharp look his way. Alarm filled her eyes. "Where are you going?"

He stamped a kiss on her cheek avoiding her gaze. She opened her mouth to speak, but he touched her lips for silence, " I'm going out to kill us a big deer. Wish me luck."

She had a way of making her face still while her eyes probed. "And where does that leave me?" He'd anticipated her next question.

"They're long gone. They won't be back."

"But I don't want to be alone," her voice leaking panic.

A block of ice hardened his stomach. "There's no other way." God knew he didn't want to do this, but what choice did he have?

"What if they do come back?" Fear ringed her eyes. "I've heard of stragglers who follow behind the army. What if someone does come? What will I do?" Her lower lip trembled for a moment.

Something squeezed tightly inside his chest. "Keep the door locked, and don't let anyone inside. Pretend you have a shotgun, and act confident."

She stood quietly a moment, her arms akimbo. "I guess I don't have a choice, do I?"

Gideon smiled, but it wasn't real.

Finally, she took his hand and laced her fingers in his. "Go. We'll be fine." Disappointment seeped into her tone.

The block of ice inside him melted. "I don't have a choice either."

*   *   *

Had Gideon known the future, he would not have been so willing to trade the warmth of the cabin for the bitter wind that nipped at his bare face. Snowflakes blew inside the fur robe and trickled down his bare skin like icy fly bites. He hunched his buffalo coat about his ears, wrapped it tighter around his waist, and tucked the bow under his left arm. Under the snow-filled sky the distant hills were like fading clouds. He wiped his watering eyes. Long even strides quickly took him out of the valley and into the dense wooded hills behind the cabin.

Two hours later, he was still leaning into the wind, but the ankle-deep snow had slowed his pace considerably. Around him, green pine branches bent low under the snow's weight as if ready to break. Tired, but confident, he counted it divine providence when he stumbled across fresh deer tracks. Thank God, the army hadn't scared away all the deer.

The bright snow hurt his eyes as he threaded his way through the trees for more than a mile. No sight of the deer. He'd left familiar territory long ago. The dense snow made every ridge and valley looked the same.

Right now, he wasn't certain he could make his cold stiff muscles draw back the bow when he did get a shot at a deer. His Kentucky rifle always shot straight and true; sadly, it was now in the hands of a British soldier. One who likely didn't appreciate its accuracy.

He looked up just in time to catch a glimpse of a deer's white tail retreat into the shadows. The wings of his heart lifted. A trickle of hope was all he had, but that was enough. Immediately, he slowed his pace and cautiously moved forward searching the trees, and listening. He needed to get within fifteen to twenty steps of the animal before taking the shot.

The deer would know it was being followed, and if pushed, it would circle behind him. He switched the bow to his left hand and nocked an arrow on the string. Bringing up the bow, he pulled the taunt string slowly to waken his muscles. After several attempts he was satisfied he could complete a full draw.

Another hour past as he continued to stalk the deer. The tracks revealed where it had been moments earlier, but he caught no sight of it. Sign was encouraging, but sign would not fill his family's' empty stomachs.

Hours of trudging through the deep snow had drained his body. The snow had stopped, and the pale rags of the evening sun was edging over the horizon. If he didn't turn back soon, he wouldn't make it home before dark. He refused to think about spending a night with hungry wolves roaming the forest. How far had he traveled from the cabin? Five miles? Likely more. The hills around him all had the look of sameness.

A flicker of white stopped him in his tracks. He strained and focused on the trees ahead. Several breaths later, he finally made out the outline of a deer nibbling on pine needles. Deer ate pine needles only when nothing else was available. It had been a hard winter for everyone.

Crouching low, he crept forward toward his prey, always keeping a tree between himself and the deer's line of sight. Soft snow crunched with every step. At least the wind was in his favor—for the moment. A nostril full of human scent would send the deer on the move again.

It took nearly a half hour before he reduced the distance between him and the deer to twenty steps. Twenty steps between food and starvation for his family. He was so close, he was afraid to breath.

The deer's head popped up suddenly, pricked its long velvety ears forward, and sniffed the air.

Gideon held his breath.

The deer stamped its foot.

Gideon remained behind two trees that had grown together and waited for the deer to look away. Finally, the deer stepped forward behind a patch of thick brush. Gideon drew the string back and waited, his bow ready.

Delicately, the deer crept back into view, its big eyes searching the foliage around Gideon. The deer's long blinking lashes softened his heart. His family needed this deer, he told himself.

Inching the bow into position, he focused on the ripples in her dark winter fur. His arms strained at the pull of the bow.

She craned her neck, and then pricked her ears again as if she sensed danger. Her movements became rigid. She froze in mid-step and bore a hole into Gideon. Her legs tensed like coiled springs ready to explode.

Gideon released the arrow.

The springs uncoiled, and the deer exploded into action. But not before the arrow penetrated the dark rippled of fur behind her front leg. She crashed through branches and brush until suddenly the forest was silent again.

Gideon's heart pounded against his chest like an overactive woodpecker. He stood poised in the snow, his feet spread apart, while he bent over and sucked in deep breaths of cold air. Thanks to God, his family would eat tonight.

Although exhilarated from the experience, Gideon fought the urge to rush at the animal. White Hawk's admonition was to always wait for the wounded animal to give up its spirit in peace. Darkness would soon be upon him, but in respect to the animal Gideon waited.

Minutes later, with only a few rays of daylight left, he approached the spot where he'd had last seen the deer. A broken line of blood led to the edge of a dry creek bed. His deer had dropped in the bottom of the creek bed. Her huge eyes stared deep into his soul. A red carpet of snow grew from under her front leg.

Only a few minutes of light remained, and he'd have to work quickly. He was much too far from the cabin to drag the deer behind him. He'd have to skin the animal and remove the meat from the bones. Doing so would give him the lightest pack possible.

He rushed down the creek bed toward the deer. Too late, he realized his foot was caught on a hidden tree root under the blanket of snow. With nothing nearby to grasp and steady himself, he plunged headlong, half rolling, half sliding toward the bottom of the creek bed.

For a moment, he didn't move. A bolt of pain shot up his leg. Blood swirled through his vision as he tried to stand. The pain couldn't be ignored. A lightning storm of images flashed through his mind. He was alone. It was getting dark, and he was miles away from another human--*continued.*

Devotions for Spiritual Growth

The following devotions are samples from my book, *Devotions for Spiritual Growth*. This book of devotions is intended to help readers develop and mature in their walk with Christ. Many of the devotions are selected events from history in which the author parallels an event with everyday life. (Available August 2018)

Don't Let the Baby Die

... regard, and wonder marvellously: for I will work a work in your days, which ye will not believe, though it be told you (Hab 1:5).

The young mother became hysterical when she found her five-year old collapsed in the back yard of their home in rural Wisconsin. Her husband quickly mounted his horse and summoned the doctor. However, medical knowledge in 1865 was limited, and by day's end, the doctor pronounced little Max Hoffman dead. With the neighbors help, the grieving couple buried their only child that same summer evening.

Late in the night, Mrs. Hoffman awakened her husband and frantically explained how she had a nightmare that her son was still alive. Her husband tried to console her and pray, but she would not be comforted. At her insistence, he had to put aside his own grief and summon the neighbors to help him open the grave. By lantern light, they unearthed the wooden casket and removed the lid.
Max had moved.

The doctor returned, and after much effort, he revived little Max. A week later, Max was back to normal and was outside playing in the backyard again. He lived eighty more years, and spent his last days in Clinton, Ohio where he would often sit on the town's park bench and show the little coffin handles he had kept. He'd explain, to anyone who would listen, how he had once died, but because of his mother's dream, he had received a second chance.
Perhaps God has given you a dream before he's given you the real thing. It is up to you to nurture that dream and keep it alive. Faith is an important element toward attaining your dream. You must not only believe in the possibility of your dream, but you must also visualize it as if you already had it.

Unfortunately, well-meaning friends and loved ones can bury

your dreams with their negativism and disbelief. Don't expect others to believe in your dream as much as you do, because God has given this dream to you, not anyone else. Make no mistake; doubt kills more dreams than failure ever does. Don't sit back and allow God to give your dream to someone else, and refuse to allow naysayers, who gave up on their own dream to talk you out of yours.

If you've given up on your dream, then do whatever it takes to resurrect it. Use your shovels of prayer and faith to scrape off negativism and doubt and get your dream out of the coffin.

It may seem difficult to keep your dream alive, but all things are possible with God. Focus on him with hope in your heart as you cling to your dream with all the passion you can muster. Keep your dream bigger than your fear and your faith stronger than your discouragement. Hold onto your dream and leave the rest up to God.

Don't downgrade your dream to fit your reality. Upgrade your dream to match your destiny.

And Jesus looking upon them saith, With men it is impossible, but not with God: for with God all things are possible. Mark 10:27

God is Always Watching Over Us

For he hath said, I will never leave thee, nor forsake thee. Hebrews 13:5

The coach kept the young football star on the bench most of the season, because he believed the athlete was not playing according to his potential. In the middle of a long practice day, the player was summoned home—his father had taken seriously ill. Disappointed in the athlete, the coach encouraged him to take as much time off as he needed. He certainly would not be missed.

Over a week later, the athlete showed up in time for an important game and asked to play. The coach kept him on the bench even though the slacker repeatedly begged for a chance to play. Near the end of game, when the team was so far behind that winning seemed impossible, the coach submitted to the young man's pleas and sent him onto the field to play.

After only seconds of playing, it was obvious the athlete had transformed. He intercepted passes, tackled his opponents without fear, and played with such enthusiasm that the rest of the team became inspired. The team played together with such unity and zeal that they went into overtime and won the game.

Inside the locker room the coach confronted the young man about the sudden change in his performance. "This is the first time I've seen you really play football," the coach said. "What happened to you out there?"

Glassy eyed, the young man looked down. "Coach, you know I had to take time off to be with my ill father. He didn't make it. We buried him yesterday."

"And I'm sorry for that," the coach said as he sat beside the player.

"But Coach, maybe you didn't know my dad was blind." The athlete's voice cracked. He wiped back a tear and swallowed. "Tonight was the first time my dad ever saw me play football."

Like the young athlete, each of us would perform better if we understood how our own heavenly Father watches over our performance each day. Since we can't see into the spirit world, our performance in life is often lackluster. We don't think our actions are important, but the God who watches over the sparrow also notices every move we make. He is fully aware of your battles and he believes in your potential.

Therefore, pick up the ball and run in the face of adversity. Tackle problems as if you can't lose. Do something that scares you. If you never risk something for God, you will never do anything great for him. Don't be a caution junkie. Without risk there is really no need for faith. So take a chance. Stop playing it safe in everything you do. After all, the real risk is doing nothing.

Your positive energy and creativity must be greater than anyone else's negativity.

Fear thou not; for I am with thee: be not dismayed; for I am thy God: I will strengthen thee; yea, I will help thee; yea, I will uphold thee with the right hand of my righteousness. Isaiah 41:10-11

WOUNDS THAT WON'T HEAL

He hath sent me to heal the brokenhearted ... to set at liberty them that are bruised ... Luke 4:28

Long before Andrew Jackson became the seventh U.S. president, he was involved in a near-death gun battle. While campaigning for Tennessee's Superior Court Judge, his opponent, Charles Dickenson, called Jackson's wife a bigamist. It was true. Rachel's first husband had failed to complete their divorce paperwork, and without her knowing it, she was married to two men simultaneously.

Determined to avenge his wife's honor, Jackson challenged Dickenson to a duel. Dickenson accepted, and the two met at the Red River in Logan, Kentucky. Here, Jackson shot and killed Dickenson, but not before taking a bullet in his chest. The doctor insisted on immediately operating, but Jackson refused, choosing to deal with the wound himself. Surprisingly, he not only survived, but he also lived thirty-eight more years with that lead bullet lodged near his heart.

Sadly, the wound caused him daily pain the rest of his life, and many believe the lead poisoning contributed to his death. His refusal of medical attention not only brought him years of discomfort, but it possibly shortened his life.

Similar to Jackson's experience, Christians tend to carry emotional wounds deep inside their hearts. These wounds aren't from guns and knives, but from the words and deeds of friends and family. No one hurts us as deeply as our loved ones.

Left unattended, emotional wounds will never heal, because the only remedy is forgiveness. Like Jackson, we too may choose to deal with wounds on our own, but it's futile. Only the Great Physician can help us forgive.

Even so, we must do more than seek God's help. We must also stop reliving the incident. When we talk about our injustice, we relive it in our mind, which is like probing an open wound. It will never heal.

Another step is to announce our forgiveness—in prayer, or at least audibly. When we speak the words, I forgive, it's as if we're giving our heart direction. It's uncomfortable at first, but saying I forgive helps release our bitterness.

Forgiving is not condoning someone's actions. Forgiveness is between you and God alone. God holds each of us accountable for our words and deeds, and alternately, he will reward every injustice we forgive. After all, in Heaven God isn't going to look us over for medals,—but like a good parent, he will examine each of his children thoroughly for scars.

The only petition in the Lords prayer that has a condition attatched is forgiveness.
Matt 6:14-15

For if ye forgive men their trespasses, your heavenly Father will also forgive you: But if ye forgive not men their trespasses, neither will your Father forgive your trespasses. Matt 6:14-15

GOD HAS A SPECIFIC PURPOSE FOR YOUR LIFE

Before I formed thee in the belly I knew thee; and before thou camest forth out of the womb I sanctified thee, and I ordained thee … . (Jerimiah 1:5).

William Cowper was forbidden to court the woman he loved. Her father thought Cowper an unacceptable suitor and would not permit his daughter to even visit the man she loved. The rejection sent William into long seasons of depression and despondency. Finally, he decided his only solution was suicide.

He ingested poison, but instead of killing him, it only made him sick. During another bout of despondency, he jumped from a river bridge. Incredibly, his clothes caught on the framework and someone rescued him. Later, he held a penknife against his chest and purposely fell on it—but the blade broke. Finally, one day he determined to hang himself in his bedroom, but while unconscious, a friend discovered what he'd done and managed to revive him.

For his own safety, Cowper's family put him in a psychiatric ward where the doctor presented him with a Bible. The book not only altered Cowper's mental outlook, but it also resulted in his salvation. As Cowper grew in the Lord, he came to understand that God had a purpose for his life. He went on to use his poetic talent to write songs and author numerous popular hymns of his day. More than a century later, two of Cowper's songs are still found in our hymnals; There is a Fountain Filled with Blood, and God Moves in Mysterious Ways."

Cowper's attitude began changing when he realized God had a reason for his existence. Confidence in God's purpose is an important element in everyone's life. You may not always see his purpose, and your best efforts may even appear a failure. Yet, God does not make mistakes. He did not make a mistake during creation, and he did not make a mistake when he created you. He put you in your location and in your generation, because this is where he intends to use you.

You are only one small part of his master plan. Even so, you are an important part. No other person can do the work God created you to accomplish. Continue to yield to his guidance, trust his management, and ask him to use you in his work.

God has a specific plan for your life, because you are his workmanship.

For we are his workmanship, created in Christ Jesus unto good works, which God hath before ordained that we should walk in them. Eph 2:10

THE MISSING PIECE OF THE PUZZLE

Ye have not chosen me, but I have chosen you, and ordained you, that ye should go and bring forth fruit, ... John 15:16

The week-long summer visits with grandmother are a special memory of my childhood. One of the last summers I spent with her was a memorable experience. The first day I arrived that summer, she presented me with a new one-thousand-piece puzzle. I had never been fond of puzzles, but she wanted to frame and hang the finished puzzle, and I agreed only to make her happy.

I worked intensely for three days to assemble the one-thousand pieces while she praised me every step of the way. Near the end, I began to worry that something was wrong. Finally, I discovered one piece of the puzzle from the exact middle was missing.

At first, I refused to abandon the project, because I had invested so much time. I improvised with parts from other puzzles to fill in the vacant spot; yet, everything I tried looked unnatural. Hand drawn pictures on cardboard and even printed substitutes only marred the beauty of the original. Regardless of what we tried, anyone who looked at the puzzle noticed the flaw right away. In the end, I completed the project using an inadequate substitute, but it never looked right. The replacement was a poor substitute for the original.

That experience often comes to mind when I pray for God's will in my life. Like the missing piece of puzzle, God has a specific purpose in his master plan for each of his children. He creates us with unique characteristics to accomplish that special purpose. Sadly, we fail to appreciate those characteristics in ourselves and sometimes even consider them as flaws.

Even so, another person cannot properly do the work for which you have been created. If you refuse to accept God's plan for your life, or if you try to change something against God's will, then you will alter the beauty of God's plan. If you give up on his work or fail to surrender to his will, you force God to replace you with a substitute. A substitute will never have the beauty God intended.

Don't underestimate yourself by comparing your abilities with others. It's your unique qualities that make you special, and being unique is a better characteristic than being perfect.

No one else can do the job for which God created you to do.

But now, O LORD, thou art our father; we are the clay, and thou our potter; and we all are the work of thy hand. Isaiah 64:8-9